T0013857

PSYCHIC SHIELD

THE PERSONAL HANDBOOK
OF PSYCHIC PROTECTION

PSYCHIC SHIELD

THE PERSONAL HANDBOOK
OF PSYCHIC PROTECTION

Your All-in-One Guide to Protecting Yourself
from NEGATIVE ENERGY,
Maintaining BOUNDARIES, and
Living in HARMONY with Others

CAITLÍN MATTHEWS

Text copyright © 2006, 2024 Caitlin Matthews. Design copyright © 2024 Ulysses Press and its licensors. All rights reserved. Any unauthorized duplication in whole or in part or dissemination of this edition by any means (including but not limited to photocopying, electronic devices, digital versions, and the internet) will be prosecuted to the fullest extent of the law.

Published in the United States by:
Ulysses Press
PO Box 3440
Berkeley, CA 94703
www.ulyssespress.com

First published as *The Psychic Protection Handbook* in Great Britain in 2005 by Piatkus Books Ltd.

ISBN: 978-1-64604-624-9
Library of Congress Control Number: 2023947774

Printed in the United States
10 9 8 7 6 5 4 3 2 1

Editorial and production staff: Shelona Belfon, Claire Chun, Yesenia Garcia-Lopez, Winnie Liu, Renee Rutledge
Front cover design: Amy King
Cover artwork: mandala © ViSnezh/shutterstock.com, swirl background © HAKKIARSLAN/shutterstock.com

IMPORTANT NOTE TO READERS: This book has been written and published for informational and educational purposes only. It is not intended to serve as medical advice or to be any form of medical treatment. You should always consult with your physician before altering or changing any aspect of your medical treatment. Do not stop or change any prescription medications without the guidance and advice of your physician. Any use of the information in this book is made on the reader's good judgment and is the reader's sole responsibility. This book is not intended to diagnose or treat any medical condition and is not a substitute for a physician.

*This book is respectfully dedicated to Dion Fortune,
a woman possessed of fine common sense and an inspirational breadth of
vision: her metaphysical pioneering
has made the path easier for all who follow.*

*This book is also for all the clients
who attend my practice.*

Contents

Reader's Guide to Using This Book

It is recommended that you read through the whole book, especially Chapters 1–6, which establish the ground rules for dealing with psychic disruption and for maintaining good spiritual health, then reference Chapters 7–15 as needed. These principles underlie specific areas where we need help with psychic disturbance. Here is a quick guide to help you find your way around this book:

- Forgetting how reality and spirit coexist? See Chapter 1.
- Needing spiritual protection? See Chapter 2.
- Always feeling vulnerable? See Chapter 3.
- Are your boundaries constantly being crossed? See Chapter 4.
- Feeling lost and confused? See Chapter 5.
- Always being invaded and influenced? See Chapter 6.
- Stuck and unable to change? See Chapter 7.
- Betrayed by your own words, or a victim of others' gossip? See Chapter 8.
- People-skills poor? See Chapter 9.
- Insecure at home or away? See Chapter 10.
- Family getting on your nerves? See Chapter 11.
- Troubled by love tangles? See Chapter 12.
- Traumas at work? See Chapter 13.
- Fear of the unseen, the metaphysical? See Chapter 14.
- Haunted by the past? See Chapter 15.

Each chapter has checklists to help you discern and diagnose what is wrong, as well as practical strategies to help you implement solutions that bring balance and healing. Answer the questions and checklists as honestly as you can: any self-deceit will only deepen confusion or worsen your problem. In applying the strategies, always ask your spiritual Advocates (see Chapter 2) for the help that you need rather than trying to deal with the problem alone. Some of the practical strategies start simply and develop through the book. Some parts of the text are purposely repetitive to remind you of what's most important. There is continual reference back and forth to different strategies and rituals.

When you pick up a book of this kind, you will find descriptions of phenomena and events that are beyond your knowledge and experience. When hypochondriacs refer to medical encyclopedias, they imagine that they are suffering from unlikely diseases when this is clearly not so. Use your common sense in this book and don't assume that every case and condition is something you will personally experience. Deal with things from the ground up, looking at obvious physical causes before you call upon metaphysical assistance.

Finally, this book provides commonsense strategies to help keep you psychically streetwise in everyday life. If your discernment of reality is impaired through mental illness, seek help from a health professional and do not stop taking prescribed medication that manages any ongoing condition without medical advice. If you are dealing with a situation threatening your physical safety, seek legal and police assistance as soon as possible. Also, some forms of psychic disturbance need expert attention and are beyond the scope of any self-help book. See the resources list on page 306 for more expert help. Each chapter ends with blueprints that help you remember the most helpful basic principles, but here are some to bear in mind as you read this book.

PROTECTIVE BLUEPRINTS TO REMEMBER AS YOU READ

1. You are never helpless, unloved or alone.

2. Your streetwise common sense is your best ally.

3. Nighttime and daytime make you feel very different about things.

4. Say "no" if persuasion or coercion is being used against you.

5. Get acquainted with spiritual Advocates and ask for their help and protection.

6. Maintain a positive attitude rather than entertaining fearful expectations.

7. If you've been the cause of psychic disturbance to yourself and others, don't harbor guilt but make the decision to change and prevent this in the future.

8. Live in the present moment rather than anticipating fearful futures or inhabiting problematic pasts.

9. You are a unique human being with a distinct role to play in the universe.

10. The ability and responsibility for stopping and preventing most forms of psychic disturbance lies in your own hands.

Introduction: Living Free from Fear

If I had five bucks for every time someone told me that they were "under psychic attack," I would be a rich woman. When I first started to see clients in my shamanic healing practice, I was initially cautious about endorsing such fearful diagnoses lest I be encouraging paranoia, for the people who complained of psychic attack would be in a state bordering on panic when they phoned me. Fear is extremely communicable, and I remember how fearfully I first reacted to these calls. But, whatever the cause of such suspicions, people were genuinely frightened and wanted help; out of their depth, they were ready to do anything to feel safe again. By getting myself and my own fears out of the way and remaining centered, I could listen to what people were telling me and begin to be genuinely helpful rather than dismissive. It may be easy to mock such fear, but every one of us has, at some time, felt genuinely attacked, invaded or unsafe in ways that transcend the merely physical.

One thing that I learned from clients who felt themselves under attack was how unprepared they were. They had no strategies. Indeed, some desperate callers had previously contacted unscrupulous "psychic healers" and been royally fleeced in the pursuit of a peaceful soul. It seemed terrible to me that vulnerable people had been further violated by such would-be "healers." How had this happened? Because they were vulnerable and fearful, because they grasped at the nearest solution and because they had no idea of how the universe works. Most of all, because *they ignored their instincts.*

Over time, I've learned that what most people call "psychic attack" is actually psychic disruption: disturbance of the soul.

Psychic disruption is the displacement or loss of soul or else an invasion taking place in the soul. We experience a sense of abnormality in which something is either missing from our being, or something alien has become part of it. Something essential has gone or something unwelcome has come. This may be accompanied by feelings of intense unease, self-doubt, fear or panic. Psychic disruption is about change or confusion in the soul: it may originate from without or from within ourselves.

Our world needs a whole new look at spiritual health for, unless we look after our souls as much as we look after our bodies, we will be ruled by fear and suspicion rather than living with confidence and strength. This book explores how you can protect your soul. It explains the dynamics of spiritual reality, how cause and effect work and how you can deal with the consequences of your actions and protect the areas you have unwittingly exposed, as well as how to cleanse, decontaminate and maintain your boundaries. It is full of simple practices, meditations and rituals that help keep your soul safe from harm. It clarifies how you think and what your intention is, and puts you back in touch with your authentic self and your sources of spiritual help. Included are checklists, danger points and reality checks so that paranoia is brought under control and replaced by calm and considered strategies. You will learn how to deal collectedly and pragmatically with disturbing influences that could send you spiraling into confusion or crisis. You will discover the mundane causes of psychic disturbance that we each brew for ourselves. Most of the psychic problems we face are motivated by human beings with few ethical or moral boundaries, as well as from our own lack of clarity. By becoming psychically streetwise and by maintaining your spiritual health, you can defend yourself against such problems.

Psychic Shield is primarily useful for daily soul maintenance in the face of psychic risk. Although you will find help in an emergency, this book will be much more helpful if you establish some good spiritual housekeeping routines for every day. Then, if something overthrows your soul's composure, you will have some strategies at hand. Please don't expect me to do all the protecting for you. You will need to renegotiate your contract with the universe and play by the rules of that contract. I can't hold you to it, of course, but the time comes for everyone when self-protective fear forces us to observe the small print of our contract very, very carefully—usually when we are in danger, in panic and desperate. To live healthily, with souls protected, means living in focus, in harmony, observant of the boundaries that keep us safe. I warn you that you will have to think more clearly because psychic health depends largely upon your intentions and motivations. If these are blurred, your life will also be so! This book can be used by anyone, regardless of spiritual background, beliefs or lack thereof. Our primary help comes from within the coordinates of our own spiritual understanding of the universe.

I believe that we have the propensity *to cause* as well as *suffer* psychic disturbance. Accordingly, this book doesn't take the dualistic stance of only helping you protect against others; it also reveals how and why you need to protect yourself and others from your own unclear intentions. It's important to know how cause and effect work. You know that if you drop a cup on your foot, it will hurt. But do you equally realize that if you angrily wish someone misfortune, your wish has an effect? Living without fear means living responsibly, so I have looked at both sides of the track—not only from the perspective of ourselves as victim but also ourselves as perpetrator. It is all too easy to become dualistic and project our own fear and selfishness upon some convenient scapegoat as the evil one. Living in balance with ourselves and each other makes us human again.

This book names and disperses the fears that bind us. It doesn't shrink from looking deeply at the sources of fear but it also gives you strategies to deal with these. Psychic protection can never be a quick-fix solution because you need to understand the nature of reality's two sides and develop relationships with protective Advocates who will boost your efforts with their own. Merely reading this book won't help you: you alone can implement the strategies and rituals. By the end of the book, you should have the equipment to become psychically streetwise enough to maintain good psychic health.

Psychic Shield has been motivated by the many people who've asked me how to live free from fear. I've repeated this advice over the years so often that I started to write down strategies, guidance and ways of coping with different problems to give them out to clients. This has been especially so for those whose feelings of solidarity and help sometimes evaporate when they return to their home or beleaguered circumstances. How do they continue to be free of fear? What strategies, prayers, ways and practices will keep them safe? This book is for them.

May you find paths to peace and strategies to strengthen your soul within these pages!

Caitlín Matthews

CHAPTER 1

Reality and the Universe

The spirit and the mind are one. Their vision is . . .
much greater than the vision we experience in the
ordinary world. Nothing can be imagined that is
not already there in the outer and innerworlds.

—Malidoma Patrice Somé in *Of Water and Spirit*

THE ANCIENT ART OF
PSYCHIC PROTECTION

What does psychic protection conjure up in your imagination?
An entranced shaman whirling to the beat of a drum? An evan-
gelical minister wrestling with the possessed at the alter? Buffy the
Vampire Slayer with stake and hammer? Or is it the exorcist struggling to subdue evil with a well-placed Bible and light-bestowing
crucifix? Isn't it interesting that few of the images that come to
mind are familiar or from our own time, except those from TV or
movies? We have grown unfamiliar with such strange skills that
have become mythologized and distant from our own society.

The art of psychic protection is not a new skill. It is a very
ancient one found in every time, place and culture. Throughout
the history of the world, ordinary people have been careful to
observe wise customs and maintain the boundaries between themselves and spiritual harm. These simple, domestic and ordinary
skills were known to everyone. And for the more difficult kinds of
psychic disturbance, we have always needed people who can stand
at the borders between the known and the unknown, to bring spiritual peace to psychic disturbance, to detect the cause of strange

happenings, to arbitrate and calm perturbations in the night, to lead unquiet spirits to their rightful place.

How on earth can we learn this ancient skill? Where can we learn and benefit from the strategies? And why should we learn it at all, you may ask? We desperately need these skills in our times because other people and factors are affecting us all the time and we don't have a clue what to do about them. We don't even have a trained set of psychic protectors to call upon anymore: they're not in any directory. This book will not enable you to set up a business as a certified psychic protector, but it does have rituals, practices and strategies that have been used from ancient times and that still work now. You learn them by implementing them.

One thing that most of our images of psychic protectors have in common is their dynamic way of dealing with psychic disturbance. Psychic protectors don't meekly apologize for existing and cast a bit of holy water about to disperse the problem; they stand firmly in a place of spiritual support and deal with psychic disturbances forthrightly and confidently.

This is why we begin this book by reminding ourselves just how reality and spirit work in this universe, and try to understand why psychic disturbance happens in the first place. Nothing can replicate spiritual confidence, but we can begin by considering our own connection to spiritual sources of help.

THE SACRED FABRIC OF LIFE

We live in an extraordinary universe that is being thoroughly explored and explained by science, but there are unseen parts that receive little study or attention. In order to understand psychic disturbance we need to consider this little-known part.

One of the major reasons we feel attacked, cursed or irritated is because of our ignorance of the sacred fabric of life. The consequence of ignoring the complete universal reality is that we become neglectful of our boundaries and careless with our energy, not noticing when someone or something has taken advantage of us.

Let's consider for a moment where we live our lives. Our universe is made up of a great web of life that has two sides to it. One side is what we call the physical world, our natural habitat, the world that we can see, feel, hear and touch with our senses. But there is also another side to the web of life. This other side is what some call the Otherworld, a mysterious realm that we cannot perceive with our senses. It is the counterpart to the physical world. It is the realm where spiritual beings such as gods and angels, guardians and ancestors exist, and it is just as real as the physical world. As you will see in this book, human life doesn't end when we die to the physical world; it continues in other ways. Life exists on both sides of the worlds as the universal energy connecting all beings, whether they are physical or otherworldly.

The existence of the Otherworld is actually well known to us. We experience it when moments of mystical insight remind us of the unified fabric of reality: when we are uplifted by a sunset or by music, when lost friends are found, when we enter into the heart of nature, when we are quiet and the universe speaks to us. Sometimes we ignore these reminders of our connection and purposely fill time and space, passing from activity to activity, flooding the silence with music, filling the dangerous emptiness with busyness so that we don't have to consider the wider reality of our lives.

Both sides of the sacred web of life are just as real as the other; both sides create a single reality that is affected by and affects all of us. Like a piece of woven cloth, one side of reality cannot exist without the other or the whole fabric falls to pieces. But now we live in a time when many people are beginning to ignore one side of reality entirely, disbelieving the Otherworld's existence because they cannot see it.

The result of this disbelief is the escalation of psychic disturbance and a corresponding loss of skill to deal with it. Ancient boundaries and respectful ways of behavior that once kept us safe are being ignored. Those who believe in only the physical world and think that they have a single chance at life are behaving as if they were the masters of the universe, living without respect for other beings and not caring about the effect that they have upon the whole sacred fabric of life.

So it is really not surprising that holes are appearing in the universal web. Through these holes come the effects of our thoughtless behavior to bother and haunt us—effects that we call psychic disturbance. As we forsake the idea of a universe with both seen and unseen natures, we find we have correspondingly fewer tools to mend the holes. None of this may seem to have anything to do with you, but when such holes open up in your own life, it becomes a matter of some urgency to find the right tools for the job before you fall through the cracks yourself. It is at such times that you realize you have a soul as well as a body.

BODY AND SOUL

As human beings we each have both a physical body and an unseen soul. Just as the two-sided universe of physical world and Otherworld create one reality, so too our body and our soul together create the life we lead. Our body inhabits and perceives the physical world through our senses and instinct, while our soul is able to visit and perceive the Otherworld when we dream, imagine or envision. Our physical instinct is the prime watchdog of our bodily powers, while the perceptions of our soul guard the seat of our integrity. By ignoring these natural wardens of our well-being, we fail to see, sense and feel what is going on around us. This is how we come to suffer from psychic disturbance.

The word "psyche" means "soul." "Psychic" merely means "of the soul" and has nothing to do with prophetic insight, which is the way we usually use the word. You perceive with your soul or psyche through your imagination and insight. This is a normal, not an unnatural, ability. "Psychic disruption" is whatever unseats your soul from its accustomed ease and grace. Each cell in your body, each component of your soul, contains embedded information about your whole being. What hurts one part of your body or soul hurts all parts of your being. We need both bodily instinct and psychic or soul-perception to navigate this universe safely.

People say that we cannot see the soul, but you have seen it many times in others or been aware of its absence. It lives in the light of the eyes, in the demeanor of the body's bearing; it is manifest in the vigor and integrity of your deeds and their outcome. If you have viewed a dead body you understand the absence of soul. You have looked into the eyes of depressed friends and been aware of how less inhabited they appear—some part of their soul is absent. You have suffered at the hands of people without integrity of soul.

Bring to mind a recent incident about which you are still feeling troubled. Remember how you reacted in your body: maybe a dry mouth, balled-up fists, a tightening or fluttering in your middle. Remember how you felt: perhaps a sense of surprise, shock, upset or anger. Let your remembrance reach deeper. Did you have an inarticulate sense of betrayal, outrage, violation, fear or an overall sense of being unsafe? This was how your soul was reacting to the incident. Although you may lack a specialist terminology to talk about the soul, you possess a wealth of metaphor and story with which to speak and dream about your soul's experience. You might say that you were "sold down the river" when someone cheated you, or felt "under the weather" when something has depressed you, or were "hung out to dry" when someone broke their promise. Listen to yourself: in these metaphors, you are describing the state of your soul. Such descriptions may not be far from the truth when it comes to finding out just how and where the soul is.

Our body and soul share a physical and a metaphysical life. "Metaphysical" just means "that which transcends the physical." As your understanding of the connections between the body and soul mature, so you grow more alert to the causes of psychic disruption and wiser about what to do about it. And, in doing so, you will be preserving and respecting the life of the whole universe, not just your own life.

THE CAUSE AND EFFECT OF PSYCHIC DISTURBANCE

All around us, every day, we see how the short-term, expedient and greedy actions of people are endangering our world from the global and political level down to the local and personal. By failing to understand how our everyday world is but one side of reality, humankind finds the universe a confusing and dangerous place. Resistance to the Otherworld and to metaphysical reality impedes our understanding of cause and effect. How we deal with the challenges of physical reality must also be the concern of all who want to live more responsibly.

All deeds, thoughts and intentions have effects upon both physical and metaphysical sides of reality. By disregarding these, we cause, and suffer from, psychic disturbance. But how can we measure the unseen effect on our lives? Throughout this book are scattered many stories of people who have encountered psychic disturbance. You will notice that each of these stories has an epicenter from which shock waves ripple out like earthquake tremors, shaking everything in that person's life with psychic disturbance. This is the result of cause and effect—something we ignore far too often.

The ripples set up from unconsidered cause and effect are what are called psychic disturbance: these ripples hit the soul first, and when the soul is disturbed, we also experience physical symptoms. If you throw a brick at a window, the glass will shatter. The physical results are clearly demonstrable. But what happens when you harbor ill-will, jealousy or resentment against another person? The metaphysical effect is just as demonstrable. How does it manifest? Well, consider those who live on the receiving end of their neighbors' racist opinions. They will tell you that it makes them feel unsafe, wary, under threat. Such resentment is experienced by the soul as a feeling of threat and by the instinct as a feeling of insecurity.

By becoming impervious to the metaphysical side of reality, we have ceased to relate what subsequently results from our unguarded acts, words and thoughts to its causation. But becoming responsible for what we say, do, think and intend, as well as for the effects they bring, is the first step to bringing peace to our lives. It will prevent us from bringing psychic disturbance to others.

We cannot stop psychic disturbance from happening, but by tracing it back to the moment that the stone fell into the pool and started the ripple-spread that you now experience, you can begin to change things with the help of your Advocates (see page 20). Better still, you can prevent causing it in the first place. Like a chess player who considers the whole board before moving a piece, you can use these questions to help you determine how any of your plans or actions might affect the universe.

- From what motivation do my intentions arise?
- What are the consequences of my intended action?
- Who or what might it harm?
- How will these intentions affect me?
- Are my intentions motivated by someone else's needs, desires, or coercion?
- Who am I trying to please/impress by doing this?

See page 265 for some more questions that help determine your effect on the universe.

We all need soul-protecting strategies in ordinary everyday life. Adrift from our soul's core, we tend to cast about ourselves for solutions, often becoming prey to charlatans who are more psychically streetwise than we are. By noticing cause and effect, we grow wiser and more careful and we will harp less upon how sources of good and evil cause psychic disturbance.

GOOD AND EVIL

The power that gives life to the universe is neither good nor evil, it just is. However, when any part of that power is in the wrong place, we experience it as an evil. For example, the love of a mother for her son can be a wonderful thing, but if a mother smothers her child in a clinging web of suffocating love, the child may experience this as an intolerable evil.

The effects of people, things, events and actions can be seen as good or bad. An axe is neither good nor bad by itself, but we consider it "good" when used to cut firewood, and "evil" when wielded by a homicidal maniac. A child's death can be seen as tragic, but the death of an elderly person suffering terrible pain can be seen as a necessary good. However, death itself is neither good nor evil. Rain that falls on gardens is seen as good but showers that cancel the high school football game are seen as bad. You will note the use of "seen as," rather than "is." We cannot deal in dualistic language or unhelpful demonization because psychic protection must be grounded in truth, not in blaming. It is intention that gives us good and evil, not gods and demons. Unclear or self-serving intentions very often overstep boundaries and create very great evils, but to say that "the Devil made me do it" does not excuse us. The process of scapegoating—casting the blame upon others—becomes clear whenever we discuss psychic disturbance. It is always someone else's fault, never our own. Conveniently, we ignore the disruptions that we have caused or colluded with. See more in Chapter 9.

They say that the road to hell is paved with good intentions, as you may well testify if you've ever suffered the high-handed "help" of someone who decided something on your behalf and cut across your own free will. You are an agent whose intentions can heal or hurt. There are no purer-than-white victims and blacker-than-black perpetrators of psychic disturbance: we all make our contribution!

Among fundamentalist religions, there is only one good and evil, nothing in between. If you're not for God, then you must be for the Devil. However, fundamentalism is not just the province of major religions. The intolerable light of some manifestations of the New Age can be equally unsparing and unhelpful, creating deep shadows of inadequacy and complacency. We cannot live at either extreme of good or evil. We can only live in a state of balance, accepting that life is full of complexities and ambiguities, of pain as well as happiness. The first way to tackle psychic disruption is to attend to our own attitude to truth and illusion.

DISCERNING TRUTH FROM LIES

The nature of truth is a great mystery. One person's truth is not always shared by others. Some matters are universally true, such as the fact that we must breathe in order to live; but it is not true to say that everyone likes chocolate or playing badminton—these are subjective preferences.

Discerning illusion from reality is essential. You can check whether what you've been told or are experiencing is true or illusory because you have the dual sensors of bodily instinct and your conscience, which is your soul's inbuilt arbiter. However, experiential and subjective states are sometimes difficult to discern. Then you may need the good advice and support of close friends to help you verify and give you a reality check that paranoia hasn't warped your judgment.

- What are your first instinctive impressions (before you second-guess the issue)?
- Is it harmful to you or to others?
- Does it make you feel connected or disconnected from your center?
- Does it offer you an ethical, viable and sustainable means beyond this moment?
- Does it make you feel glad and quickened, or depressed and deadened?
- Are your thoughts and feelings about this your own or are they those of others?

WHO ARE YOU?

"So much of the harm we inflict on ourselves and others stems from the fact that we don't remember who we are," says dreamworker Robert Moss. Do you know who you are? If you don't, it's time to find out, because you can only protect something when you know its true nature. We are skilled at self-deceit, camouflaging our true nature even from ourselves. Some people have very low self-esteem and have trouble finding themselves because they have become eroded, while others have an ebullient, overassertive personality that may mask the fear within: these self-perceptions distort reality.

Regardless of how you define yourself, you are worthy of love and respect. That means having self-respect and holding to your deep center. If you evacuate the center of yourself, you risk inviting something to set itself up in your place; if you beat yourself up and denigrate yourself, you contribute to being self-divided. But if you can identify and value who you really are, your sense of self will help protect you from unwonted intrusions. Explore:

- How do you define/describe yourself?
- What is the essence of you?
- What makes you tick?
- What do you like about yourself?
- What do you not like about yourself?
- Are you the same person you were 10, 20, 30 years ago? In what ways are you currently changing?
- What of yourself do you show to others? What do you hide and why?

YOUR OWN CONNECTION TO THE UNIVERSE

In trying to define yourself and the space around you, you've probably discovered that many important facets of your life mirror back to who you really are. You are not alone in the universe. You are accompanied by those whom you love, the environment in which you live, your work and the things that make life worth-while, like music, books, sports, pets, friends, art, etc. Each of these important connections is a blessing in your life, giving you the gifts of love. The most connected people are the most resilient to psychic disturbance because each of these connections grounds them and holds them securely. Psychic disturbance most often affects those whose connections are few, those who feel solitary and sealed off from the universe, and those who have been violently parted from their connections by changing circumstances. Try this exercise:

1. In the middle of a large piece of paper, write your name. Draw lines radiating from it, making yourself the meeting place for all the major connections that meaningfully make you part of the universe. At the end of those lines write down what connects you strongly to the universe and contributes to your well-being (e.g., my mother, my horse, the tree in my yard, roses, cycling, my children, my husband, etc.).

2. Consider each of these connections from your own standpoint and appreciate what gift they each give you. Then consider yourself from the standpoint of each of the connections you've named: what gift do they receive from you? Look again at the questions above. How do you see yourself now?

3. What intelligence or spirit maintains life in all these connections? To whom or what do you turn for help when any of these connections is broken?

TAKING UP YOUR OWN SPACE: ENERGY FIELD AND AURA

Everyone has a unique space in the universe that they fill by reason of being alive. This space goes everywhere with you. When you feel expansive, it expands, when you feel threatened, it contracts. In congested cities, you draw your space closer; in the country, you let it unfold and breathe. This space has both physical and metaphysical existence about you because it is made up of both your instinctive energy field that surrounds your body and your aura that extends beyond it. You can feel in your energy field when someone is staring at you and also when someone is directing attention toward you from afar—you find yourself thinking about that person but often dismiss this thought as irrelevant. The space of your own energy field is your natural boundary. You can tell when someone invades it or when you have let down your protective defense because an internal alarm bell sounds. Your aura extends a little beyond your energy field and surrounds it. Your attitude is signaled in your aura and other people pick up whether you are confident or ashamed, strong or vulnerable. You don't have to be able to see auras to pick up someone's intentions and attitude.

Our unique space in the universe is shaped by the way we live, by actively engaging with life or by our passive attitude to it. There will be people who don't want you to assert your own space but who prefer you to be their victim, dependent or scapegoat. While you are harnessed to or in bondage to another person, you are not taking up your own space; someone else is taking up your space. Conversely, it is possible to swamp the space of others and over-whelm them by the sheer weight of your presence, ego or attitude. Sometimes you are so highly dependent upon a person or insti-tution that you are spared the trouble of filling your space at all. This is how you can become invisible in our society, disregarded and passed over because you have not attended to yourself, your connections or your boundaries.

- How do you fill your unique space in the universe? Describe this space to yourself. What shape, texture or quality does it have?
- Is your unique space larger or smaller than it was when you were young? What has changed this?
- What significant factors alter, warp or affect your spatial sense?
- Close your eyes, relax, breathe and be still. Become aware of your own personal space about you made up of energy field and aura. Extend that space a little to make more room. Now try contracting the space, bringing it closer to you. Find what is comfortable for you. When you have a strong sense of your personal space, experience its perimeter as sparkling, astral

electricity that runs continually. Explore the vitality of your space.

· Draw an outline of your body on paper. In another color, draw your energy field around it. In a different color draw your aura around the energy field. What is held in the space between your body outline and your energy field, or held between energy field and aura? Draw whatever impressions, symbols, objects and qualities that you envision or experience. Some of these belong there; others may not. See Chapters 3, 4 and 5.

CODE OF HONOR

One of the most important protections against being a source or vessel of psychic disturbance is to maintain and live by your core principles. If you know where you end and the rest of the universe begins, you will have established a key boundary to keep yourself and others safe. Compromising your core principles puts you in harm's way. Honoring them protects you. The way you keep your code of honor protects others as well as yourself.

Honor is a word we don't hear very often in our greedy, self-serving society. Upholding our personal code with honor helps us live harmoniously with our environment and not to be so fixated upon ourselves. Answer the following questions to discover what your code is. If you can't answer the first of each pair of questions, then answer the second of the pair first and you will find the boundary of your code:

1. How do you respect all forms of life? –In what ways do you wish others to respect you?

2. Which for you is the truth? –How do lies and dishonesty arising from others hurt you?

3. What actions, words, thoughts and intentions of yours give life? –How do the actions, words, thoughts and intentions of others give you death?

4. What central light do you live by? –What wisdom shines from within you?

5. Which rules of living are unbreakable in your code? –Which abuses against life most upset you?

6. What ways are personally best for you? –What ways must you avoid?

7. What motto or slogan or symbol exemplifies your personal honor? –With which mottos, slogans and symbols of others do you most resonate?

8. Which laws, principles and structures would you affirm/ abolish if you were empowered to govern your country? – Which laws, principles, structures need radical revision?

9. Where/in whom is your love bestowed? –From whom/where do you receive love?

10. In what ways do you serve the universe? –How does the universe serve you?

TEXT OF HONOR

Yuri, a recovering alcoholic with a severely addictive past, creates his own code of honor, keying it into his cell phone, where he can flash it up during the day to remind and encourage himself. Like a warrior in armor, he knows this code reinforces his protective boundary and keeps him safe from within as well as from without. Here it is:

1. Don't drink alcohol today.

2. Always speak and do the truth.

3. Keep my promises.

4. Take time to make decisions and not rush into things.

5. Don't buy things I don't need.

6. Avoid casinos and gambling.

7. Phone Jack when I feel old habits returning.

8. All life is sacred.

9. Put my children's welfare first.

10. Leave the world better than I found it.

BLUEPRINTS FOR BEING REAL

1. The whole universe shares one life.

2. Reality has two sides that are equally real: the physical and metaphysical.

3. Psychic disturbance affects the soul and the body.

4. Energy follows thought. What you intend is what you get.

5. When life-energy is in the wrong place, you experience it as evil.

6. We are all responsible for our actions, thoughts and intentions.

7. Your personal code of honor protects both yourself and others.

8. Taking up your unique space in the universe respects the life you live.

9. When you define yourself, you define your safe boundary.

10. Psychic protection is an ordinary skill for everyday life.

CHAPTER 2

Finding Spiritual Protectors

We are born with counterparts in other places and
times, and in other dimensions of reality. When we
encounter them through interdimensional travel,
they become allies and sometimes teachers.

—Robert Moss in *Conscious Dreaming*

KEYS TO THE SOURCE OF LIFE

Psychic protectors are able to work and live confidently because
they are supported by their spiritual protectors. When you want
to deal with psychic disturbance efficiently, you will also need
the insightful wisdom of spiritual protectors, as well as your own
human common sense.

We live in a time of spiritual fracture, where many people have
turned their backs on spiritual matters at the same time as jetti-
soning religion. But, at the same time, many are experiencing a
great spiritual longing for certainty and guidance. As a result of
the vacuum left by religion, many individual ways of exploring
spirituality have arisen, revealing that we can be people of spirit
without being religious. Whether you are at home in your spiritual tradition or whether you are exiled from it, whether you are
actively seeking a spiritual abode or are a spiritual nomad, does
not matter. For this book to be of most help to you, you need to
consider your view of and connection with the Source of Life.

The Source of Life has been called by many names and been
personified as a supreme divinity who is male, female, neither or
both. Our Source of Life is just that—a living source of vitality—not
vindictive, ready to punish or zap you. Imagine what is best and
most wonderful, an abiding presence that always accepts you the

same whatever the circumstances, and you have an understanding of your Source of Life. No one can be separated from the Source of Life, because each living organism shares its life. The life of the universe runs indivisibly on both sides of reality, throughout all things, and its central mainspring is balance, not punishment for sin. How have we lost this simple understanding? Our loss of the sacred, our misapprehension of the divine, are largely due to the relinquishing of spiritual power into authorized hands; it has become channeled down narrow and dogmatic teachings, which have diluted our view of the vitality of the Source of Life over centuries. But when we take back our spiritual vision under our own authority, we regain an authentic understanding; we find no punishing tyrant, but an unconditional love of life that accepts us the way we are. Some of us grew up with burdensome images of the divine or else experienced religion as guilt-provoking. We are sometimes separated from grace by fearful images, rather than fallen from it. Reconnection with the Source of Life heals us. Disconnection from it makes us separate and unhappy.

W. H. Auden wrote, "All imaginations do not recognize the same sacred beings or events, but every imagination responds to those it recognizes in the same way ... (with) a passion of awe." Spiritual affinity is formed by the attraction of resonant and like-souled beings. You must follow the spiritual way that is best for you. And although you may not be able to live under the influence of another's spiritual belief, yet most of us are agreed on the fundamental principles that maintain life: balance, truth, wisdom, understanding, mercy, justice, harmony, beauty, strength, inspiration and love.

Explore how you experience the Source of Life:

- What do you call and how do you understand or perceive the Source of Life?
- What outworn concepts, pictures, symbols, representations and qualities have obscured your view of the Source of Life? Let these go freely.
- What is your contract with life?

- What sacred duties maintain that contract?
- What harms or blocks that contract?
- Does your vision of the Source of Life have a name or symbol associated with it, even if you can't imagine it?

You may find it helpful to return to these questions and meditate upon them. The Source of Life itself may be a mystery too vast to be encompassed by your imagination, and you may find it easier to scale down your perspective and look nearer to where you are now. Please do not disconnect yourself from the religion or spiritual tradition you've been following if it provides you with the help and support that you need. Find ways of incorporating your core beliefs with the suggestions in this book, using your common sense as well as your inspiration. The guiding law of the Source of Life is harmony and balance. Whatever feels harmonious to us is also beautiful. When psychic disturbance strikes, your own sense of balance and harmony is lost, so it's essential then that you are able to locate a center of balance that will not fail you while you are readjusting yourself. The keys to your personal spiritual affinity with the Source of Life lie within and about you as reminders of where the door to your connection may be found.

- How do you envision the Source of Life? If you cannot find your Source of Life in a conventionally divine image, then look about you in the world and see what connects you most strongly to a sense of beauty and harmony. Maybe for you it's triggered by the sight of geese in flight, or perhaps it's found in the musical patterns of Bach's "Goldberg Variations"? The form doesn't matter, only that it gives you a sense of deep connection, inspiration and balance.
- Contemplate the nature of your connection to the Source of Life and allow this connection to provide you with a simple but powerful symbol. For example, if the wild geese move your soul, maybe your symbol is a chevron or V-shape that glows with power. This symbol is both the key to your soul and the way into the Sanctuary of Life.

A SPIRITUAL DONUT

Kerry's childhood Episcopalian faith fell away some time in her teens and she's felt no great connection to it since then. However, after a breakup with a particularly resentful boyfriend about whom she has nightmares, she feels unsafe and in need of spiritual protection. Alienated by conventional religious icons, she has no sense of a Source of Life. Looking at what moves her in nature, she immediately thinks of the cliff where she walks the dog and where she goes for cheering up. But how can this place become a key to the Sanctuary for her? Lighting a candle, she sits in meditation. Nothing comes, so she asks the cliff to show her what symbol it might take for this purpose. She has the impression of a piece of chalk with a hole in it. Opening her eyes, she draws a simplified symbol of what this looks like on paper—a bit like a donut. Dismayed, because this symbol doesn't feel very "spiritual" to her, she tries the Sanctuary meditation below. The piece of chalk very quickly turns into a pulsing shape of rainbow light. The donut symbol elongates and becomes a key to open the door. Inside the Sanctuary it feels so safe that she knows she will come here when she sleeps. The Source of Life feels all about her here. She now feels that her funny key to the Sanctuary is like the password to her computer files: no one's going to guess it or break in.

SANCTUARY OF LIFE MEDITATION

This meditation helps establish a presence in your life that will cast out fear and doubt. It can be done all at once or in parts if you wish. Practice it often in the good times so that it becomes easy to access in the bad times. If this is your first meditation, then use all your senses to experience what is happening; allow the meditation to unfold without worrying about whether you are making it happen. Repeat and let it build.

1. Close your eyes, relax, breathe and be still. Sense, see and feel the nature of your personal key-symbol to the Source of Life. Be aware of its unique quality and signature. Tune in to whatever makes it harmonious and beautiful. Now be aware of your key turning into light and color and shaping itself into an actual key within your hands. With this key you can

open the door to the Sanctuary of Life. Practice this a few times. When you finish, allow the key to return to its own form again and thank it for helping you.

2. Close your eyes, relax, breathe and be still. Sense, see and feel within your hands the key that you found before. Be aware of an urge within your key to find the door that it opens. It moves in your hand and draws you forward, like a divining rod straining toward water. Allow yourself to be led by your key, for it is only trying to come into contact with the source of harmony and beauty. It leads you to a door and the key leaps gladly from your hand into the keyhole.

3. Take your own time, breathe and gather yourself. Open the door only when it feels right for you. Experience what lies beyond the door, knowing that this place and presence is the Sanctuary of the Source of Life. All living beings are welcome here. In this place of supreme harmony and balance, you are held securely. Spend whatever time you need here.

4. If you are feeling vulnerable, ask for a beam of protective light from the Source of Life to fall about you, enclosing you in a mantle of light that is also loving and strong. This mantle of light offers you safety and protection in times of danger, reminding you of the Source of Life that keeps the universe in balance, and this Sanctuary beyond the door is where your soul can always go to be safe when you sleep. The mantle encloses your body, energy field and aura. Don the mantle of light wherever you are every day.

5. If you are feeling dirty or polluted, the mantle of light can become like a crystal shower of cleansing water that thoroughly removes residues and pollutions.

6. When you leave the Sanctuary, give thanks. Return through the door, wearing your mantle. Turn the key to close the door, taking the key back with you. As before, allow your key to return to its usual form, with thanks.

In this meditation, you may experience a distinct sense of presence rather than see a being. The Source of Life touches us each in different ways because we are all uniquely seeded with the gift of life. Spend a little time each day in communion with that feeling or presence and experience the difference in your life. Life loves life. You are included within that love, even though you may feel loveless and lonely now. But just as you when you spill mercury from a thermometer into a dish, and the little blobs of mercury gravitate toward each other to create a larger blob, so it is with us when we are scattered and separated. The Source of Life always loves and welcomes you back into balance because your soul is part of the eternal spirit. Love is nothing less than the union of spirit with another aspect of spirit. It calls and reaches out to us eternally and makes us whole once more in the sacred fabric of the universe.

SPIRITUAL BACK-UP

Whether you have a formal religious background or your own spiritual understanding of the universe or not, in psychic protection it is necessary to have spiritual back-up as well as physical support. You live in physical reality and cannot be fully conversant with metaphysical reality. For that you need Advocates or spirit friends who live in the Otherworld. We live in a spirit-filled universe that shares the vitality of the Source of Life. Within the Otherworld are other life forms that are not human: the spirits of nature, fairies, guardians of places, angels, gods and spirits, as well as what we may call ancestors—people who were once incarnate humans and who now live in the Otherworld as saints, wise ones, teachers and guides. Both sides of reality are populated by a variety of different life forms. And just as we choose to associate with those friends with whom we feel affinity in our world, so it is in the Otherworld. In daily life, we all make a conscious choice to be with or avoid certain individuals in a streetwise manner. This rule is exactly the same in metaphysical reality.

Recall, for a moment, when you first met someone who is now a good friend. How did you recognize this person as a potential friend? Was it the way she lit up and engaged with you? The way he naturally understood you? Probably what you both experienced was a mutual recognition of the other, a sense of soul-likeness. The way we recognize our spiritual back-up team is exactly the same. It is a friendship waiting to be recognized.

Everyone—even people with no spiritual beliefs—have spirit-companions and protectors who are sources of spiritual help and nurture. This friendship may manifest in our lives as a love of music or nature, an abiding trust in a deceased relation or a sense of guidance from a saint or angel. Spiritual protectors may include divinities, ancestors, angels and spirits of place or nature. By identifying our spirit protectors, we will discover how they can help us deal calmly and effectively with all that disturbs our peace. Such spirit protectors are your Advocates, those who have your soul's good at heart and who may also act as your soul's teachers. We may have many such Advocates.

When experiencing psychic disturbance, the sense of being separate and isolated can be overwhelming. You may long for someone to help you but be intimidated by fear of mockery into concealing your problem. It is inadvisable to deal with your problem alone without an Advocate to accompany you. An Advocate acts as an active messenger and protector as well as giving you the equivalent of a rearview mirror to be aware of helps and dangers when your own sight lines are restricted.

For some people, the notion of spirits or otherworldly life forms is the stuff of horror stories because they have been told that all unauthorized spirits are wrong. Religions tend to emphasize just the heavenly inhabitants while horror stories only focus upon the dead and upon demons, werewolves and other ghastly denizens. The Otherworld is not so black and white. Because it is part of the total fabric of life, it houses spirits of many kinds and conditions. The ones we want to associate with are those who have loving affinity with us.

Becoming spiritually streetwise means recognizing spirit friends and discriminating just who shares soul-affinity with you. If you have a profound religious faith, then you will undoubtedly strengthen your bonds of friendship with major figures of your faith, inviting Jesus, Moses, Mary, Mohammed, Saint Francis, your guru, your teacher or whoever walks with you to protect you. If you have no clear sense of who your Advocates are, then be assured that you too have a spiritual back-up team and that you are authorized at any time to ask for the help that you need. You have only to ask. You can call on your Advocate when you feel in danger, such as when walking through troubled streets, when you wake and sleep, when you want to share something wonderful, when you need help or advice, or when you need inspiration and encouragement.

We become visible and present to our Advocates when we pray or meditate, when we turn our minds and hearts and souls toward them. They become present to us through our imaginations, taking forms that will be resonant with our understanding.

FINDING A GUARDIAN ADVOCATE MEDITATION

Every human being needs at least one friend. In combating psychic disturbance, we need both human support and metaphysical assistance. Many cultures believe that the individual soul has a companion or guardian angel who acts as an Advocate. To find your Guardian Advocate, use this meditation. Advocates can take many different forms, such as the spirit of a tree, plant, animal, wise ancestor, mythological being, angel or other spirit. But it will not be someone now living.

1. Close your eyes, relax, breathe and be still. Focus on your energy field and aura about you, expanding and contracting it until you are comfortable. Bring to mind a place in nature where you are completely at home and happy. While remaining within your own space, experience that special

place before you. Say, "In the name of the Source of Life, I call upon my Guardian Advocate to please meet me here."

2. Sense, see and feel what happens next, without trying to direct what happens or imagining a result. Stay neutral and attentive. If someone or something shows up, ask, "Are you my Advocate?" You may sense, understand or hear answers. On first view, you may not have a clear sense of your Advocate's features, but tune into the quality of how he or she feels and seems to you. Your Guardian Advocate may or may not give its name. Ask, "How am I to address you?"

3. Ask, "If you are my Guardian Advocate, please give me help/advice about [whatever is troubling you]." Note this advice or help, apply it if it feels appropriate and see if it is useful. This will help build trust between you. Don't write off the advice as the product of your own brain. In further meditations, get to know your Advocate more. You may also find others ready and willing to befriend you. It is possible to have more than one Advocate.

4. If you experience something that frightens or challenges you, stay within your energy field and make the astral perimeter of your aura crackle with sharp, warning light, like an electrical fence. Call upon the Source of Light to help you meet your Advocate and don the mantle of light.

5. Thank your Guardian Advocate for showing itself. Return to your own time and place, reestablish your ordinary consciousness. Note down your experiences.

6. Repeat this meditation until it becomes familiar. If you don't find an Advocate the first time, don't give up. Keep asking it to show itself.

ANGEL BY THE WELL

Shannon's background is Baptist and although she has strayed from its fold, this faith still unconsciously informs her life. Since she was a little girl, she has had the sense of a guardian angel nearby to whom she addresses quick "help me" prayers when she has difficulties. But now some unpleasant and rowdy neighbors make her life hell, driving her to seek out a more personal and conscious relationship with her guardian. Her favorite place is a holy well about five miles away where she often goes to sit and think. Closing her eyes, she brings this place to mind so strongly that she can feel the cold stones where the water gushes out and hear the bees in the nearby flowers. She calls upon her Guardian Advocate to meet her here. Nothing much happens at first, but she begins to be aware of a presence that makes her feel safe. It is more of a feeling than a seeing. She meditates two or three times, experiencing this same feeling of safety before she begins to be aware of a male figure who looks like a wingless angel. He has a vigorous aspect, not like a vapid stained glass angel at all. She asks if he's her Guardian Advocate and he nods his head, saying, "Yes, I've been with you a long time."

The answers happen deep inside Shannon. She asks his name, and he replies, "Call me Michael." She then asks for help with her neighborly dispute. "Don't deal with it alone," he tells her. "Inform the police. Before you sleep, call on me and I will be on watch. When you have to pass your neighbors on the street, I will be at your side." Her Advocate has given her permission to seek help; without this encouragement, Shannon might have just put up with the unpleasantness. The police monitored the situation; after receiving complaints from other neighbors and an incident involving officer intervention, the rowdy family is evicted from Shannon's neighborhood a few months later. Shannon formally accepts Michael as part of her life, one who is always there to help and encourage her.

DISCERNMENT OF SPIRITS AND FREE WILL

"Question the spirits to see if they be of God" is St. James's good advice to anyone who explores the world of spirit. Recognizing who our Advocates and companion spirits are is a big step to finding help and support in metaphysical matters. Always remember that it is love and affinity that draw us together. Never believe that you must be subject, docile, overly reverential, unquestioning or frightened in the presence of your Advocates. As a human being, you retain your free will at all times. This means the ability to say yes or no to things. Streetwise psychic protection begins with respecting your own free will.

Our true Advocates and allies have no agenda to enforce upon us. They only want our good. They do not coerce, persuade or intimidate us. They will also give us space and leave us alone unless we actively ask for their help or intervention. They do not ask us for anything in return, but, as with all friendships, you will want increasingly to bestow your trust and affection on your Advocates for the love they have shown you. This is how friendships are forged over time. Until that trust is formed, use your discernment wisely. You will encounter other Advocates of yours through this book. Use the checklist below to help you discern any new ones you meet:

- Ask if the being before you is your Advocate. If it isn't, it will probably go, or ignore you.
- Ask your Advocate for the help you need and check the results.
- If your Advocate suggests something you disagree with, challenge it and ask how such advice would be useful.
- Question your Advocate and discuss any course of action before taking it.
- Do not give yourself into the hands of any spirit without challenging its identity and intentions.
- Do not assume a passive or unquestioning attitude.

This advice holds good for all encounters with Otherworldly beings. It is by these means that we tell friend from enemy.

SHRINES AND RITUALS

In combating psychic disturbance, it is helpful to have a focal point in your own home where your spiritual back-up team has its physical abode. This is especially important when you are feeling displaced, fearful, suspicious or panicky. A shrine is the physical seat or dwelling for a spirit. Create a shrine for your Source of Life to help that presence become stronger to you and in you. Make a space for it in your house. You only need a clean shelf or surface. Place something on your shrine that represents your Source of Life—an object that you associate with your source. It doesn't have to be representational, nor does it have to offend or upset others. Light a candle or tea light in a secure holder and spend a little time each day in the presence of the source. The flame itself can act as symbol of the Source of Life. If you have a fireplace, it may be that your hearth becomes the shrine—the warmth around which everyone can gather.

Throughout this book, there are ritual outlines that help you implement the changes and healing that you need. By performing rituals we acknowledge and consciously enter into a unified reality where we ask for and affirm the help of our spiritual Advocates, confirming our desire and need for change and making the pathway down which it comes into our world. Your intentions will also feel more concrete when you do these simple intentioned acts. Of course, by performing ritual you are acknowledging that there is an Otherworld, and that may be challenging for you, especially if you formerly believed no such thing. But by creating a shrine and by performing ritual and meditation, you are making real the Otherworldly help that will protect you from psychic disturbance.

SHOWING UP—REPETITION AND THE ART OF PERSEVERANCE

Whatever you want to achieve in life, whether it is learning a foreign language, reforming a bad habit or getting to know someone, you have to show up. Perseverance and persistence are sadly neglected in our society where everything is about instant gratification. Showing up is being faithful to yourself, to the Source of Life, to your Advocates and to your own code of honor. It is one of the major weapons in your arsenal. Laziness, neglect, inertia and giving up easily without effort are human weaknesses. Your own faithfulness heals the self-betrayals that you have inflicted upon yourself.

It is said that we need to repeat something at least twenty times in order to establish a new habit or to help erode and replace an old one. In the work of psychic protection, repetition is your friend. Don't be lured by novelty into neglecting the practices you have begun.

"The world of the spirits is not a place, but a frequency," writes shaman Daan Van Kampenhout. If we keep tuned into the frequency of our spiritual allies, we will always receive clear transmission in times of trouble.

BLUEPRINTS FOR SPIRITUAL CONNECTION

1. You cannot be separated from the Source of Life.

2. You have spiritual Advocates who protect your soul and well-being.

3. Connection with spiritual protectors will give you back-up against psychic disturbance.

4. Your unique connection to the Source of Life is a dedicated waveband that you alone are wired to pick up.

5. Your personal understanding of the Source of Life is authentic. No one can alter or deny this.

6. Advocates are recognized by their soul-affinity with you.

7. Ask for the help you need from your Advocates.

8. Trust between you and your spiritual protectors increases with time and use.

9. Meditation becomes clearer through practice and repetition.

10. You contribute to the well-being of the planet by the way you live.

CHAPTER 3

Streetwise Psychic Protection

With limited knowledge and distorted
perceptions of the spirit world, many people
leave themselves open, creating their own
vulnerability as part of creating their own reality.

—William J. Baldwin in *Healing Lost Souls*

BEING STREETWISE TO THE PRESENT

This chapter gives you some fundamental psychic first-aid strategies to help keep you focused and protected. If they seem basic or obvious to you, don't discard them because of that. The most helpful strategies are simple and undramatic, and we forget to use them at our peril.

To protect ourselves most efficiently from psychic disturbance we must be on the ball. If we continually allow our consciousness to lapse into a trance, we may well stray into dangerous regions. Staying alert and paying attention to what is going on will help prevent us from causing or encountering psychic disturbance. Living unconsciously, wandering through life like cows monotonously chewing the cud in a meadow, we can create the optimum conditions for psychic disturbance. Our unguarded living becomes a playground for opportunists, intrusions and power-thieves.

Where do we go when we drift off? Most often it is somewhere else in time. We are often so busy living in the past or fearfully or hopefully anticipating the future, we lose the present moment. We cease to be streetwise in that very moment. For some people, the present moment feels scary and so they hide in the past or future. Impatience is the thief of the present. It will lead you into the future.

For the course of one day, keep a log of just how you focus your consciousness. How much time did you spend daydreaming, being unfocused, self-absorbed, unconscious of what was going on around you? How much of you runs on automatic? What internalized concerns are continuously claiming your attention? What things trigger your distraction? Which old scenarios keep claiming your attention? What future events are distracting you from the present moment? Spend five minutes practicing being in the present moment. Extend this for longer periods each day. If you zone out on trips or in meetings, when you're bored or tired, then make sure that you alert your Advocate to be on guard and warn you when to come back online. Make regular self-checks and reality checks at intervals throughout the day. Practice engaging totally with what you're doing. Take downtime at times and in places when you can control your circumstances.

SELF-CHECK

We all like to look in the mirror before we step out of the door to ensure that we are tidy and presentable. This self-check does the same thing for your state of being. Perform it regularly and it will become just as habitual.

- How is your breathing? Reenergize by breathing more deeply.
- Where is the tension held in your body? Breathe, stretch, massage or exercise it out.
- Are you centered in your body? Become aware of where your consciousness currently is.
- How are you feeling emotionally? What emotions have you suppressed or which are riding you?
- What is your mind doing? Be aware of what subtextual concerns are filling your mind.

REALITY CHECK

Learn to focus on what's going on around you, so that at any given moment, you can discern what different signals you're receiving:

- What is going on right now? What's the story here?
- What undercurrents, tensions, dynamics or anxieties am I experiencing here?
- What is irritating or worrying me?
- What warning signs are my instincts telling me about?
- What lies, half-truths, illusions and fantasies are at play here?
- Who is causing me to act up, exaggerate, be submissive or uncooperative?
- Whose plan, opinion or mind game am I colluding with or combating?
- What is causing resistance in me?
- How am I being true to my code of honor (page 17)?

A LUCKY ESCAPE

Brian bought a new red Mini Cooper, even though he'd had many dreams warning him about a fatal accident in such a car. Brian was lucky that his Advocates were on alert: he only managed to drive three miles from the dealership before the new car broke down. When he returned to pick up the car, it had been stolen. He arrived at our session boiling over with rage, having had to catch a bus. Brian had never considered dreams seriously, thinking they were all nonsense. However, after assessing what was going on and the way in which he continually risked his life every day by way of mind games of "do or die," he felt a lot better about the car's loss. When I asked if he had felt any qualms when paying for it, he nodded reluctantly: he had chosen to ignore his instinct. We both felt he'd had a lucky escape.

INSTINCT

If you ask most people whether they knew they were making a bad decision at the time, a large proportion will tell you "yes." Their instinct warned them and they chose to ignore it, like Brian.

Awareness of our instinct is on the wane, as we forget that we are human animals. Instinct is the doorbell that rings when trespassers approach. It is that gut feeling that we have been violated in some indefinable way that makes us sick to our stomachs. If intention is the key to the door, then instinct is the doorbell. If our intentions are unclear and our instincts out to lunch, then our door is wide open for others to cross the threshold.

We human animals are not so instinctively alert as our creaturely cousins who can detect adverse weather patterns, fires and earthquakes long before we can. Being psychically streetwise means listening more deeply to the subtle messages of our body and soul instead of ignoring or discounting these signals that are almost outside the range of our contemporary indifference.

Of course, our normal sensory array can become faulty if we are fearful, ill, hormonally imbalanced, under the influence of alcohol or drugs, or suffering mental disturbance. These conditions can distort our experience and mask our instincts. The more out of alignment with reality we are, the more distorted our experiences. If this is the case with you, look at the grounding procedures on page 37.

The infinitesimal messages that you receive to take an unscheduled diversion when you're driving, the reminder to take an umbrella or to buy an extra bag of flour at the supermarket usually turn out to have been true. Remember, if we can't pick up and act on these seemingly unimportant signals, then we will be equally unable to distinguish the lifesaving instruction to catch a later train and avoid the accident or to move from the spot we're standing at where the steel girder is about to fall. Distinguishing instinctive signals may save your life or at least avert a great deal of trouble.

- Today note down any subliminal instinctive messages you pick up on and check them against what subsequently happened.
- Note how you experience instinctive signals in your body, soul and mind: what sensations, impressions or thoughts accompany them?

• During your self-check, try setting up a low frequency boundary around you by visualizing an electrical charge surrounding you. This will help you catch instinctive signals more easily.

LOST IN SPACE

Elaine was a woman with multiple serious problems who had spent the best part of her life in the Otherworld rather than in this one. After our first, rather heavy session, I suggested that she do something gently grounding for the rest of the day—to walk in the park or read an enjoyable book. Later that night she phoned back, saying she'd felt too tired to do much and she'd been reading. "Something good?" I inquired. "Meditating the Qabalistic Tree of Life," she replied, "I've just got to path twenty-two." I suppressed a groan. Elaine was so used to being out of her body that she had no idea of how to be in it. She'd just turned to a metaphysical book, which would help her vacate her body all over again. We spent the next hour discussing what grounding really meant.

GROUNDING PROCEDURES

For people like Elaine, who have suffered violations and dangers, being out of the body is a natural state because it feels safer. A significant portion of their souls (see below) has learned how to find safety away from assault, which is a legitimate way to survive when your body is endangered. They usually have a safe place to go. But they have a tendency to "live beside themselves." Before we explore psychic disturbance in detail, let's focus on how we come down to earth and ground ourselves. Use one or more of these to ground you:

- Do the self and reality checks (see above).
- Practice your well-being breathing pattern (see below).
- Bring your mind back to your body by concentrating on physical sensation. Fuse your mind with your body.
- Recall your purpose and intention.
- Be aware of the connections that keep you centered in the universe (see page 14).
- If you're overtired, rest or sleep.

- Eat some substantial food, drink something warming.
- Clap your hands, stamp both feet.
- Walk in nature, being aware of yourself in your environment.
- Do some mechanical or repetitive task that involves your body (weeding, cooking, addressing envelopes). Concentrate on what and how you are doing it.
- Speak to a friend on the phone and get another reality check from your friend.
- Leave off all metaphysical practices except your core spiritual practice.

We were all born with our common sense, but when psychic disturbance is escalating along with fear or panic, we can engage in extreme forms of behavior that don't help us. Here are a few reminders that will ground you. Remember that changing and healing isn't an "instant fix" but arrives by incremental steps over time. You will need to return to this list a few times. These common-sense measures will help you deal with the confusion of psychic disturbance:

- Don't struggle or deal with things alone. Get help.
- Challenge and question rather than be passive toward circumstances, environments or people. Blind acceptance endangers.
- When seeking advice, choose whatever is best for you, and suits your nature, character and preferences.
- Practice being in your body, not floating beside it or always daydreaming. Do some exercise or see a cranial therapist to help ground you.
- Stop ill-wishing or detracting others by gossip.
- Deal with problems appropriately and pragmatically, starting first with the frontline approach: so take criminal matters to the police, addictions to addiction support, family fallouts to family counselors, etc.

- Don't try and heal all ills only by psychic or magical means; draw upon other, more ordinary forms of support in addition.
- When consulting a healer, psychic or diviner or someone qualified to help your psychic problem, do not try to combine different strategies or to follow the advice of more than one person at a time.
- Sometimes you just need to talk to someone you can trust such as a close friend or a counselor.

BREATH OF LIFE

Breath is the primary sign of vitality. Fear and panic go straight to the breath, so learn to breathe in ordinary, peaceful times and you will be able to manage times of fear better. There are significant connections between brainwave frequencies and rates of breathing, as you will see below. The quicker and more shallow your breath, the less able and more scattered you will feel: the deeper and slower your breath, the more connected and resourceful you will be. Our customary breathing pattern is present in active attention, but also present in states of tension, anxiety and alarm. It corresponds to the beta brainwave frequency over 13Hz. This breathing pattern ties up energy, making you feel heavy and apathetic. We usually breathe to this pattern: Inhale ½–1; Hold in 0; Exhale ½–1; Hold out 0. These numbers refer to a moderate counting, not to seconds of time.

To energize and cleanse yourself, breathe out, exhaling all that is stale and fearful to detox your body. Breathe in the radiant vitality of the universe to revitalize you. Experience all in-breaths as coming from the Source of Life. Exhale all fear and panic on your out-breaths. Practice in your spare moments. Deepen it by imagining your breath coming in and out through every pore of your body. This is better than a shower! Each of the breathing patterns below has a fourfold pattern of inhalation, holding the breath in, exhalation and holding the breath out. Don't strain at these. Ensure when you practice your breathing that your torso is upright and supported so that your diaphragm is able to control your lungs. Keep your shoulders low and don't strain with your throat or neck. Focus on the source of your breathing as coming from your deep belly rather than from your upper chest. Practice some of the following breath rhythms:

- Well-Being Breath helps regulate pain and get control of panic, which corresponds to alpha brainwave frequency 8–13Hz, giving relaxation and well-being, and making you alert and balanced: Inhale 8; Hold in 8; Exhale 8; Hold out 4.
- Positive Breath helps you start trusting your own perceptions and transmutes negative doubts into positive energy, which mixes alpha and theta brainwaves of 6–10Hz: Inhale 4; Hold in 8; Exhale 8; Hold out 4.
- Creative Breath helps you connect powerfully with creativity, intuition and allies, corresponding to theta brainwaves 4–8Hz, associated with hypnagogic imagery experienced on the verge of sleeping, reverie, drowsiness: Inhale 4; Hold in 8; Exhale 16; Hold out 4.
- Sleep Breath helps give quiet sleep and trustful dreams, resulting in delta brainwaves below 4Hz: Inhale 4; Hold in 8; Exhale 32; Hold out 4.

Visualize breathing in through all the pores of your skin. If you are in pain, visualize breathing air into that part of your body. On your out-breath, sigh or sing a single tone.

THE MULTIPLE SOUL

Psychic disruption is the displacement or loss of soul, or else an invasion taking place in the soul. Whenever we experience a sense of abnormality in which something is either missing from our being or something alien has become part of it, we feel that something has gone or something unwelcome has come. This may be accompanied by feelings of intense unease, self-doubt, fear or panic. Psychic disruption is about change or confusion in the soul: it may originate from without or from within ourselves.

How can it be possible to lose your soul? So far we have talked about the soul in the singular, but in traditional shamanic cultures, soul is understood to have multiple parts. To keep things simple, I offer the following definition based upon my own shamanic experience. If this doesn't fit your own beliefs, please treat it as a working model that helps gives shape and focus to the parts of your soul that may be susceptible to psychic disruption.

1. **Vital or Animal Soul** is associated with the lower body, below the solar plexus. It governs vitality and physical health, and its mode of understanding is the sensations, with instinct as its chief faculty. Its metaphysical counterpart is usually an Advocate in animal form, an animal companion. After death, the Vital Soul returns to the well of souls from which all life forms draw their cellular memory. Encoded in the Vital Soul are the memories of nature, landscapes of power and the modes of survival. The Vital Soul is active in every person born. Children's souls retain a lively connection with the Otherworld until their fontanelles (soft spots) close up, around age five to seven; it's noticeable from the way they possess a spontaneous innocence, sense of wonder and creative play. The way in which the Vital Soul is nurtured in childhood is very important in the subsequent development of the individual. Some people mostly inhabit their Vital Soul and try to ignore the other parts. They feel closed down and uninterested in metaphysical things.

2. **Personal or Ancestral Soul** is associated with the upper body, between throat and solar plexus. It governs emotional and psychic health, and its mode of understanding is the emotions, with imagination as its chief faculty. Its metaphysical counterpart is an Advocate in humanoid or other spiritual form. After death the Personal Soul returns to ancestral realms in the Otherworld, becoming an Ancestral

Soul and may be encountered by others as an ancestor with a distinct personality. Encoded within the Ancestral Soul are the personality traits formed by life experience, the memories of the bloodlines, the family gifts and evolving patterns of maturity. The Personal Soul has to be awakened and matured. This usually happens through the initiation of the emotions, which render us more sensitive and aware. It begins to develop its capacity when the fontanelles begin to close up, and goes on maturing until our early thirties when it is mainly formed by life experience. The extent to which we engage our creativity in daily life is an important factor for the Personal Soul, as are the life experiences of love, sorrow, joy and pain.

3. **Wisdom or Eternal Soul** is associated with the head. It governs wisdom and spiritual health. Its mode of understanding is through thought and the spiritual intelligence or conscience, with insight as its chief faculty. Its metaphysical counterpart is the Advocate who takes the form of a wise teacher. After death, the Wisdom Soul reincarnates into other forms, retaining certain memories, gifts and dispositions, which may accumulate or be forgotten, according to the use made of these gifts in the next or former life. The Wisdom Soul encodes the eternal soul's spiritual mission or life purpose, which will reincarnate in order to manifest through many lives. The Wisdom Soul is present at birth but dormant until we actively begin to seek our spiritual path and our connection to the Source of Life. This isn't necessarily when we join a religion but when we begin to seek our spiritual direction! The Wisdom Soul may be so deeply sheathed in some people that they never fully recognize it. Some discover their Wisdom Soul in their teens or later in middle life. There's often a sense between the ages of thirty to sixty of something taking root that feels "new." This is the germination of the Wisdom Soul leading to a full flowering,

when people often experience a deep connection to their life's purpose.

Some people refer to the Wisdom Soul as the "Higher Self," but I don't care for this superior term. All our souls are fully meshed within us and each is as important as the other. We all continually receive flashes of insight from the Wisdom Soul, which illuminates how we see the world; this is what people call "mystical experience." In rare individuals, all three souls are active in such a way that they are recognized by spiritual mentors as "enlightened ones."

The physical locations associated with the souls are resonant with the kinds of signals our bodies make when our souls suffer disturbance. Thus, we may press our hands to belly, heart or head when distressed with psychic disturbance. These bodily locations are validated by diverse traditions from ancient Ireland to Chinese Taoist belief.

You will notice that each different soul part has its metaphysical counterpart in the Otherworld. Since every part of the universe shares a common life, it is not surprising that our multiple soul is supported by an Advocate appropriate to its condition. Advocates uniquely resonate with each soul part.

The idea of a multiple soul helps us answer the common question about how it is possible to metaphysically contact ancestors who must surely have reincarnated in another life by now! With this model, you can see how part of the soul becomes ancestral and another part becomes reincarnated. So, as a pianist, you might seek to contact the Ancestral Soul of Mozart and receive his instruction, but you might be unable to locate the reincarnated Wisdom Soul of Mozart who may now be rejoicing in a new life.

After death, the multiple soul divides, rather like a space shuttle taking off from Earth. The Vital Soul is our power-pack and returns to the pool of life. The Personal Soul goes to swell the ranks of the ancestral guardians and becomes an Ancestral Soul. The

Wisdom Soul alone voyages on to its destination. See Chapter 15 for more about the soul after death.

HOW PSYCHIC DISTURBANCE AFFECTS OUR MULTIPLE SOUL

How we manage our souls enables us to live better lives and avoid entanglements and confusions. But because most people are unaware of how they are behaving, believing and relating, psychic disturbance can affect our multiple soul in distinct ways:

The Vital Soul draws upon the physical nurture of our environment and is responsible for our physical vitality. It is susceptible to power-loss, power-theft and invasion of its space. We will deal more particularly with these problems in Chapter 4.

The Personal Soul draws upon the emotional nurture of relationships with people in our lives as well as upon creative sources that feed the soul's life purpose and ancestral factors. It is susceptible to influences, intrusions and soul-theft. We will deal with these problems in Chapters 5 and 11.

The Wisdom Soul draws upon the Source of Life and the Otherworld for its nurture and seeks to experience participation in wise living and spiritual practice. It is that inviolate part of our soul that cannot be injured, cajoled or deceived. However, there are some circumstances when we can hazard our eternal soul: specifically when we willfully break our contract with the Source of Life and betray fellow creatures and beings. The chief law of the Source of Life is balance. In order to make good, we must come into balance. This is why the path of reincarnation is often seen in the East as the path of karma or the cleansing balance, which must result from unheeded cause and effect. The Source of Life is wise and loving, but also just and merciful, and gives opportunity for those who have hazarded their Wisdom Soul. Those who have broken their contract of life must return to mend it through the course of life itself. Only the Source of Life can bring balance. Our main task is the balanced regulation of our own lives—not the lives of others. See Chapter 15 for more on reincarnation.

Fragments of our Vital and Personal Souls can stray off, become lost, wander aimlessly, become stuck, predate, stalk, possess or become detached from us. We cannot deal with more serious aspects of soul-loss, which go beyond self-help, here, but throughout this book, you will find practices that help you manage your souls and become more aware of them.

VULNERABILITY THRESHOLDS

Our susceptibility to psychic disturbance is increased when we cross any of the following vulnerability thresholds. These create cracks in our boundaries through which we may lose power and soul, become susceptible to energy intrusion or both.

- Stress
- Sexual or violent abuse
- Overstimulation
- Sudden psychic awakening
- Failure to make regular self- or reality checks
- Coercion of or by others
- Indecisiveness
- Illness
- Insufficient information
- Bereavement
- Imagination run wild
- Accidents
- Blind acceptance of face value
- Betrayal
- Expediency
- Hospitalization
- Laziness
- Loss of job
- Neglect of boundaries
- Sudden shocks
- Fear of losing face
- Addictions
- Immaturity of soul
- Traumatic episodes
- Apathy and inertia
- Assault or violence
- Defeatism
- Extreme emotional upset
- Compromise
- Exhaustion
- Depression

SYMPTOMS OF PSYCHIC DISRUPTION

The following checklist includes the major symptoms accompanying psychic disruption. Keep a log of your own experiences. If you have fewer than five symptoms, study the strengthening strategies in this book. If you have five or more, then it is time to deal with the problem. If you have eight–ten, look at Chapter 5 and take action. More than ten, you should go and see a shaman or psychic healer and seek assistance.

- Sense of impending dread, oppression or groundless fear.
- Vitality depletion, nervous exhaustion, soul disquiet.
- Disrupted sleep patterns—sleeping like the dead, unable to sleep, nightmares.
- Heightened sensitivity to more than daily reality.
- Feeling empty or hollowed out.
- Feeling full, burdened or seething with too much stuff.
- Dulling of senses.
- Ache in the solar plexus as if you were being hollowed or sucked out.
- Doing things involuntarily or contrary to your normal preferences.
- Marked and uncharacteristic changes of behavior.
- Lack of interest in daily life.
- Sense of aimless drifting.
- Sense of indifference to anything.
- Inability to gather the scattered self together.
- Memory blanks of significant magnitude, not just forgetting a word or name.
- Anxiety or depression that comes on suddenly without known cause.
- Uncharacteristic desires or cravings.
- Addictive behavior.
- Drastic mood swings; being up, then down.
- Sense of inner voice or compulsion urging you to do things against your will.

- A succession of low-grade illnesses or ailments, which never clear up after decisive treatment.
- A pattern of disturbance that recurs at the same time of day, week or month.
- Serial sequences of things going wrong, runs of bad luck.
- Being overwhelmed or fearful of others and their influences.
- Fearful of being alone.

Many of the symptoms above can be caused by ordinary, physical conditions entirely unrelated to psychic disturbance, such as being overtired, long periods of stress and isolation or temporary detachment from normal life patterns. Check carefully before leaping to the wrong conclusions.

IMAGERY, METAPHOR AND THE IMAGINATION

What we think of as imagery and metaphor often expresses the truth as we experience it, but we will often discount or ignore this vital information because we have been taught to distrust the imagination. This book has many practices that encourage you to use your imagination as a strong searchlight. Use all your senses to perceive what you are being told or shown; don't just try to visualize. Learning to trust the imagination is based upon using it and finding how it can help you. If your imagination is a fantasy-factory, go to Chapter 7 to find helpful models.

Literal-mindedness will not help you here. Engage with the metaphor, the image, the feeling, the inkling that is just within your grasp. Use your subtle senses, not your everyday senses. Follow the story or scenario that's unfolding within you. If an understanding forms in your mind, or a sense grips your body, follow its meaning without shouting it down with your disbelief. You and your senses are a valid source of wisdom. You don't need to depend on experts to trust and validate your understandings.

A very good source of core images and metaphors arise in your dreams, which you should regard as a primary source of diagnostic information about your psychic condition.

Sometimes the stories that we tell ourselves merely reinforce the disturbance. See Chapters 7 and 8 for ways of dealing with this.

PSYCHIC ATTACK

Dion Fortune was one of the few metaphysical writers to inquire into the motivation for a genuine psychic attack. In *Psychic Self-Defense* she wrote: "If a person can offer no valid explanation as to the reasons for the attack that is being made upon him, nor as to its cause or origin, we can probably rest assured that it originates in his own imagination." Psychic attack can't come out of nowhere. It has to have an origin from outside of you, and you must have done something or been involved in something to merit such attention. You must ask yourself:

- Who resents you or your attitude?
- Whom have you offended?
- Who envies your gifts or achievements?
- What were you doing, thinking or planning when psychic disruption began?
- In other words, precisely who and what caused this psychic disturbance?

Where do psychic attacks emanate from? Who makes them and why? Western society is not exactly top-heavy with sorcerers and spell-crafters, although there are certainly many people who wish to manipulate the universe for their own purposes, but they aren't necessarily sorcerers. Sorcerers are those who manipulate the universe in personally beneficial ways for themselves or for others who pay them. Ethical metaphysicians—people who engage in spiritual transactions, like shamans, healers, magicians—cooperate with the universe to bring balance.

Psychic disturbance generally arises from the displacement of the flow of life caused by ordinary people who are resentful, want to have their own way or to get even. Most times, such disturbance is not even malicious, so much as careless and thoughtless. Genuine psychic attack of a sorcerous nature has to be laid with malicious intention and be maintained with energy. Most people do not know how to do this or sustain it, as it is exceedingly draining for anyone to keep this up over a long period. People do not need to be sorcerers or skilled in magic to ill-wish you. Even members of your own family who love you may be capable of causing psychic disturbance inadvertently by continually crashing through your personal boundaries, by obsessing about something in your space, by being intrusive or psychically dependent on you, by living off your life-energy. They do not do this maliciously or with any thought of harming you, but because they just don't know any better.

Even when we acknowledge the sacred fabric of life as a two-sided reality we may have difficulty in believing in and recognizing the signs of psychic disturbance. We revert to a one-sided point of view and second-guess what's going on, rationalizing and dismissing symptoms. If you are experiencing something and it's affecting you, then these effects are real and palpably manifest. There is no smoke without fire.

One of the first hurdles for anyone suffering from psychic disturbance is their own and others' lack of belief in the reality of what is happening. The biggest reality check that you can get around psychic disturbance is the witness and belief of others. Your witness must have some perception of the two sides of reality and be open to sharing a version that is different to their own.

These questions will help you focus on what's really going on:

• **What makes you feel you are at risk?** If you are experiencing unease or disquiet or radical changes for no apparent reason, then something is happening. But it may not necessarily be due to psychic disruption.

- **When did it begin and what was happening at that time?** What changed things? What new contracts, associations, conflicts, traumas, conversations, violence, arguments, fights, agreements or life changes have you undergone immediately prior to the onset of these symptoms?

- **How did you feel before and how are you now?** What factors changed things?

- **Are your current symptoms experienced now (or have they been in the past) by other members of your family or group?** See Chapter 11.

- **Write down the significant changes you are experiencing,** including in your health, ideas, motivations, desires, dreams, behavior and life patterns.

- **Is there a discernible pattern, picture or story building up?** How have you explained this new pattern to yourself? What is the story you are telling yourself?

- **What are your dreams currently about?** If you can't remember much of them, what themes or images seem to recur? These are highly relevant.

- **What health changes are you experiencing?** Be aware that some prescribed medications can change your perceptions of reality considerably.

DEFENSE STRATEGIES FOR PSYCHIC DISTURBANCE

If you feel that you are under psychic attack or suffering psychic disturbance:

1. Eliminate any obvious and physical causes. Jon began a series of meditations with an ethical teacher. After a week's trial, he complained of psychic disturbance. Every time he sat down to meditate, the wardrobe moved in an uncanny way all by itself. Fearing he had stirred up malign forces, Jon appealed to his teacher, who came to his apartment. She soon discovered that the floorboard on which Jon's chair was positioned was the same floorboard on which the wardrobe

stood—it was his own weight that caused the "psychic phenomenon"!

2. Get adequate rest as well as physical exercise and eat a regular, balanced diet. Delicate, physically vulnerable people are more susceptible to feelings of psychic disruption, especially if they stay indoors all the time and have protein-light diets. Eat a balanced diet of foods that ground your physical body rather than ethereal diets that send you out of it. Jennifer insists on fasting on a metaphysical weekend course instead of eating the plain vegetarian food provided and sees frightening visions. Glen is frequently constipated for days at a time and becomes oppressed by feelings of guilt and inadequacy, which vanish after he has emptied his bowels.

3. Remain grounded in this world and avoid practices that send you out of your body.

4. Keep your sense of humor and proportion by meeting up with grounded friends. "The devil, that proud sprite, cannot bear to be mocked," said Sir Thomas More.

5. Break ties and links with opportunists, would-be colonizers and opponents. Send back or destroy gifts or objects given to you by such people. Cut the supply line to energy thieves. See Chapter 6.

6. Restore your own vitality and soul-power by reconnecting to the Source of Life and filling up with power. Keep your bottle filled up. See Chapters 4 and 5.

7. Cleanse thoroughly and repair damage with help of Advocates. See page 113.

8. Keep a log of all events or changes, so that you can look over it to check any patterns or improvements.

9. Seek the help and support of friends and family. Don't try to manage all alone.

10. Avoid completely any alcohol, drugs or stimulants, except prescribed medication.

11. Before sleeping, practice the Sanctuary of Life meditation (page 23) and sleep safely within that hallowed place of safety. Remember, only you have the key to the Sanctuary.

RETALIATION AND DEFENSE

Life is not fair. Those who are instrumental in making us suffer or causing us pain are often those against whom we spend a lifetime in unconscious retaliation. If an authority figure—parent, teacher, doctor or employer—caused you difficulties when you were younger, you may well develop a disproportionate dislike of authority and react in retaliatory ways that only serve to bind you to that perceived aggressor. Much teenage rebellion stems from this source. It takes a lot of energy to maintain resentment—energy that might be better spent in more productive ways.

When you are threatened, do you take evasive action or meet the threat with force? Real warriors only use force as a last resort. Sometimes discretion is the better part of valor. Retaliation only works to bind us more closely to our opponent, which is the last thing that we actually want. Separating ourselves from enemies and disengaging hostilities brings us peace. See Chapter 7 for finding lasting means of forgiveness.

Defense against psychic attack should never include any form of retaliation or personal intervention on your part. Leave the administration of justice in the hands of the Source of Life and your defense in the hands of your Advocates.

SEALING THE ENERGY FIELD AND BLESSING THE AURA RITUAL

Many animals have resilient skins or feathers, which help deflect water, wind, cold or heat. We can emulate their resilience by sealing our body field and aura (the soul field) from intrusion or disquiet:

1. Bless some ordinary tap water poured into a small bowl by saying over it with outstretched hand: "May this water be

blessed by [name your Source of Life or Advocate] to be a powerful protection against all harm." Be aware of the power of your Source of Life and Advocate as an active agent of life and vitality.

2. After your bath or shower, take the blessed water and anoint the crown of your head, brow, lips, heart, solar plexus, navel and perineum/genitals, palms of hands and soles of feet with a drop of blessed water, saying, "I anoint myself in the name of [your Advocate or Source of Life] that no malign spirit or intruder may enter or influence me. This body is sacred to [your Advocate or Source of Life]. It crowns my head, protects my brow, guards my breath, sits in my heart, shields my center, observes my beginnings and endings, protects my man/womanhood, assists the work of my hands and walks with me wherever I go." Be aware of the Source of Life sealing your energy field.

3. Dress yourself in clean clothes. Stand, extending your arms outward to shoulder level and with legs firmly on the ground with your feet apart. Be aware of your energy field completely encircling your body to a yard beyond fingertips, toes and head. Say, "I seal my aura and bless my souls, in the name of [your Source of Life or Advocate]."

- Take right hand to your brow, saying, "In the name of wisdom."
- Take right hand to solar plexus, saying, "In the name of love."
- Take right hand to right shoulder, saying, "In the name of justice."
- Take right hand to left shoulder, saying, "In the name of mercy."
- Extend arms outward again, saying, "Of the Eternal Source of Life."
- Be aware of yourself entirely surrounded with the mantle of light and of your aura sparkling with vitality, saying, "Nothing can separate me from the Source of Life."

You can use this formula of anointing and blessing at any time. You can also use the aura-sealing (number 3) by itself as a prayer in times of need. Before you seal your aura, always cleanse yourself of any unwanted residues by breathing them out at least three times. See Chapter 6.

When you find yourself in danger, whether physical or psychic, immediately become aware of your energy field, breathe into it and blow it up around you to the greatest extent you can. Be aware of it in orbit around your body, as if you were the sun and it was the solar system, completely encircling you. It rotates and makes a boundary between you and all harm.

SPIRITUAL ARMOR RITUAL

This protection can be used when you know you are going into difficult circumstances that may get to you.

1. Breathe your fear out as you exhale; breathe in life with every inhalation.
2. Call on your Source of Life with cupped hands. Sense, see and feel a silvery-metallic light filling your hands—this is liquid armor that you can smooth on around you. Raise your cupped hands over your head and smooth the liquid armor over the sides of your body with both hands. It encases your energy field and aura.
3. With one graceful motion of your hands, lean down and scoop up the liquid armor from the puddle on the ground in front of you and smooth it over the front of your body and over your head to fall behind you.
4. You are now surrounded and protected by a completely flexible spiritual armor that molds to your every movement and that will mirror back to the sender whatever comes against you. Say aloud, "I am protected by the Armor of Light on every side. No harm will I give, no harm will I receive."
5. Practice this in ordinary times and circumstances, so that when you need it urgently, you can perform this protective ritual easily and quickly.

6. When you remove yourself from danger, unpeel the armor plating from your body field, starting at your feet where you crack it open with both hands. Then raise your arms and allow your Advocate to lift the armor off and return it to the Source of Life. Give thanks for the protection.

MAKING A TALISMAN

Talismans and amulets are spiritually charged protective symbols that we see around people's necks or wound around the rearview mirror of their cars. Some of these are genuine religious emblems, like the ubiquitous silver St. Christopher medallion. Protective talismans have been traditionally made out of precious metals or stones, or from natural substances. The creation and wearing of amulets is hedged with credulous superstition. Physical amulets offer no protection whatever unless they are imbued with belief in what they symbolize and are empowered by prayer and blessing. Talismans protect us by strengthening and reminding us of the power of the Advocates who walk with us and of their power within ourselves. While a talisman is a strong reminder of the help that attends us at all times, it doesn't mean that it does all the work. You still have to pay attention, take care and be alert.

Making and empowering your own talisman is better than one made by someone else. Because many people require talismans at a time when they feel vulnerable, they will often take their protective emblem to a person of power—a priest, witchdoctor or shaman—for blessing. But you can both make and bless your own:

1. Close your eyes. Relax, breathe and be still. Be aware of your energy field.
2. Call on your Guardian Advocate to be with you and ask for the design of a protective talisman. Allow the design to come to you by whatever array of senses you normally use: you may feel it, have a spatial sense of it, it may appear as a blueprint in your brain or consciousness.

3. Confirm with your Advocate by describing what you've been given: "So is this five-pointed star my talisman?" Thank your Advocate.
4. Your talisman needs to be in an easily portable form. Check what kind of material it will be made of. Craft, draw, embroider or paint it.
5. When it is finished and before you wear it, visit the Sanctuary of Life and ask for a blessing to imbue it with protective power (page 23).
6. Whenever you wear or view your talisman, repeat this blessing.

If you see a suitable talisman in a shop and decide to buy rather than make one, ensure that it is a new one and not secondhand, because you want to imprint your own blessings into it, not evict those put there by others.

Remember that talismans do not work forever. As your circumstances and clarity of outlook change, so your need for it may diminish or fade. It is good to return your talisman to nature when its need is over, by burying it in the earth, burning it or casting it into the sea or a large river. See the Decommissioning Objects ritual on page 273. For ideas about the diversity and efficacy of talismans see *Body Guards* by Desmond Morris.

SAFETY, SECURITY, CHANGE AND DISRUPTION

When you are in the middle of psychic disruption and you begin to get to the bottom of things and apply remedies, you may find that instead of things calming down, they may get more disrupted. While this phase shouldn't go on for a long period, it is normal to expect some upheaval when you are getting straight. Remember moving? It takes a lot of work packing, unpacking, cleaning, dusting and fixing. Only when things are in their rightful places can you begin the work of homemaking.

When people demand safety or security they often mean they want things to stay as they were, in customary or familiar lines. We can become addicted to safety, never risking ourselves and never changing. Change must first sweep its broom before peace prevails. We live in security and in safety-conscious times when legislation wraps us in Bubble Wrap, which only serves to provoke in us intense feelings of insecurity. "When you protect something, the thing you are keeping safe decays," says African shaman, Malidoma Somé. We were born to live freely and interact with the life-energy that flows through us. However, when we go into security-mode, we may inadvertently create a toxic field when life struggles to survive in us. Studies suggest that human beings need measured risks and some uncertainties in order to live freely and that a totally safety-conscious society is frequently crime-ridden.

Change happens. Nothing in this book will help things stay unchangingly the same. We must learn how to balance and roll with the punches of life. You can't fix things permanently because life is mutable and changing. "Self-improvement can have temporary results, but lasting transformation occurs only when we honor ourselves as the source of wisdom and compassion" (Malidoma Somé again). Finding the courage and conviction that is within can help us become mature, while seeking to be constantly coddled and comforted can keep us naive and childish.

However, the love of our Advocates and the Source of Life will never change. These will help us find the calm center when all around is in turmoil.

MORE HELP NEEDED?

If you experience extreme symptoms of disruption that you feel cannot be dealt with alone, seek help as soon as you can. The Resources list on page 306 will help you. If your sense of reality is becoming unhinged, there may be other things going on. Do not discount ordinary explanations and sources of help—your doctor, your closest friend or your family. Go there first, for these are your frontline defense allies. Do not seek to deal with physical symptoms only by spiritual means. This checklist gives a rough guide to the kind of things you should not ignore or seek to tackle unaided:

- Inability to look after yourself normally (keep clean, deal with the daily grind, budget or care for dependents or pets).
- Extreme isolation from friends, family and sources of contact.
- A permanent state of panic or fear for your own survival.
- A listless or torpid condition in which you want to do nothing but sleep.
- Being continually aware of commands in your head that threaten your well-being or that of others.
- Suicidal thoughts.
- A self-absorption that excludes all other people, beings and events from your world.
- Overwhelming tides of emotional anguish, murderous hatred, consuming guilt, vindictive jealousy, etc.
- A sense of things rapidly spiraling out of control.
- A burdensome sense of oppression that makes you feel heavy.
- Enveloping feelings of depression.

You may also be aware of these symptoms in others. The first warning sign may be when you become aware of just how distant and at odds with normal perceptions and shared values someone has become. You may also notice that the person:

- Looks less "inhabited" or appears coarse, wild or unkempt in appearance.
- Speaks disjointedly and without enthusiasm or can barely string words together.
- What they say makes little sense.
- Is full of flights of impossible ideas or fancies and speaks unstoppably.
- Behaves in ways that cause public embarrassment.
- Fails to hear what you say and has difficulty understanding even simple speech.
- Makes you feel very unsafe to be in their presence.

Such people need professional help and care, and should not be treated by spiritual means alone, although this may play an important part in the support and rehabilitation of grave mental illness or psychic disruption.

MAINTAINING YOUR SANITY

Remember that while you are undergoing the trials, anxieties and confusions associated with psychic disruption, you are still yourself—a human being in a state of transition and development. When you are blown off course, you need to get a fix on where you are and ride out the storm as best you can. Psychic disturbance may give you an opportunity for becoming more consciously focused in your life, helping you to live with greater depth and connection. It can call forth an underdeveloped soul into greater maturity and discernment.

To keep a sense of your true self while you are being blitzed by conflicting factors, you need a strong support network of both physical friends and family, as well of spiritual allies and Advocates. These are part of your frontline defense. Also:

- Simplify your affairs.
- Downsize your workload.
- Avoid large gatherings of people.
- Avoid overstimulating events.
- Create a sanctuary of peace for yourself.
- Clarify yourself and your situation in silence.
- Keep close to supportive friends.
- Avoid the company of influences and people that escalate psychic disturbance.

HOW WE CAUSE PSYCHIC DISRUPTION

Psychic disruption is not just something we experience; it is also something we cause. We don't have to be malevolent in intent for this to happen. Unless we can see how we stand in the chain of cause and effect, we cannot truly call ourselves psychically responsible or spiritually aware people. We all like to be seen in a good light and will endlessly manipulate the evidence and appearances to produce this result, but the truth is that we all have self-serving intentions. The following actions and attitudes can precipitate psychic disruption:

- Stepping over boundaries without invitation.
- Neglecting psychic hygiene (see Chapter 6).
- Refusing to change.
- Holding on to the power and soul of others (see Chapters 4 and 5).
- Being careless of our words, deeds and intentions.
- Having our own way no matter what.
- Being convinced of the rightness/justice of our cause.
- Being a do-gooder with meddling intentions that fracture boundaries.
- Being inactive or passive when we should be active.
- Letting things slide.

If you are currently suffering psychic disruption, you might want to ask yourself, "What is my responsibility in causing this?" not to invoke guilty feelings, but in order to examine the chain of events leading to this problem so that you can gain clarity and avoid it happening again.

BLUEPRINTS FOR PSYCHIC PROTECTION

1. Call upon Advocates and the Source of Life for immediate aid.

2. Pay attention to your breath.

3. Keep a sense of proportion.

4. Retain a sense of humor.

5. Check what's really going on around you by questioning and paying attention.

6. Be aware that conditions change and so must your defense strategies.

7. Use your intelligence and discernment.

8. Ground and center yourself rather than following the confusion.

9. Validate your lifesaving instincts by acting upon them.

10. Be attentive to the present moment rather than the past and future.

CHAPTER 4

The Boundaries of Power and Energy

Energy is eternal delight.

—William Blake in *The Marriage of Heaven and Hell*

THE FLOW OF LIFE-ENERGY AND POWER-LOSS

Life-energy is the power that vivifies the universe. It flows in all places and beings, bringing vigor and health with it. When that flow is impeded, we recognize it as being out of balance or unhealthy. Life-energy is the vital current that keeps us alive and healthy. When we are in harmony with our energy it is easy to keep clear boundaries, to live with clarity of purpose and responsibility for our actions, words and intentions. When we are out of sync with our energy, we can end up throwing it about, manipulating others with it, giving it away or losing it. Unless energy is freely flowing, our lives feel stuck or lacking in power.

Power-loss is the first symptom of psychic disturbance. It can be caused by lack of order, neglect of proper boundaries, through putting up with unethical or manipulative behavior, by neglect of appropriate rest or nurture, as well as through power theft or relinquishing of vital power, but most of all it is caused by *failure to listen to our instincts*. Sometimes our power can be stolen or siphoned off to help maintain dependent or power-hungry people and situations. This usually happens without malicious or conscious intent. Power-thieves live by stealing someone else's energy; this causes them mental paranoia and massive personality distortion, while leaving the victim/s weakened or powerless.

Power-theft can occur to both individuals and countries who suffer from manipulative governments and repressive regimes; national solutions may involve exile or revolution. Symptoms of power-loss include:

- A sense of inertia and powerlessness.
- Severe reduction or loss of energy.
- Feeling disconnected from loved and familiar things.
- Feeling out of control in or unequal to normal tasks.
- Inability to maintain boundaries.
- Recurrent mishaps or continual bad luck.
- Struggling to catch up with oneself.
- A series of low-grade illnesses.
- Being fixed in workaholic patterns.
- Living in a fearful or suspicious way.
- Continually being taken advantage of by others.
- Low self-esteem and self-depreciation.
- Panic attacks.

Some of these symptoms can be experienced at the same time, often accompanying more manifest physical symptoms, such as illnesses of many different kinds.

POWER-LOSS CHECKLIST

The following questions should help you gauge your current energy alignment and help you recognize danger signs as well as find your boundaries. Some questions concern not only your own power but also the ways in which you may be manipulating the power of others.

1. Do you continually push yourself beyond your physical limits into exhaustion or collapse? How are you making similar unreasonable demands upon others?

2. Do you maintain your code of honor and personal standards of behavior in the face of opposition or peer pressure? Do you infringe or cause the infringement of others' codes and standards?

3. Do you maintain your basic rights, needs and desires or abrogate them at the behest or need of others? How are you trespassing on the rights of others?

4. When did you last check on the motivations that fuel your life, work, relationships, hobbies and so on? Are these power-connections between you and your gifts still operative?

5. How do your personal circumstances and home environment reflect your present power alignment? Does outer disorder reflect inner disorientation?

6. Are you allowing others to encroach upon your environment, time or resources without conscious permission? How are you encroaching upon those of others?

KEEPING THE BOUNDARIES

To some degree, we all cooperate in our own power-loss. Instead of noticing the signs and being alert to the potentialities of each moment, we have all taken wrong decisions, which have led to power-loss. Our society does not value instinct, but it is a vital tool for self-survival and we neglect it at our peril. This is why we need our Advocates so badly, because they will help us keep the boundaries of our own life safe from incursion or danger.

Unfortunately, our society encourages us to "give away power" nearly every day; we are programmed not to resist giving up our rights, our boundaries, our integrity and spiritual authenticity in a variety of ways. We are constantly being encouraged to overwork, to expend our efforts on others' behalf, to give our essence. It is worth remembering that we each have free will and that if we wish to maintain our boundaries clearly we must exercise it. When we fall into recurrent cycles of unfortunate situations, we lose power and need power-retrieval. We can limit future power-loss by:

- Obeying our code of honor.
- Returning to the sources of our power.
- Attending to our essential needs before those of others.
- Removing ourselves from situations and people who cause power-loss to occur.
- Finding and listening to our Advocates.

When we fail to use our free will—when we are manipulated or coerced into something against our better judgment—then we suffer the consequences.

Learning to say no, to draw the line, to defend ourselves against strong-willed others or people in authority is very hard. That is the time to call upon your Advocate and ask it to help you with as much trust as you can.

KEEPING CONNECTION

The power lines and telephone poles that stride across our land carry power to where it is needed. When storms come, they can get disconnected and blown down. If you have suffered the loss of one of your major power-connections recently, you too may feel as if your electricity has been cut off. The list of power-connections that we have in the universe (page 14 and above) demonstrate whence we receive our nurture. These reciprocal links of love and affection are our power lines.

A daily spiritual practice is not just the duty of religious or believing people, but of all living beings. It is possible to be a person of spirit but not a card-carrying member of any spiritual institution. Your personal spiritual practice may be completely individual and unique to yourself. We keep good connection with the rest of the universe by simple rituals that spring from our own understanding, preferences, orientation and world view. In every twenty-four hours you can make a small space in which you freely offer back thanks for the power that flows into you.

The rhythm of the whole universe is based upon the tides of giving and receiving, which enable life to flow and not become stagnant. We cannot always be receiving or we become too full. The rhythm keeps us healthy: animals eat and excrete; vegetation grows and decays; tides ebb and flow; seasons follow their cycle; the stars wheel in their courses. We are all too aware of how imbalance enters into our world and the effect it can have; ingratitude, ignorance of these rhythms and failure to connect are now causing global changes in seasonal patterns.

Finding our own way of giving thanks and reconnecting with the tides of the universe, we strengthen our life, health and belonging to the earth, while acknowledging the sacred relationship of our soul to spirit. We can focus our prayer of thanks at our shrine, or we may prefer to stand in nature to speak our heart. One person will want to dance or sing; another to be still and silent. Times of connection will show themselves: at dawn, noon, twilight and midnight; before beginning or upon ending something; on greeting and farewell; while working, before resting, on waking. The manner, form and content do not matter, only your good intention. Strong connections keep our power vigorous and our souls serene.

GIVING BACK POWER RITUAL

We all want to appear better than we really are. In order to do so, we steal power and energy from people, groups and family members. Despite the fact that the life-energy of the universe is freely running through us, we get panicky and needy, we feel small and lost, and we want that little bit more confidence. Power-theft happens when we take something that doesn't belong to us and that hasn't been offered freely. Ordinarily we enter into all kinds of agreement about power-lending with those whom we love and support—this is a normal contractual engagement with loved ones. (We'll explore the complexities of families and relationships some more in Chapters 11 and 12.) We also draw freely upon places in nature. Again, this is one of the more important connections that we have with the universe that supports us; the exchange is our love of those places. It is the same with our Advocates: where there is a mutual respect and love, then life-energy ebbs and flows in balance.

Power-theft happens when someone is using you as an extra battery and you haven't invited them to do so, where there is no reciprocal arrangement. The power-loss checklist above is also intended for potential power-thieves like ourselves. Look it over and join the club—we've all stolen power before, but we can become more aware of what we are doing and stop it. The consequence of hanging on to other people's power distorts our own energy field and makes us feel heavy and unwieldy in soul.

1. Relax, breathe and be still. Establish your body field (page 52).
   Breathe in and out of it, using the Positive Breath pattern: Inhale 4;
   Hold 8; Exhale 8; Hold out 4. Keep this going for a few minutes. Call on
   your Guardian Advocate to help you.

2. Now begin to sense where your body field feels distorted or heavy,
   and where there are connecting tubes, straws or wires leading out of
   you into someone else; be aware of what you are holding in your body
   field that doesn't belong to you. Parts of your body field may feel like
   an octopus with many arms. You don't need these connections or the
   burden of stolen energy any more. You might be aware of an associate
   whom you've been cultivating for his useful connections, a friend on
   whom you've been leeching and not really reciprocating with, a family
   member who's been not just supporting you but warehousing your
   energy, an ex-lover whose image has been keeping you feeling young
   and lovely, a celebrity over whom you've been obsessing. Where have
   you been feeding illicitly without consent? If it helps, draw your body
   field and the lines that come out of it and where they connect without
   consent.

3. Without beating yourself up—because most people unconsciously
   practice this from time to time—breathe the energy you have taken
   back down those connecting tubes in turn to each of the sources
   you've found connected to you. Apologize and thank those from whom
   you've taken, bless them. When you've done that, retract the tubes,
   straws or wires, and breathe right through your body field so that it is
   whole again. *Remember not to cut links with those with whom you have
   a healthy and reciprocal relationship!*

The results of this ritual will be astonishing to you. You will not only have a more lively sense of yourself but a lot of your personal energy will now be free to pursue legitimate pursuits and activities. Those from whom you've stolen power will feel free and more energized.

FEAR AND PANIC

Every day we have lots of little fears: "Maybe she won't like me" and "What if I miss the train and arrive late?" We also harbor some big ones: "What will the medical tests reveal?" and "What will happen if I lose this job?" The way we cope with fear and keep it at bay impacts our bodies and souls.

The primal purpose of fear is to protect us from dangers that will harm us. If we never experienced fear, we would not survive long. But when fear becomes the master, you become the slave.

The adrenaline activated by fear can either help you flee or else, like an engine flooded with gas, you can stall and become rooted to the spot. Excessive and unused adrenaline needs expression or it goes inward, causing confusion and depression, psychic disturbance and paranoia. Fear erases memory, creates gaps in consciousness and locks up our will to live.

Fear is frozen power. Power is frozen fear. When fear is present, power is locked up. When power is flowing, fear is asleep.

Extreme fear is the first sign that something isn't right. Don't ignore this sign or allow it to disempower you into silence and passivity. Don't become a victim of fear by dwelling on it or following it. Fear, suspicion and doubt divide us from ourselves. If we are one in our souls, we cannot be divided from ourselves. Rather than hiding or running from fear or battling with it, the best antidote is to replace fear with power, strength and vitality:

- Breath is your frontline defense against fear and panic. Establish a strong Well-Being Breath pattern: Inhale 8; Hold in 8; Exhale 8; Hold out 4. You will soon come back to yourself.

- Immediately call upon your Advocates and the Source of Life for help rather than trying to cope alone.

- Gather your power (see below) and souls (page 91) to you.
- Do not dwell on the fear nor allow it to invade you even more. Use your mind skillfully to consider something strong and invincible. Invite Advocates to enter the place of fear and take up the space instead. Put power in the place of fear.
- Say, "I have fear, but I am not my fear. Feelings of fear are what I am experiencing. Greater and more powerful than the fear are [names of your Source of Life and Advocates]."

THE MAGPIE'S WARNING

Elizabeth had never had much of a life or even a job of her own. She lived at the beck and call of her husband and of various "friends," who called her up to listen to their complaints and problems. After a shamanic course, where she made contact with her power and her Animal Advocate, she went home where her husband began to outline the weekend's visit to the golf course that he'd planned for them both. Rebellion stirred and she found herself thinking about the magpie that had come to be her Advocate. It seemed close to her and very agitated. She found herself responding to her husband with, "That may be what you're going to do, but I shall be staying home." It was as if the bird had spoken for her and defended her boundaries for the very first time! Her husband was considerably peeved, for she had never answered him back before. Elizabeth began to be even bolder, and when her "friends" called, she cut the calls short. She started to enjoy being self-directing and less dependent or depended upon and got a volunteer job that she loved. Her power had truly come back home in the form of the magpie's warning.

CALLING OUR POWER HOME RITUAL

Power-retrieval reconnects us to the Source of Life from which we have been disconnected, so that we can responsibly maintain the boundaries of our lives again. Restoring power is our first concern in cases of psychic disturbance, preceding any other kind of work, since, without access to our vital energy we cannot recover our direction in life. The primal way we call our power home is to find the guardian of our Vital Soul, which governs our vital power; this guardian is usually in the form of a spirit animal who is our Animal Advocate.

Animal Advocates are spirit-companions in animal shape. They are reminders to us of the wisdom in our bodies, guardians of our survival who help boost the signal of our instinct and physical vitality. If the Guardian Advocate you found in Chapter 2 is already in animal form, that's fine. Animal Advocates and allies in other spiritual forms are as much our friends as the people in our address book, except that Advocates live on the other, unseen, side of reality. They love us and are concerned for our well-being, wanting only the best for us. If we attend to their wisdom, which we do by listening to our deep instincts and our truthful needs and desires, we will find that we are able to live in much better alignment with our power. The nature of Animal Advocates is different from person to person: the animal spirit chooses you, not you the animal! However, the animal that comes is often one that you have always felt warmly about.

1. Aloud, in your own words, make a firm intention to re-erect your lifesaving boundary of instinct, to avoid giving power away so freely, and promise to abide within its limits. State that you reject all power-thieves and will not place yourself in their hands again. Repeat your code of honor (page 17). Call upon the Source of Life and your Guardian Advocate to be with you.

2. Relax, breathe and be still. Establish your energy field and aura. Now stand and face each direction, one at a time. Be aware of the pathway leading between you and that direction. Say, "I call home my power from the East [then, South, West, North, Below and Above]." Feel all the vital power that is astray coming home to you from each direction. It may come in symbolic forms or as a gift. With outstretched arms gather it up and gently bring it home by placing both hands over your belly, just below your navel, and feel the power passing into your body.

3. Welcome your power back by breathing and smiling into your lower belly. Feel the vital power growing warmer the more you smile at it. Love the vitality that flows within you as you breathe it round your body. Smile and breathe.

4. Now ask that your Animal Advocate, the guardian of your power, reveal itself to you. You may already have been aware of some animal as you

gathered up your power. Now sit quietly and let it show itself to you, using the discriminating questions that you used on page 28. When you've established who it is, gather it to you in the same way.

After power-retrieval, it is courteous to welcome your Animal Advocate back and to keep in close communication with it. Enjoy some physical activity—dancing, swimming, running, walking—and introduce it to your body. Feel what it is like to have your animal on board with you.

When power returns, you are able to take up the reins of daily life with more strength and confidence. This restoration may be delightful to loved ones or sometimes distressful to those who have enjoyed interesting others with the power they have formerly stolen. Such manipulative power-drainers suddenly discover that their supply lines are cut off. See Chapter 6 for strategies for dealing with power-theft.

"TRIES TOO HARD"

At ballet class, the teacher praises young Zoë for her high leaps but draws her aside after class to say, "But don't make dancing so full of effort. Your face was screwed up with determination when you leapt. Think of a deer leaping: use the earth to propel you." The teacher knows that Zoë's effort isn't just showing up on her face, but also in her internal organs, muscles and bone structure, putting a strain on her whole body. She is a courageous and hard-working student, but, sooner or later, this much effort will begin to drain off her vital energy and sabotage any dance career she might pursue. A dancer must have not only skill and determination, but also the ability to renew her stamina that comes through the right temperament. Effortlessness can only arrive when Zoë learns how to draw upon the free flow of energy that arises from the dance-forms and her practice: as long as she is trying to work from personal effort alone, she will not create a circuit of exchange.

LEAKY ENERGY AND OTHER POWER PROBLEMS

Watch the hawk fly: he doesn't frantically beat his wings to keep aloft but he uses the thermals to underpin his flight. He cups his wings to grab air and gain height or change direction, but most often he cruises. Sometimes we overexert ourselves by choosing to do ordinary things in the most difficult ways. Having formulated the intention to do something, we take the hard route of forcing all our powers to its accomplishment. Having achieved it, we no longer have the capacity to enjoy it. This kind of effort depletes our vital organs, drains our will to live and wastes the power of our Vital Soul.

If you leave your car headlights on overnight, the chances are that you will face a dead battery in the morning. If your vitality is always switched on and running, then you will suffer depletion and exhaustion. Immune system diseases like chronic fatigue syndrome and other energy depletion disorders are caused by involuntary leakage, by our collusion with power-thieves and by overwork. Energy-leakages also occur in people whose passion and will to live have become lowered by circumstance or illness.

One of the most common causes of energy-leakage is our disconnection from sacred reality. The reason why people try too hard and invest all their power is because they don't trust the universe enough and feel they personally have to supply everything. This is why we must remain in close contact with our Advocates, because they share our life and walk with us. Different things change our energy field:

- Unclear divisions can lead to lowered thresholds. Remember to make a clear division between different activities. Everyone knows how difficult it is to move from an argument into a task requiring close concentration; you need to defuse the anger before working or your anger will continue to draw power out of you toward its object. See Chapter 3 for more on grounding procedures.

- When energy is not in a circuit you get inertia. This happens when you become congested with too much stuff and when you fail to be reciprocal with the power of the universe. We deal with that problem more fully in Chapter 6.
- When our intention leaves an opening. If your intention is to be defeatist, victimized or fearful, opportunists will notice this message in your aura and take advantage. See Chapter 7 for more on how to strengthen intention.
- When our passion, desire or libido go into overdrive and don't turn off, we leak energy. See Chapter 12.
- When we are being overly scrupulous, painstaking, workaholic, dutiful or overly dedicated, we use too much power and drain. See Chapter 13.
- When we exercise we stimulate and re-create the circuit of vitality in our body fields. The key to energy leakage is rest, cessation and sleep. Psychic disturbance enters most easily when we are depleted and tired, when stamina has deserted us. Sleep is when we naturally refresh our energies. Whatever your workload, family responsibilities, housework or commitment to hobbies, you have to turn off, take rest during the day and sleep every night. Too many of us go on to our reserve tank to keep going long after we should have taken rest, leaving ourselves open to depletion. Keep your tank filled up: a half-empty tank leaves room for unwanted guests. Energy leakage is also caused by overstimulation.
- Use most lunches and breaks at work to stop and rest, rather than shop every day.
- Finish one task before starting another. Have a break between tasks.
- Cultivate some quietness by turning off the television or music rather than having them on regardless of whether you are watching or listening.
- Take off at least one day in every seven to ten for recreational pursuits instead of work.
- Turn off cell phones or pagers when you need to be private and rest. Don't give people continual access to you.
- Discharge residues and stresses by breath and relaxation. See the easy technique below.
- Withdraw your attention from whatever is depleting your power.
- Sleep for at least seven hours a night.

Because your body is always in a circuit of energy with the planet you can draw upon the natural power of the earth to help boost your energy. For a quick and easy method of rebooting your energy levels in cases of need, you can use your hands like jumper cables:

1. Sitting or standing, place your right hand upon your sacrum, just above where your buttocks start, and place your left hand upon the crown of your head, the place where your hair radiates out.
2. Remain sitting, or, if you're standing, walk up and down, keeping your hands in place for three minutes.
3. Repeat this, placing your left hand on your sacrum and your right hand on your crown, for three minutes.

DISCHARGING STRESS FROM A FRAUGHT ENERGY FIELD

When we become fraught with undischarged worries, heavy with grief, pain or problems, or even full of lovely dreams that we never fulfill, we begin to experience the way in which the power of life turns inward and burdens us. This can cause untold psychic disruption. Discharging our pain and grief and expressing our innermost hopes and dreams can help us avoid this. If we begin to inhabit our problems, angers and frustrations, they will become part of us and soon you will have colonists inhabiting you. See Chapter 6 for more advice. Here are some ways of discharging stress:

- Reconnect with nature and the stars above and around you.
- Keep things in perspective by giving yourself a reality check—where are you in the situation?
- Be compassionate to yourself. Accept for yourself the advice you give to friends to relax!
- Forgive yourself. One failure doesn't stigmatize you forever as a failure.
- Delegate tasks to others rather than trying to cope.

- Don't make things worse by dwelling on the hassle and working it up into a full-blown crisis.
- Stop blaming others and take responsibility for the tasks you've taken on.
- Consider what you can stop doing and lighten your load.
- Allow yourself a good cry or laugh.
- Say "no" to a task too many.

For all of the above, and to discharge whatever is stressing your energy field, become aware of every pore in your body as a gateway. Breathe in for a count of 4 through the open pores; as you hold in your breath for a count of 8, close your pores momentarily; then open them and exhale powerfully for a count of 8; hold out for a count of 4. Continue this circuit of breath until you feel your pores opening wider and more easily. All air coming into you brings with it a cleansing light. All exhalations convey away any residues that have made your energy field heavy, sad or painful.

RESTFUL SLEEP

When patterns of psychic disturbance are held in your body field, it's often hard to get to sleep. Try the following practice or study the releasing strategies in Chapter 6:

1. Discharge stale energy and stress before lying down.
2. Bless your aura with a prayer for protection and sleep. See Chapter 8 and page 52.
3. Lie on your back, placing both hands over your navel, and contemplate the power held in your energy field as centered there.
4. Allow any thoughts, fantasies or fears to pass. Don't chase or follow them, but return to your contemplation.
5. Gently focus your mind upon your Advocates with love and gratitude, slowing your breathing down to the Creative Breath pattern of Inhale 4; Hold in 8; Exhale 16; Hold out 4. This will enable you to reconnect with Advocates and alert them to the fact that you wish to sleep.

6. Gradually take your breathing into the deeper, Sleep Breath pattern of Inhale 4; Hold in 8; Exhale 32; Hold out 4. Allow yourself to drift off, trusting your energy to circulate your body all by itself while you rest.

THE HEALING ELEMENTS

Our own energy is part of a much larger continuum of vitality that powers our planet. The regulators of that vitality are the elements of air, fire, water and earth, which are the creators and transformers of life-power. They can help us to cleanse, heal and bless. Wind, sunlight, fresh water and the stability of the ground beneath our feet are how we experience these elements about us, while within our bodies, our breath, blood and body-heat, moisture and the physical frame of our bones are how we experience them as part of us. From these everyday powers, the universe is woven together. When psychic disturbance shakes us, the elements can lend us power to clarify, cleanse, heal and bless our situation or condition.

We are drawing on the powers of the elements whenever we ground ourselves and find a framework of stability; whenever we seek the warmth, the comfort of supporters; when we attend to our breathing; and when we wash away what is entangling us. The elements also have their own spiritual powers that give life and strength, as well as the ability to cleanse and clear: air, fire, water and earth also represent the powers of life, light, love and law. "Law" in this sense means the pattern, order and boundary of the universe. Here are a few simple ways in which you can draw upon the powers of the elements to cleanse and strengthen you when psychic disturbance threatens.

TO CLEANSE AND STRENGTHEN WITH AIR AND THE POWER OF LIFE:

• Stand in a windy place and allow the wind to blow away all that bothers you. Visualize any entanglements loosening and blowing away to the ends of the universe.

- Use a bunch of dried herbs, smudge stick, incense stick or cone to cleanse your energy field or a room, first dedicating the herbs to this cleansing.
- Visualize a handheld psychic vacuum cleaner to suck up residues that have become attached to you during the day. Give the psychic vacuum cleaner to your Advocate to empty!
- Light some incense and place it on the ground so that you can breathe in its smoke and permeate your body with the Power of Life. Allow the breath of the Source of Life to inspirit you with every in-breath; allow all that is impeding your life to be breathed away with every exhalation. Be blessed by the precious and preserving air.

TO CLEANSE AND STRENGTHEN WITH FIRE AND THE POWER OF LIGHT:

- Stand in the rays of the sun and feel its warmth penetrating to the core of your being.
- When you have to dispose of objects that have entangling associations, burn them in a bonfire in your yard or in a grill to help sever connections. You can also write on a piece of paper the feelings, connections, fears, etc., that you wish to be transformed.
- Visualize a great flame of blue light into which your Advocate leads you safely. This cleansing fire has the power to burn away all entanglements and confusions.
- When you pray or meditate, dedicate a candle to represent the power of light. Cup your hands over the flame and spread that warmth and light over your body field, and be blessed by the precious and preserving fire.

TO CLEANSE AND STRENGTHEN WITH WATER AND THE POWER OF LOVE:

- Stand outside when it's raining, or in an outdoor pool or in the sea. Or stand in the shower, if you can't go outside. Experience the cleansing waters washing away all that is dirty or polluting.
- When you've been in places and with people that have left residues with you, immediately wash your hands in cold water. Later bathe in fresh water with a handful of cleansing herbs and salt.

- Brew some herbal tea to drink. Place cleansing herbs in your bath to wash away impurities.
- Bless some pure drinking water. Dedicate it to represent the power of love. Drink it down and be blessed by the precious and preserving water.

TO CLEANSE AND STRENGTHEN WITH EARTH AND THE POWER OF LAW:

- Stand in a place that you love on the earth. Send that love down in the earth and draw it up again through your feet. Feel impurities and attachments being drawn out of you down into the deep earth. Focus upon your love of the earth.
- Bless a bowl of sea salt. Keep some of it in a little bag in your pocket. When you've been with people who've been exploitative or in places that feel psychically polluted, rub some of the salt over your hands so that nothing can adhere to you.
- Find a stone (not a crystal) that you really like and can hold easily in one hand. Sea-smoothed pebbles are good, but any small stone that you find lying on the ground will serve—especially if it comes from your special place. Carry it with you and let this stone be your grounding touchstone that always reminds you of enduring earth when you are getting overexcited or out of yourself. It will help you draw your power back into your body. Dedicate it to represent the power and wisdom of earth's law and be blessed by the precious and preserving earth.

RADIATION OF LIGHT RITUAL

Use this method when you need to radiate strength, confidence and joy without being shielded. Like filling up your car with gas, this practice will fill you up with protective strength.

- Standing up tall, feet firmly on the ground, with your hands facing up and arms bent at the elbow, call on your Source of Life and on your Animal Advocate's power to strengthen you. If you can face the sun outside, even better, but close your eyes and feel the sunlight enhancing this practice.

- Feel a powerful beam of warm, golden light streaming from your Source of Life that connects with your solar plexus and begins to fill you up with golden, powerful light.
- As you feel the flow beginning to stop, bring your hands to cover your solar plexus and seal it thankfully within you.
- Breathe the golden light around your entire body and being, visualizing its warm strength radiating through you by the pumping action of your breath.

SURVIVAL AND FLIGHT: WHEN BOUNDARIES ARE NOT ENOUGH

Sometimes it is impossible or too challenging to maintain the boundaries of our power within certain circumstances without infringing our self-respect or risking our lives. When your boss asks you to work overtime a couple of nights a week, that may be beneficial to you both; however, if he begins to coerce you into working four nights of overtime a week and suggests that your job is up for grabs if you don't, then you must consider your health or how important the job really is in the long term. If your partner is violently abusive to you and you stay on for the financial security or for the children's sake, you are seriously infringing your own power. Power is life-energy. When your life is in danger, the option of flight must be taken very seriously. When you are in an untenable position and change feels impossible, choose change every time. You will release the energy to live and defend your rights again. The painful stability that you are choosing to inhabit in untenable situations will begin to crush the life out of you, starting first with your power, then your soul. What remains is a body in thrall to a set of impossible circumstances.

THE WILL TO LIVE: CONSERVING AND SPENDING OUR POWER

Much of this chapter may strike you as very selfish. What about the needs of others? What about the needs of the planet? When you are dealing with psychic disturbance, focusing upon self-survival becomes the primary task. For many people brought up to put others first, it comes as a bit of a shock, perhaps, but if you are unable to function, you're not in a position to help anyone else.

The way in which we guard and trust our power depends upon our will to live. Are we passionate enough about living, or do we not care how we live? What are you living for? How you engage with your life is reflected in your health and energy. Living with vigor and passion affirms your will to live. Living in victimhood, self-pity or inertia is living at low ebb; it will eventually kill us by making us vulnerable, undercutting our will to live. Passive living weakens us, allowing gloom, doom and disaster to pollute our body field and leaving us floating and drifting through life, under the spell of others' enchantments and susceptible to negative influences. Hoarding power will do you no good: you will just get congested with psychic constipation.

Be as filled with your passions and gifts as you can, according to your capacities. This will ensure that nothing else can invade you. When times are good don't be afraid to spend your power generously. It will come back to you again. That is a law of the planet. Being positive and active brings the enchantment back to life better than being defensive. Live as if you mean it.

BLUEPRINTS FOR HEALTHY ENERGY

1. Maintain a positive attitude by affirming and practicing your gifts.

2. Listen to your instincts and preserve your boundaries.

3. Live vigorously.

4. Exchange fear for power. Put power in the place of fear.

5. Acknowledge your own needs, abilities and limitations.

6. Keep connected to your support network of friends and family.

7. Keep connected to your spirit Advocates and to the Source of Life.

8. Return the power you've stolen from others.

9. Call home the power that you've lost.

10. Reciprocation is the key to the ebb and flow of universal vitality.

CHAPTER 5

Soul-Care

It is noble for a man to grip tight his soul's casket, hold
his spirit fast, let his thoughts be what they may.
—"The Wanderer," Old English poem

POWER AND SOUL

What is the difference between power and soul? Power is our life-energy and it is shared equally by our body and souls. Our body is the physical vehicle of our power that operates in the physical world; our souls are the spiritual vehicles of our power and they operate in the metaphysical world. Because physical and metaphysical worlds are meshed together at every point in the universe, we cannot strictly separate the Otherworld from our world—it is all about us. Normally and naturally, we use our souls to travel about and check things out while we are awake in our physical body. You send bits of soul to check out whether the gas station is still open, if your child's out of violin classes yet, whether you turned off the oven, how your sister in Australia is doing after her operation. You've thought about your ability to do this as "merely imagination," but your souls can travel and experience things. In this chapter we'll look at soul-care in some detail because we live in a society that ignores the soul, tolerating spiritual flab, intellectual sloth and psychic ambiguity. These three neglected areas are breeding grounds for psychic disruption. As we come to understand our souls, so we will learn to see the ways we can avoid enmeshing ourselves in psychic turmoil.

SOUL-FRAGMENTATION

Our multiple souls each have many parts with separate functions. We send soul-parts out skillfully to perform various tasks for us, but we don't think about how skillful we are being. In the last chapters we spoke of the Vital, Personal and Wisdom Souls and of the possibility of losing parts of our soul. Just as we can lose power from our bodies, so too we can lose power from our souls. Everyone experiences minor soul-fragmentation at times and comments upon it, as when we are tired ("I'm completely out of it"), angry ("I was beside myself with rage") or disoriented ("I feel spaced out").

Soul-fragmentation is caused by loss of self-esteem, bereavement, abuse, job loss, extreme shock, accident, rape and other incidents. It is evident in people who have been spiritually neglected or maltreated; in those whose decisions, self-motivation and resources have been colonized or appropriated by others; in those who suffer from burdensome ancestral bequests that cascade into the current generation. It can also occur when you are in entangled relationships; through anger, frustration and disappointment; through intense longing and desire; after periods of hardship when no help or relief has come. Soul-fragmentation is always accompanied by power-loss, which is why it is important to attend to your power-connections first, for if these are not dealt with then returning soul-parts will have no scaffold or support.

Soul-fragmentation can range in intensity from minor accidents in which a soul-part is ejected through shock of impact, right through to a traumatic episode where we don't seem to heal afterward, or even a major accident that leaves the subject in a coma. Death is the ultimate soul-loss, since all life-power leaves the body. When a significant soul-part has been ejected or left, we instinctively seek for something to take its place, which is why soul-loss is often accompanied by a sense of being obstructed with something that has taken up residence in our body field or everyday life. When human beings lose a vital part of themselves, they resort to other substitutes to "fill the gap," which is the root cause of all addictions. We will look more at what may enter the soul and need eviction in Chapter 6.

Soul-fragmentation explains why many long-term problems and illnesses have been deemed impossible to alleviate. The reason is obvious when we understand the concept of soul-loss, since it is impossible to heal *something that is not present!* Most serious soul-loss is seldom curable by therapeutic means, since these ignore the spiritual cause of the problem and address only psychological or physical levels. For many people, it is often a great relief to be able to put a name to their trouble. Soul-retrieval restores the straying soul-part and our will to live.

Where do soul-parts go? Most often, soul-parts seek a safe place in the Otherworld. In cases of extreme bereavement, a soul-part may follow the deceased to the land of the dead. In cases of abuse and coercion, a soul-part may be retained or imprisoned at the abuser's pleasure and be stuck between the worlds. In cases where the will to live is low, the soul-part may be wandering further away from this world in search of another place to be. In cases of sudden shock, a soul-part may remain near to the epicenter of the trauma. These constitute more serious soul-loss conditions. However, in most cases of minor soul-fragmentation, a soul-part remains close by and can be called home.

We are interested here in how psychic disturbance affects our souls. This is not the place to deal with major soul-loss, which should always be referred to an experienced shamanic practitioner. Some people ask, "Why can't I do it myself?" Minor soul-fragmentation can be dealt with some success by yourself, just as you are able to bind up your own sprained ankle. However, dealing with serious soul-loss unaided is like trying to do your own brain-surgery.

Symptoms of soul-fragmentation include:

• A lack of connection with life, an inability to be present, a sense of numbness, apathy or deadness.

- Feeling scattered and unable to get back to your center.
- Memory blank-out after trauma, accident or abuse.
- Addictive patterns.
- A sense of something missing, a sense of searching.
- An inability to retain a job, a relationship or sustained interest in any project.
- A sense of isolation, loneliness or disconnectedness with what normally brings you delight.
- A failure of physical or psychological therapies to bring any significant improvement.
- A sense of being elsewhere.
- A lack of joy and access to the emotions.

Some of these symptoms may be experienced together; one or two may be prominent. The following diagnostic questions may help you locate what soul fragments you have mislaid and through what cause:

1. What are you always longing for but never finding?
2. What are you grieving for?
3. What shock, abuse or event is still rocking your boat?
4. What are you exiled from?
5. With whom do you have unfinished business?
6. How has your loss affected your health?
7. When did you last experience joy?
8. What success has eluded you?
9. When did you lose inspiration?
10. Whose envy, enmity, spite or cruelty echoes in you still?
11. Where are you located in your dreams? What stories do they tell?
12. What quality, faculty or ability did you once have that you lack now?

These questions may point to a quality you lack or have been looking for. It isn't necessary to fully identify missing soul-parts in order to get them back again.

LOST IN THE GARDEN

Lizzy's life had been disrupted ever since she got pregnant at 16 and her strict parents threw her out of the house. A string of abusive boyfriends and two more children left her unprepared and unsupported. I saw her after her own daughter had fallen pregnant at 15, when Lizzy realized that the same situation faced her again and that it was time to do something about it. Issues of abandonment, betrayal and powerlessness over-whelmed her but therapy had been unfruitful. She was still looking for a sense of safety and family inclusion. Lizzy's soul-loss was evident in her dull, joyless eyes and inability to focus upon the matter at hand. She chain-smoked so badly that she needed to go out twice during our ses-sion. With my own Advocates to help me, I searched the Otherworld for Lizzy's lost power and soul. They led me to a suburban yard where, under a tree, I found the lost soul-part, a younger-looking Lizzy. My Advocates told me that this was the yard of her parent's house and that she had been trying to return home but had finally given up hope of a welcome. I also found her Animal Advocate, a fox. The fox had an abundance of good suggestions and power, and encouraged the lost soul-part to come with me. I explained to the soul-part that Lizzy was needing her back so that she might live with joy. The fox promised to accompany her always and bring back her sense of fun and adventure. Returning from the Otherworld with the soul part and the fox, I sang soul and power back into Lizzy. She experienced a sudden surge of hope as I was singing over her, validating many of the things I'd experienced on my Otherworld journey. She is now making better progress since this reassimilation of soul and power, able to speak her mind and feeling more confident. By standing up for her daughter and not abandoning her, Lizzy also feels that she is redeeming part of the great wrong she herself experienced.

HOW TO PREPARE FOR SOUL-RETRIEVAL

Just as soul-fragmentation is a universal condition resultant from our isolation from nature, our disconnection from each other and our neglect of spiritual practice, so soul-restoration is part of our reunion with life. It helps to maintain the following attitudes:

• A sincere desire to be whole again.
• An ability and willingness to retain the soul-part/s retrieved.

- An understanding that retrieved parts may sometimes briefly evoke difficult memories, feelings and physical sensations for a while.
- An intelligent and loving acceptance of the retrieved soul-parts so that you can live a whole life.
- An understanding that integration of soul-parts can take a few weeks, and will always involve considerable changes in attitude, which will affect the course of your life.

You can actively prepare yourself to receive any missing parts by courting them in the following way:

- First call home your power (page 69).
- Light a candle at twilight. Spend at least ten minutes each day singing to any of your missing soul-parts, or by thinking of them returning and how this will complete your life—this sends out a clear signal that you want them back!
- Meditate on the parts and qualities that you lack and envision them coming back home.
- Formally break ties (in actuality or through simple ritual) between yourself and anyone who has been responsible for curtailing your freedom. See Chapter 6.
- Sometimes soul-intrusions have to be removed before soul-parts can come home. See Chapter 6.

Doing some of the actions above may cause spontaneous soul-retrieval. Sometimes something happens to clear a pathway between ourselves and the missing soul-part and we are able to receive it back with grace and love. This can happen while reading an insightful book, while having an ecstatic uplifting of spirit or when in communion with the healing power of nature.

THE SOUL-SHEPHERD

In Chapter 2 you discovered your Guardian Advocate, the Advocate who watches over you always and acts as a companion when you go into the Otherworld during your dreams, meditations and rituals. In Chapter 4, you found your Animal Advocate. Now you will find the Soul-Shepherd: this is an Advocate who accompanies the parts of your multiple souls that travel forth into the Otherworld. The Soul-Shepherd's job is to round up soul-parts that have strayed and bring them home safely. Like all Advocates it has your soul's well-being at heart at all times. This Advocate may appear in a variety of forms: it may be a wise ancestor, a spirit in humanoid or animal form, but, very frequently it takes the form of a being with both human and animal characteristics or a fusion of species. This is not as monstrous as it sounds. Very many divine beings have taken part-animal, part-human forms: the Egyptian and Hindu deities, for example, who have animal heads and human bodies, or the Greek god, Pan. One of Jesus Christ's many titles is "the Good Shepherd." Soul-Shepherds are, as their name suggests, used to herding or tending souls of all kinds. They are stern in defense of souls under threat and compassionately protective of those that stray. They can go into places and situations that would be dangerous for us, but not for them. Here's how to contact the Soul-Shepherd:

1. Relax, breathe and be still. Establish your energy field. Call your Animal Advocate to be with you.

2. Bring to mind the highest natural land feature near you: a hill, cliff or mountain. Together with your companion animal go in meditation to that place. Your animal leads the way and shows you where to find the Soul-Shepherd. In every locality where s/he can overlook the terrain, the Soul-Shepherd can be found. Follow your Animal Advocate's lead. Use the same discriminating questions for meeting your Advocate to ascertain the Soul-Shepherd (see page 28).

3. Be aware of the Soul-Shepherd in whatever form s/he takes. In her/his hand is a staff of some kind. All those who want her/his help must touch the staff. Do this now, especially if you intend to call soul-parts home, asking for the Soul-Shepherd's help. As you touch it, you may be aware of music in the form of a tune or resonance that echoes deep in your body.

4. The Soul-Shepherd sees you and your need. S/he blesses you with a light touch of the hand or by touching your shoulder with the staff. (And may also touch and bless your Animal Advocate as well.) This

touch is the sign that the Soul-Shepherd will come to you at time of need and help you. You will only have to call. Receive that blessing and knowledge with confidence.

5. Thank the Soul-Shepherd and return to your own time and place.

GATHERING YOUR SCATTERED PSYCHE RITUAL

When we have been at difficult, exciting or overstimulating events, we often feel ourselves scattered or fragmented at the end of the day. It is essential, especially after a long run of such upheaval and excitement, that you take time to gather yourself together again. A good indication of your scattered condition is your dreams, where you will sometimes locate yourself in the place or with the events and people who have drawn parts of your soul and power. You may also experience a tape-loop (see page 135) running through your consciousness: note where its route takes you because these are the places and events where fragments of your souls have gone. Write down any dreams you have so that when you gather your scattered soul-parts you can call them home from that location or event. It is not essential to find the Soul-Shepherd before you call or sing home your soul-parts, since any one of your other Advocates can do this job if you ask them. If you have only found one Advocate, then that one will help you. Use this method for non-serious soul-straying when you need to gather yourself back again:

1. First call home your power (page 69).

2. Aloud, in your own words, make a firm intention to care for your souls as lovingly as you know how.

3. Relax, breathe and be still. Establish your energy field strongly (page 52), and call upon your Guardian and Animal Advocates. Be aware of their presence.

4. Now call upon the Soul-Shepherd to help find the soul-parts that are lost, missing or strayed. From wherever s/he currently is, s/he comes with her/his staff to lead souls home.

5. Facing the directions in turn, calling or singing out in turn, "I call my souls home from the East, South, West, North, Below, Above. May they find me wherever they may have strayed." With eyes closed, experience a pathway between you and each direction. Throughout this part, remain receptive and centered with your Guardian or Animal Advocate. *Do not travel down the pathways yourself. It is the Soul-Shepherd or one of your other Advocates who goes to collect them.* If any of your soul-fragments are stuck or slow, your Advocate gives them a hand to return to you. Sense, see and feel their return and embrace them before turning to the next direction.

6. When all six directions have been addressed, say, "I welcome my souls home in peace and tranquility."

7. Bless and seal your aura by making the crossing sign (page 52). Thank your Advocates and record your experiences.

THE PIPES OF PAN

Six months after a serious traffic accident, Nicola's physical injuries have healed, and X-rays have shown she has no concussion, but she is still out of focus and disoriented. When she reads about soul-loss, she immediately knows with certainty that she has lost a soul-part. She prepares carefully and sings her soul home with the help of her allies. Doubtful about her own voice and ability to sing for a long time, she begins to sing one note. After a bit, the note turns into a tune and she is immediately aware of the Soul-Shepherd setting off to find her soul-part. He looks like a kindly figure of Pan with a twisted hazel stick in his hands. He strides away into the West, where there is heavy rain. Her song gets louder as Pan struggles through the weather. Holding out his stick, Pan calls the soul-part by playing on his pipes. Nicola's song has become the tune he is playing. Out of the West, the form of Nicola's soul-part emerges, drawn by his piping. The soul-part grasps Pan's stick and together they return down the western road. As Nicola embraces the soul-part, she experiences a quiver of excitement and recognition.

Afterward, she feels tired and drained, but she sleeps secure in the knowledge that she is no longer divided from her soul. The next day, she lights a candle to thank Pan, because she was too excited yesterday. After a few weeks, her sense of disorientation has vanished as the soul-part becomes fully assimilated.

SINGING THE SOUL HOME RITUAL—SOUL-RETRIEVAL

In cases of minor soul-loss, where a soul-part is not just straying but absent, you can sing it home using the same basic method as above. This is a very powerful way for missing soul-parts to return. Don't be put off by the idea of singing. This isn't grand opera or a performance, just the sounds that you can naturally make if you sustain your breath and stop using your tongue, teeth and lips to form words. If you can speak, you can utter sound, believe me. Pitch your voice in your middle register where it feels comfortable:

1. Follow the same instructions as for the Gathering your Scattered Psyche ritual, above, but remain seated upright and be aware of the directions around you. After calling your Advocates to you, ask them to help find the soul-part that has been lost or missing.

2. Tune into the three locations where your Vital, Personal and Wisdom Souls reside: in lower belly, chest and head. Begin to perceive a common unifying note that expresses all your souls and sing that note out aloud. Don't turn your attention to anything until that sound is established. Let the note sound freely; if it wants to change and begin a musical phrase or tune of its own, let it. If words come, let them. If they don't, just hold your mouth in a shape and sound that feels right. Follow the flow and keep singing. If self-consciousness distracts you, remember that you are helping create a pathway for your soul-part to come home. The sounds don't matter, but your intention does. Keep going.

3. The choir of your souls is now singing through you. This is the pathway of the search and you are going to keep it going while your Advocates help you. When the Soul-Shepherd or whichever of your Advocates is ready, s/he will use the path of your song to go find the missing part. Stay centered. You may be partially aware of where the Soul-Shepherd is going, but your task is to keep singing and not be drawn away from your center.

4. After a period of singing lasting anything from ten to thirty minutes, you will be aware of the Soul-Shepherd's return. In his/her keeping will be the soul-part and possibly a symbol of your power. Keep singing and open your arms to receive what is coming back to you. Embrace and

enfold what is returned to you to your heart. Stop singing. Allow your breath to distribute the soul-part and any gift into your being.

5. Welcome the soul-part and any gift home. Ask the Soul-Shepherd and Advocates for any information they may have to convey. Attend to the returned soul-part and register its feeling, frequency, quality. Remember, you are welcoming home your essential soul-parts—not the trauma or pain you suffered when they left. If you experience a shadow of the trauma, refer it immediately to the healing of your Guardian or Animal Advocates.

6. Record your experiences. Thank your Advocates. Immediately following this ritual, spend the ensuing part of the day and the next few days in ordinary, non-demanding activity or rest. Avoid confrontational situations where power-loss or soul-threat may occur.

THE EFFECTS OF SOUL-RETRIEVAL

Soul-retrieval will enable you to be the person you really are, and that will mean *change*. It often brings:

- The return of honesty and awareness, of a sense of personal responsibility.
- The realization that abusive relationships and addictive patterns must be treated in a radical way, that you need expert help and support. This is the time to seek formal therapy (in the case of addictions) or professional assistance (if you are suffering from domestic violence, for example).
- A sudden distaste for old habits and patterns, which before soul-retrieval may have been your mainstay.
- An acceptance and valuing of yourself.
- A sense of being more present in your life, rather than always "observing" yourself.
- A closer connection with your sensations, emotions and intuitions as a renewed surge of life-energy begins to flow through you.
- A sense of being full of power.
- A relieved disconnection from connections that have disturbed you.
- The arrival of fresh perceptions and possibilities that overturn old impossibilities.
- An appetite for new horizons and more adventurous outlooks.

Soul-retrieval is sometimes followed by a short period of emotional intensification: tears, physical disorientation or blocked-out memory bleed-through are some short-term and temporary effects. This will not last. You are now hosting soul-parts that have been dislocated from everyday life for a while. Live gently and with intention, be aware of every small action you perform, and reintroduce the returned soul-parts to your everyday life. As they learn how you live, so you will also be learning about the returned soul-parts.

Full integration may take several weeks. You will organically become aware of this integration yourself, but the strongest validation is when other people begin to notice how much improved/different/happier you are. If you are recovering from or still dealing with a long-term condition, don't give up the medication, support, therapy, etc., without the advice of your therapist/doctor/practitioner.

People often fear that their soul-part will stray off again. If you truly welcome it home and are determined to live in better balance, of course it will not go.

RETURNING STOLEN SOULS RITUAL

Everyone wants to be bigger and better than they really are. We don't mean to steal souls, but we do, retaining them long after the need to do so has passed. Soul-theft usually occurs unconsciously when you have been in a dependent or abusive relationship. It is very rarely consciously malicious. Examples of soul-theft might include: when relationships break down and one partner announces "I'll never let you go!"; when a child's vitality or spontaneity is sapped by an impatient adult; at death, when the living one has unwittingly become dependent upon the dying one and still clings on. (See Chapter 15 for more about issues around death.) Such cases require our Advocates to cajole or entice the soul-parts back.

We all customarily hold on to soul-parts of those whom we were once mutually contracted to, such as ex-lovers, as well as to other people, associations and groups with whom we have no more to do. Clubs and groups have their own group-soul, which we'll look at in Chapter 9. These can also be given back. By ties of affection, advantage and opportunity, we try to maintain the soul-nurture that those old associations gave us, even though those groups and individuals no longer wish association with us. Our own neediness argues that we must retain these connections and so we lock them up in a safe place. These souls help us hang on to our old image of ourselves, keeping us ever young and untouched, or so we think.

A good example of where this sort of soul-retention is seen is in the character of Miss Havisham in Charles Dickens's *Great Expectations*. Jilted on the day of her wedding and suffering immense soul-loss, she sits among the decay of her wedding breakfast still dressed in bridal array until her old age, maliciously harboring her disappointment and spite and stealing the souls of young Estella and Pip, so that her revenge infects and blights the next generation. We must have compassion for the soul-thieves because they themselves are the victims of soul-theft, caught in a long chain created by need, soul-loss and confusion.

Although you may deny that you've ever retained a soul for your own purpose, please think again as you look over this checklist of questions:

- Of those you no longer associate with, who are you still depending upon and for what?
- What old relationships are you still hanging on to?
- Who are you still punishing for doing you wrong?
- What old groups, clubs and associations do you claim connection with to give you status?
- What soul-nurture have you derived from all of these connections? What are your needs now?
- How are these associations cramping your development?

These are a chastening set of questions, I know, because we must all answer them honestly if we are to be free of the psychic disturbance that soul-retention wreaks upon our lives and upon the lives of others. In order to move on and to liberate the lives of others, let those souls go home now:

1. Before you begin, write the name of every person or group whose soul-parts you know you must return, each on a separate slip of paper. If you've forgotten names, write "my old boyfriend from work" or "the woman I cast aside" or whatever. Note that this method works for all kinds of soul-retention. If the owner of the soul-part is dead, it still works. You will also need a bowl.

2. Relax, breathe and be still. Establish your body field (page 17). Breathe in and out of it, using the Positive Breath Pattern: Inhale 4; Hold 8; Exhale 8; Hold out 4. Keep this going for a few minutes.

3. Center yourself and be aware of the directions about you, behind, before, left and right, above and below. Call your Advocates to come and be with you to help strengthen and support you. Be aware of your animal before you and your guardian behind you. Call upon the Soul-Shepherd to be near.

4. Take up one of the pieces of paper, saying, "I have kept the soul-part of [name] but now I give it back to her/him." Press the piece of paper to whichever part of your body you feel you have stored this soul, transfer the soul to the piece of paper, then offer it to the Soul-Shepherd. S/he takes the essence of the retained soul-part and takes it back to its owner down one of the pathways of the directions, while you put the piece of paper itself into the bowl on the floor. Say, as you place the paper in the bowl, "I freely release [name]." Stay centered and allow the Soul-Shepherd to do the work. Call upon the support of your animal and upon the loving wisdom of your guardian, while each soul-part returns, especially if you experience feelings of loss, anger or sorrow. Tears are a very appropriate cleansing at this time. Repeat this procedure with every name you've written down. Apologize and thank those from whom you've taken; bless them.

5. Now take the bowl to a safe place where you can burn the pieces of paper. This doesn't harm anyone because the soul-essence has been returned. This final act clears and cleans everything. Throw the ash to the six directions when the fire is dead.

Remember not to return souls with whom you have *a healthy and reciprocal relationship*—for example, you will certainly have a mutual exchange of soul-parts with your partner or children, which is normal and natural! See Chapter 12 for more on soul in relationships.

PSYCHIC SURVEILLANCE

It's an anthropological observation that people in traditional societies believe that cameras steal their souls. However you feel about that, it is certainly true that whenever we go shopping at the mall we are all under the surveillance of security cameras and that our images are stored on video for at least a few days before the tapes are reused. This security-conscious surveillance makes many of us uncomfortable. However, there may be more intrusive things than video cameras and satellites to be concerned about that may endanger our souls.

Because our souls have the ability to travel about, it is more than possible that you have experienced or are practicing psychic surveillance. This is when you send out a soul-part to check up on someone else. All mothers do this naturally when they are parted from their children, but usually in shortwave blasts of attention, being also aware when a child is in danger, even though they may be on the other side of the planet.

Full-blown psychic surveillance is seriously disturbing. You may experience it with a jealous lover who, even when he's not with you, seems to know what you're doing. If you've angered someone, you can feel the blast of her searchlight rage. Celebrities suffer this kind of continual surveillance on both physical and psychic levels, when fans obsess over their pictures, or dream of having sex with them. The symptoms are usually a sense of being watched, of looking over your shoulder, of being followed, but when you go to look, there is no physical person in sight. Here's how to deal with psychic surveillance:

- Reinforce your energy field and visualize a low-frequency electrical charge of white starlight through it (see Chapter 1). This will boost your early-warning system that someone's trying to get through.
- Don't forget you come with your own bodyguard: your Animal Advocate is the best guardian of your soul, acting as watchdog (or whatever species walks with you) to warn and to guard you.
- Call upon the Soul-Shepherd to watch over you and see off any would-be intruders.
- Use the Spiritual Armor ritual (page 54). The armor will mirror back the watcher's own gaze.
- Regularly check and clean your soul cauldrons. (See page 99.)
- If symptoms persist, ask Advocates to wield the Knife of Separation (page 120).

If you discover that you've been a psychic snooper, then don't beat yourself up but make a firm resolve to stop doing it. Other people's business is not yours. There are more strategies for dealing with would-be psychic intruders in Chapter 6.

POWERS OF THE THREE SOUL CAULDRONS

Each of our three souls has a home in our bodies. These may be seen as a set of three interconnecting vessels or stacking cauldrons in which each of our souls are nurtured. They work subtly and affect each other. Vital power irrigates all of the cauldrons and connects them. The cauldrons are the reservoirs where soul-nurture is stored and remembered. The capacity of each person's cauldrons is immense: this is how we can contain the whole universe in our souls. The three cauldrons are subtle, not physical, reservoirs. You will not find them in an anatomy book, but they are known to metaphysical wisdom throughout the world. They are where the subtle alchemy of our souls is brewed. None of the three is better than or "superior" to the others, for they work in concert. We have to attune to our souls and their power, learning how to access our capacity and how to manage it. This subtle management of these reservoirs is what makes us really streetwise in soul-care and teaches us how to avoid psychic disturbance.

The cauldrons can fill and empty. When we fill our cauldrons with stuff or unconsciously store things there or when we have uninvited guests in our cauldrons, we become aware of psychic disturbance and confusion. When we have leaky power or soul-fragmentation, our cauldrons begin to empty and we feel depleted, fearful and anxious.

The way we live impacts upon our souls and bodies, as instinctive diagnostician Caroline Myss tells us, "Biography becomes biology." Sooner or later, any lack of flow in our power, passion and intentions will cause the physical symptoms of illness. Our accepted model of physical health regards illness as emanating from environmental, genetic or outside factors, and physicians often treat the symptoms rather than the cause. In the spiritual model of health, illness is experienced as the bodily manifestation of misplaced spirit that has lodged and is already resident in the subtle bodies; treatment begins by going to the seat of spiritual causation. Shamans would speak of "spirits of illness," while psychologists talk of "subconscious predispositions" and physicians of "bacterial microorganisms." But, as Malidoma Somé wisely says, "Illness is a physical manifestation of a spiritual decay."

Our psychic health hinges upon two key factors. Most psychic disturbance works by way of repercussion upon a vulnerability where a hole opens and power or soul can be lost, or else arises around an area of blockage, which becomes the catalyst where power or soul retention cause confusion and delusion. Repercussive and intrusive soul-disturbance is generally caused by outside factors, with some help and collusion from us; but psychic disturbance arising from blockage is usually self-generated. *Thus we are responsible for creating much of our own psychic disturbance, though we invariably project the blame upon an outer set of factors.* By paying attention to the state of our soul cauldrons, we can prevent much of this happening.

CLEANSING THE CAULDRONS

Leo is a workaholic line-manager with a complex life. He is often exhausted and aware of being held together by willpower alone, a fact obvious to his employers, who send him on a stress-management weekend. He begins to appreciate meditation and to realize how work is impacting upon his body, mind and soul. He practices the Soul Cauldrons Meditation. The Vital Soul Cauldron deep in his belly feels full of rubble, like the undigested remains of fears for his very survival. His Animal Advocate is a chimpanzee who very playfully tosses out the bricks and hoses down the cauldron, filling it up with clean water.

The next time he meditates, Leo concentrates upon the Personal Soul Cauldron. His solar plexus feels both hollow and aching, making him feel like the scarecrow in *The Wizard of Oz*. The humiliation of being so out of control that he has to be sent on a course rankles with him, though he acknowledges that he needs helpful strategies. The middle cauldron appears to be on its side and leaky, so he calls upon the Soul-Shepherd to fix it. His Soul-Shepherd is a good-tempered giant who draws the broken edges of the cauldron together while singing a rhythmic song. Unconsciously, Leo breathes to this rhythm. As the Soul-Shepherd works, Leo is aware of a new warmth and resilience in his solar plexus.

On the next occasion, Leo concentrates upon the Wisdom Soul Cauldron, first of all checking in with the two lower ones into which he breathes, feeling the revitalization. His head feels like Grand Central Station, criss-crossed with warring tensions and unresolved plans. The Wisdom Soul Cauldron seems to be upside down. He is cross about this, because he craves perfection, but his Guardian Advocate—a priestess who resembles the supporter of a Greek temple—stands by. She lays a hand upon his brow to calm him, encouraging him to concentrate upon the lower two cauldrons and the strength and stability that has been returned to them. Letting go of his opposition, Leo allows her healing power to come through. Briefly, he experiences the three cauldrons upright and in harmony. Over a period of two months, he keeps up his meditations and is a changed man, able to take rest, defer decisions and say no to tasks he would once have tackled head-on regardless.

THE SOUL CAULDRONS MEDITATION

In order to help regulate our soul cauldrons, we need to become aware of both the leaks and the blockages. Balance and flow are the natural conditions of life-energy. When blockage and stagnation occur, when energy pools, when it grows static and disturbed, we experience both physical and psychic distress. Likewise, when we are leaking power or allowing soul-parts to stray, we are creating a dangerous vacuum. This chapter and Chapter 4 have equipped you to deal with these problems. Tune into your body and souls now. As you work through the meditation, which you can do a section at a time or all at once, consider the following questions for each cauldron:

- What does the cauldron look, feel and seem like to you?
- Is it upright, leaning or turned over?
- What feels blocked or static within it?
- Where does it appear leaky?
- What's inside it?

Note that if you find that the Personal Soul Cauldron is on its side in this meditation, don't be alarmed, for this cauldron is the busiest. It moves about a good deal and collects ingredients for soul-nurture. If it is upside-down, this is normal after any upset or disturbance. Allow the Soul-Shepherd to deal with this. In many people, the Wisdom Soul Cauldron is upside down and has been so from birth. It gradually turns upright as we begin to not just receive wisdom, but to store and use it—let it be; your Guardian Advocate will know when it needs to be upright. In this meditation, all cauldrons become upright for a brief time. The more you practice this meditation, the better aligned the soul cauldrons become:

1. Sit comfortably. Relax, breathe and be still. Establish your energy field (page 17) and seal your aura (page 52). Be aware of the earth beneath you, supporting you.

2. Breathing into your lower body, become aware of the Vital Soul Cauldron in your belly. Place both your hands on it. Be aware of the powerful life-energy that this cauldron supplies to you. Ask the questions above. Allow all that is clogging up this lower cauldron to be emptied out: concerns and fears about family affairs, money, sex, power, self-esteem and worries about the everyday struggle to survive. Let these go now. If the cauldron is leaky, call upon your Animal Advocate to repair it. If it is leaning, be strongly aware of the earth beneath you and the power of gravity. Breathe the power of gravity into the cauldron to stabilize it. Now breathe the power of life back into the cauldron to revitalize it. Feel the warmth of your breath rising up and heating the middle cauldron above it.

3. Breathing into your upper body, become aware of the Personal Soul Cauldron in your chest. Place both hands between solar plexus and heart. Be aware of the passionate power of life that this cauldron supplies to you. Ask the questions above. Allow all that clogs this cauldron to be emptied out: concerns and fears of emotional and creative origin, issues about decision and choice, frustrated passions and desires, issues about relationship entanglements. Let these go now. If this cauldron is leaky, call upon the Soul-Shepherd to repair it. In whatever position you find your cauldron, send your breath into it with love and joy. Feel also the safety and support of the lower cauldron beneath it. The gift of the power of life rises and helps turn the middle cauldron upright. Feel the warmth of your breath rising up and bringing love and joy to the upper cauldron.

4. Breathing into your head, become aware of the Wisdom Soul Cauldron in your head. Place one hand with your fingertips upon your brow. Be aware of the wise and discriminating power of life that this cauldron supplies to you. Ask the questions above. Allow all that clogs this cauldron to be emptied out: fears about knowing enough and being good enough, obsessive and circular thoughts, issues surrounding stale beliefs. Let them go now. If this cauldron is leaky, call upon your Guardian Advocate to repair it. In whatever position you find your upper cauldron, send your breath into it with peace and tranquillity. Feel also the safety and support of the lower cauldron and the lively joy of the middle cauldron beneath it. These gifts of power and joy help turn the upper cauldron upright.

5. The three cauldrons are now upright and their triple soul-power is becoming aligned. Now open up to the greater wisdom of the Source of Life that is always available when you are focused and still. This wisdom fills the Wisdom Soul Cauldron with crystal water, without any effort on your part; it is a wisdom that doesn't have to be striven after. As it fills the upper cauldron so, this wisdom flows over the sides into the middle cauldron below, and so on into the lower cauldron. As the waters of wisdom pool about your feet they become infused with cleansing truth. Breathe in and gather the waters of truth and wisdom upon your breath to create a circuit of wisdom, passion and power in your cauldrons. Allow your breath to pick up the rhythm and pattern of this flow and allow it to bathe you as long as you need.

This meditation can be profitably repeated many times to help strengthen and coordinate your Soul Cauldrons. I know that if I allow myself to get physically, psychically and mentally run down, and out of tune with my souls, I may experience green slime in my lower cauldron, psychic spaghetti in my middle one and the beginnings of a scuzzy fungus in the upper one. This meditation always realigns me as well as cleaning, repairing and filling me up again.

SOUL-NURTURE

We wouldn't expect to be able to go long without refueling and resting our bodies with food and sleep, so how is it that we believe we can go on indefinitely without soul-nurture? We can nurture our three Soul Cauldrons in simple, everyday ways:

• Nourish your Vital Soul Cauldron and tank it up with strength and stamina by spending time outside in nature, walking in the park, eating fresh food that still has vitality in it (notably absent in highly processed foods), living with relish and delight, being in the present moment, exercising or dancing, cultivating your family and garden, spending time with your Animal Advocate in meditation and finding out how to maintain your power-boundaries with skill.

• Nourish your Personal Soul Cauldron and tank it up with passionate power by engaging with and exercising your emotions, living passionately to the full, practicing your creative gifts, meeting with and enjoying the company of friends, honing your imagination, meditating with the Soul-Shepherd and finding out how to manifest your inherited and natural skills with joy.

• Nourish your Wisdom Soul Cauldron by exercising your intelligence and discrimination, seeking out and studying what interests you, maintaining your spiritual practice with delight and thankfulness, meditating upon your Guardian Advocate and finding out how to manifest your life's purpose in service to the universe.

BLUEPRINTS FOR A HEALTHY SOUL

1. Take a period of silence and mindfulness each day to refresh your soul.

2. Clarify your soul by considering motivations and clearing out stale agendas.

3. Gather your souls together at the end of each day.

4. Take proper rest after overstimulating or challenging events.

5. Keep connected to the Soul-Shepherd.

6. Live with power, passion and intention.

7. Liberate soul-parts that you may be retaining.

8. Be circumspect not to psychically snoop on others.

9. Keep your Soul Cauldrons clean and aligned.

10. Nurture your souls with the food they most desire.

CHAPTER 6

Uninvited Guests

The best defense against the spiritual
intruders is awareness of the condition and
strengthening the "spiritual immune system."

—William J. Baldwin in *Healing Lost Souls*

PSYCHIC HOUSEKEEPING: SPIRITUAL HYGIENE

Welcome to the most powerfully transforming chapter of this book! If you thought you could ignore the cleaning duties when it came to spiritual matters, the truth is, you're mistaken. Here you will learn about psychic housekeeping and the art of spiritual hygiene.

As a species we veer between being mucky and dirt-tolerant or squeamish and dirt-intolerant. Whichever end of the spectrum you gravitate toward, believe me when I say that dirt is dirt and disorder is disorder whether it lives in this world or the Otherworld. Disorder happens when things get out of their rightful place: the lovely Venetian crystal glasses on your dresser can become disordered when deposited carelessly on your sofa with dregs of cheap red wine and cigarette ends inside them. Dirt is what builds up the minute you've finished cleaning, and builds up and builds up. The classic sports car stored in your garage may be worth a bit, but neither you nor anyone will be driving it anywhere if you haven't cleaned it for the last eight years, because it will be full of spiders, mice, and other uninvited guests who've made their home in it since you obviously don't need it.

The primary attitude of the housekeeper is one of orderliness and matter-of-factness when dealing with dirt and disorder. Housekeepers also need patience, because dirt doesn't suddenly stop happening. Dealing with psychic dirt and spiritual disorder requires exactly the same attitude. Of course, there are people who blanch at cleaning a toilet or retch over cat-vomit, but even they can clean up if equipped with plastic gloves, a long cleaning implement and some disinfectant. Be pragmatic as you read this chapter rather than alarmed because you are the housekeeper of your souls. What you invite in and what accumulates in them is your responsibility.

The condition of our souls is dependent upon spiritual hygiene. We are all accustomed to physical hygiene: we wash our hands after using the toilet, we disinfect the mop after cleaning the floor and we put antiseptic on our cuts. Spiritual hygiene works exactly in the same way but because we have discounted the Otherworld, we forget to observe its rules. Thus, we forget to decontaminate ourselves after a fierce argument, or after being with a slimy salesman, or after witnessing a car crash. We take their residues with us.

One of the biggest myths about psychic disturbance is that it is always caused by other people, but it is more true to say that most of it is caused by our own lack of spiritual hygiene. Here are a few guidelines for maintaining your own spiritual hygiene:

- Maintain the boundaries of your power and souls by taking responsibility for them.
- Be careful who or what you invite into your physical, emotional or mental space.
- Make clear distinctions between each activity, set of emotions or thoughts, so that your power, soul or mind doesn't flow into and become part of other areas like wet paint.
- Inhabit your body, soul and mind attentively and with vigor.
- If you encounter people, events or situations where you feel polluted, clear any residues immediately (page 109).
- Keep connected to spiritual Advocates and the Source of Life with regular meditation, prayer and practice.

FINDING YOUR OWN CENTER RITUAL

We live in a world where we are subject to sudden urges and influences, where opportunists cruise looking for the big chance, where dependents' expectations drag us down, where we are continually knocked off center by the events of the day. Sometimes it is hard to sleep because so much of these distracting occurrences whiz through our being like rush-hour traffic, giving us no rest, and confusing our understanding so that we can hardly distinguish between us and them. We feel as if we were in a food blender with all these things, whirled round by a giant centrifugal force.

Malidoma Somé reminds us, "No one's center is like someone else's. Find your own center, not the center of your neighbor; not the center of your father or mother or family or ancestor but that center which is yours and yours alone." If we live within and from our own center we will not be pulled into the gravitational field of someone or something else. We find our own center by going within and exploring the landscape that is already there. Finding our center requires that we sacredly inhabit the present moment. If we live in the mundane present, we are often concerned by what people think of us or how we will appear to them and the effect we are making. The sacred present is quite different from this. It is a living state of awareness wherein we are neither in past nor future, nor yet in daydreams or drifting consciousness.

Practice this every day, at least once in the morning and once before sleeping. When centering becomes habitual, you will be able to snap into focus as necessary. You can use it wherever you are. In this meditation, you become the center of the natural universe. But don't feel that this is too grandiose for you. Permit yourself to take up your own space in this universe. If you become knocked off center by something, immediately flash up the coordinates of this meditation and return to center again.

1. Stand upright. Become fully aware of your body by breathing into every part of it. Establish your energy field with your vital breath.

2. Next begin to align yourself at the center of all that is whole and holy in the universe. Be aware of the truth of the earth beneath you and the wisdom of the sky above you. Feel a connective power link that runs straight through your body from heights to depths, from depths to heights. This link never leaves you wherever you are, even though you may be on the fourteenth floor above the ground. Feel the roots of this power link extending beneath you to the earth beneath. Feel its branches extending into the heavens above. From below and above you receive both physical nurture and spiritual sustenance. Be a part of this universe as a living, moving tree of connected, blessed vitality.

3. Be aware of each direction around you: before, behind, left and right. Feel a connective power link running through you from front to back at the height of your navel, and another such link running through you from side to side at the same height. These power links connect to the four directions and help stabilize and balance you wherever you stand on earth, in whatever direction you turn. Feel your center of gravity as being in your lower belly. You can visualize it as a kind of Hula Hoop about your body.

4. Face each direction in turn. Visualize a pathway between you and each direction: north, south, east and west. Be aware both of what physically lies in those directions by way of the natural land features in the country in which you are living (the ocean, a mountain, a river, a wood, etc.), but also of the blessing that comes from the direction you are facing. In each of the four directions and connected to the four elements are the protective powers of the Source of Life: these can appear as guardians, angels or protectors in each direction. You decide which compass directions these powers stand in because these change depending on where you are upon earth. Here is a brief guide to some of the spiritual patterns by which we can recognize these powers throughout the universe:

These powers help sustain your whole being. With closed eyes, be alert to how each direction appears, feels and seems to you. Over time you will find this part builds very powerfully.

5. Now, feeling your connection in all six directions, turn your awareness inward to the deep place inside yourself where your three souls live along with the cauldrons that hold their power. Experience each of the cauldrons and their power as an energy field that permeates and envelopes your body. Enter into the very center of yourself and be

seated on the throne of your Personal Soul. From this seat, enter into a profound stillness and attention where you are perfectly centered. If distracting thoughts arise, reconnect yourself with the six directional powers and the pathways that connect you, and go within once more.

6. Finally, visualize the vitality of your energy field and the supple strength of your souls as one being of light as you stand/sit at the center of the universe. Gradually allow your attention to flow forward from the seat of your soul and open your eyes to perceive and engage with the universe.

7. Once you have tried this a few times, you can extend the practice of centering by singing the note of your soul in the directions so that you tune the universe and yourself into one harmony. This practice can also be done as a moving or walking meditation in any place so that you experience your centeredness as you walk, perceiving your connection as a vibrant mesh that moves with you like a garment you are wearing. Over time, you will become much more tuned into what is right or wrong for you, the kinds of places and situations to avoid, since this practice boosts the instincts and perceptive faculties of the soul.

UNINVITED GUESTS AND HOW WE LET THEM OVER THE THRESHOLD

We unconsciously let "uninvited guests" over our threshold. But when we have actually opened the door and put out the welcome mat to them, is it any wonder they make free with our offer? These uninvited guests are the roaming spirits of people, substances, thoughts, feelings, fears, etc., that come into our energy field and soul cauldrons. These range from minor residues and attachments that are merely hitching a ride, to more serious colonizers, opportunists and intrusions, which have penetrated deeply into our souls and are busy drawing off our power for their own purposes. Intrusions are residues that become inhabitant in our body field; they want to have access to our vitality, passion or mind.

All uninvited guests need an open invitation to come in, a gap or space to settle in and then some nourishment. Such an opening may come when our thresholds are lowered and when we are suffering power-loss or power-leakage. The space vacated by a lost or straying soul-part can make a home for an intrusion. The nourishment that we provide to intrusions is supplied from our own power and vitality, from our emotional engagement with the intrusion, and from our mental acceptance of and collusion with it.

Intrusions may range from small intrusive fragments that are embedded in our being and cause us minor discomfort, to more serious colonists that alter our behavior in significant ways. Remember that intrusions can become attached to us from the need to survive, out of love or dependence, and not just out of malicious or exploitative motives. Intrusions are entanglements that warp the web of life, confusing us by the pressure they exert upon our own life's weaving. The following factors endanger our souls by lowering our thresholds of resistance and allowing gaps for intrusions to enter:

- Being "out to lunch," continually daydreaming or inattentive. See Chapter 2.
- Having little sense of self or of self-worth. See Chapters 1 and 7.
- Ignoring or denying our instincts. See Chapter 1.
- When an anesthetic, drunkenness or overdose sends us out of our body.
- Being away from home and familiar things. See Chapter 10.
- When we come under the influence of the group-soul of a crowd. See Chapter 9.
- When in contact with charismatic or unscrupulous people. See Chapter 9.

RESIDUES: WHAT YOU PICK UP DURING THE DAY

Residues are leftovers, dregs, fluff, strains or traces of something. You know all about residues already from cleaning your own home, but every day we pick up residues in our energy field too. These are made up of other people's psychic stuff, the events of the day, the places we've been. As with house-cleaning, if you don't clean residues regularly, you get ground-in grime, bacteria and infection. You don't want to take residues home.

All residues and intrusions exist in spirit form. However, just because we experience residues and intrusions as an evil doesn't make them evil. They are just in the wrong place.

- Cleaning residues is something you can do at the end of every day while you wash and shower. As you wash your body, let your Advocate loosen and stroke away any residues attaching to you. These all go down the drain.

- After you've become aware of residues, immediately shake your hands and feet as if they were very wet and you were trying to get dry again. Do this outdoors in places where they can disperse, or else open a window if you're indoors.

- Remove stale air from lungs by breathing right out. Suck your belly toward your backbone to help expel air.

- Detoxify your body by a simple twenty-four-hour fast. Eat normally but without alcohol between 6–7 p.m. On rising next day, drink a glass of warm water with the juice of half a lemon in it. Do the same at lunchtime. Eat a light, meatless meal in the evening.

- When you pass water or defecate, expel any impurities and residues from your system and flush them away.

- If your energy field has obvious residues in it you may be very aware of them as aches or fullness in different parts of your torso. If you have the physical urge to pull these feelings out, first call your Advocate to put shielding gloves upon your hands. When you've got the gloves on, begin to tease, stroke and pull out whatever is there. Your hands will probably be working a few inches from your body in your energy field. The stuff you've pulled out should be shaken away from you. Your Advocates remove these residues safely from the vicinity.

- The magician, William Gray, used a little saying to help rid himself of residues:

  "Leave me without delay. Whatever should not stay.
  Away from me proceed all I no longer need.
  Let this release cause inner peace."

SYMPTOMS OF INTRUSION

Physically it is easy to identify what is not of us. However, it is less easy to tell when we have a psychic intrusion. Check if you feel:

- Displaced from your center (as if you were pushed to one side).
- Inflated, blown up (physically or in your being, mind or soul).
- Burdened by unknown heaviness.
- Over-full or stuffed with things that don't discharge themselves.
- Unable to shake off the influence or presence of someone.
- Unsatisfied by the goodness of either physical nurture, or emotional or spiritual benefits.
- Unable to take full pleasure or enjoyment in things (for no good reason).
- Afflicted by uncharacteristic desires or urgings.
- Aware of a subtle or alien intelligence that influences your decisions, tastes, emotions, etc.
- A sense of something foreign occupying your space.
- Aware of a mental image or the voice of someone dictating how you should behave.
- Aware of something alien in your energy field.
- A sense of being watched or manipulated by someone.

Remember that you may feel these symptoms of intrusion not only from being invaded by other people but also from your own personal psychic turmoils that have been left to brew unchecked. We need to be very clear that intrusions are nothing more than life-power in the wrong place. If we demonize them, we begin to fear them, giving them our power, and then they will have power over us. Intrusions must be dealt with as vigorously and forthrightly as you clean your floor, sink or toilet.

THE WATCHER

As a child, Sharon had been sexually abused by a priest whom her family trusted, but she never told anyone. Even as an adult, she felt his presence always near her, watching her. In the paper one day, she read that this same priest had been accused of abusing several other children in that parish. One of his victims had brought a successful case against him. Now that he was serving a long prison sentence, she assumed that this creepy feeling of him watching her would go away, but it didn't. She eventually came to me to ask what was going on. I explored Sharon's energy field and discovered a secret room within it where a series of photographs of Sharon hung from the wall opposite a chair. As I watched, an elderly priest came and sat on the chair and masturbated while ogling the photos. Two of my Advocates came and firmly escorted him away from the room and back to where his body was. My Animal Advocate told me to take down the photos, tear them up and set fire to them. I was reluctant to do so at first, but as we watched them burn, there emerged from the flames a single image of Sharon as a girl. This was the image of Sharon's soul part that the priest had stolen. We had removed the intrusive watcher and also found an essential soul-part for Sharon. She has subsequently seen a therapist to help clear out any residual trauma of her early abuse, and she no longer has the sense of being watched.

RELEASING INTRUSIONS RITUAL

Intrusions come in when we have lost power or soul. *Sometimes power and soul will not return to us unless we first remove the intrusion.* This is because the intrusion colonizes the space left by lost power or soul. The healing process is one of substitution: when the intrusion goes away, your power and soul can come home. Use this in combination with Chapters 4 and 5.

1. Invoke the Source of Life to aid and protect you. Center yourself. Establish your energy field (see Chapter 1). Sense, see and feel it as a bubble about you.
2. Now call your Advocate/s to help you clear your personal space of any residues or intrusions. Become aware of your Advocate beside you. Your spirit-companion now extends a loop of his/her own body field around your bubble, so that it surrounds your space.
3. Become aware of whatever is alien within your own body field, without engaging with it. Your Advocate sucks through any residue or intrusion and removes it safely from your body field into his/her own.

4. When you are aware that the intrusion has left you, check in each of the six directions to see if there is any power or soul that needs to return to you. (See page 69 and page 91).

5. Directly afterward go into your shower of light to clean yourself and invoke the Source of Life to bless and strengthen you (page 24).

REPAIRING THE BODY FIELD RITUAL

After you've expelled intrusions from your body field, it will need immediate repair, so that it can knit together again and not be susceptible to any further intrusions:

• Breathe into every part of your body to relax. Establish your energy field.

• Call your Advocate to take you to the Sanctuary of Life (page 23). Enter with your unique key.

• From the Source of Life a fine thread begins to flow toward you. Your Advocate guides the thread toward any tears or gaps in your body field and begins to weave them into the whole fabric. The fine thread keeps coming until the Advocate is satisfied that there are no holes.

• Be aware of the fabric of your body field as being denser and more resilient than light; feel its substance cloaking you like a new garment. Now breathe it nearer to you until it molds about your body and feel how your energy field and your body are of one substance.

• Thank your Advocate and the Source of Life. Ask them how you can best maintain your resilience and what you need to avoid to prevent further tears.

THE EFFECTS OF CLEARING RESIDUES AND INTRUSIONS

When minor intrusions and attachments move on, they often do so abruptly, leaving you with a feeling of lightness, the sense of a burden lifting. More rarely, you may experience some very physical effects that might initially appear alarming. When serious and long-term intrusions leave, the residue of their toxins also leaves you. Your body wants to seriously help these go entirely and you may find yourself experiencing vomiting or nausea, purging or diarrhea, low grade fever, weight loss or a sense of your body shape having somehow changed, or fatigue. All these effects should subside within twenty-four to forty-eight hours. After the removal of intrusions, drink a glass of pure, clean water and eat lightly some hours later. Bathe and cleanse yourself physically and psychically. See the Cleansing of the Elements starting on page 76. Look after yourself, seek comfort and quiet solitude. Sleep and be free from your burden. Give thanks to the Source of Life.

ADDICTIONS

Addiction is a form of intrusion that has colonized the space a lost soul-part has vacated. The onset of addiction is rarely noticeable, since most start as innocent pleasures that we enjoy. We become aware that we have an addiction only when we cannot do without the substance or behavior and that we need to use or do it to excess. As we neglect essential parts of our soul or when we lose contact with the central supports of life, we allow our pleasures to colonize those empty areas. Addictions need a void in order to colonize and will frequently take the opportunity to invade when a soul-part is lost. Whatever we invite to fill the space will grow to huge proportions if unchecked until our pleasure enslaves us. When we lose love, we comfort eat; when we suffer disappointment, we drink alcohol; when we can't relax, we smoke. Addictions can take many forms: substances, foods, shopping, gambling, sex, behavior, work.

Recreational drugs lower our resistance and open our souls up to intrusion, as well as messing with our minds and nervous system. The substance of every drug has not only a chemical signature that affects our physiology; it also has a spirit that affects our souls.

Of course, some people have to take regular medication to manage physical or psychological conditions. For them, such medication must become allies, and they may need to enter into a deeper alliance with the spirit of these substances in order to live. See page 159 for ways of blessing your medication. It is inadvisable to take sleeping pills and other addictive forms of medication on a regular basis because these can lower bodily resistance and create energetic and psychic vulnerability.

Each of the three soul cauldrons is susceptible to addictions. When significant soul and power have leaked away they can be replaced by the following kinds of addiction:

- Vital Cauldron: substance and sexual addictions.
- Personal Cauldron: emotional addictions and attachments.
- Wisdom Cauldron: compulsions and obsessions, distortions of belief, spiritual sources usurped by idols or substitutes.

This book cannot cover issues of serious addiction, but we can all do with some help with our minor and habitual ones:

- Admit that you cannot cure this all by yourself. People who believe that they can are kidding themselves. Approach the Source of Life and your Advocates to help guide you.

- Seek the help of an addiction support group. To kick this habit, you need human allies to give you support and encouragement, as well as to provide practical models for maintaining a balanced life. Get this help going as essential preparation before you use any of the methods described below.

- Begin to avoid the places, people and circumstances where your addiction flourishes. Clear your home of any hidden substances.

- Perform the Releasing Intrusions ritual (page 112), immediately followed by power (page 69) and soul-retrieval (page 91). Repair your energy field.

- Even when you've been successful in all the above, you will still be left with your habitual pathways to the addictive substance or behavior. These habitual pathways are so well trodden that they are easiest to walk along: any new strategies you wish to implement will eventually create a new pathway, but you will have to repeat this at least twenty times before it begins to feel habitual. This is why you need so much help and support.

- If you fall off your new pathway, start again by centering yourself and repeating the above.
- Take it one day at a time and don't set yourself impossible goals.

POWER-THIEVES

We have already explored how we involuntarily steal power from people around us and how we can let it go again, as well as how we can call our power back. How can we prevent power-theft from happening to us?

Many people are unconscious power-thieves because they themselves have had their own energy poached by others, while some may be particularly dependent or have little idea how vitality works on a circuit of give and take. You may recognize power-thieves after the event when you realize how exhausted being with someone has made you; you may even have one in the family. Here are a few strategies to counter power-theft:

- If you touch, shake hands or have been in the company of a power-thief, shake your hands down immediately and go and plunge them into cold water. Carry blessed salt with you to cleanse and ground you; sprinkle some on your hands and rub them together.
- Cleanse your energy field of residues.
- If you know you have to be in the company of a power-thief, then do not look them directly in the pupils but in the whites of their eyes, or direct your gaze slightly to one side of their head. Do not stand with your torso directly facing them, but slightly angled. Cross both arms or one arm over your solar plexus, as this is a primary "drinking" point for power-thieves.

Dreamworker Robert Moss writes of a woman who reported that she felt her batteries had been drained. She said that "she felt that someone was sucking energy from her abdomen, as if through a straw. When I asked her to find the person at the end of the straw, she identified a grasping, needy relative who was stealing her energy without returning it. We proceeded to cut that unhealthy link." See page 120 for the Knife of Separation Ritual.

OPPORTUNISTS AND COLONISTS

Opportunists are those who seize any chance to steal what is not theirs; they are would-be colonists who seek an invitation to move in and live with you. It isn't always easy to discern them, for they are often plausible people who seem "so nice" that you want to be reciprocal and accommodating to their desires. But, be warned, opportunists want a comfortable life and their model is the feudal system: make others work for you, so that you get the largest share of the labor and leave just enough for your slave to live upon. Frequently we give ourselves into the hands of opportunists and become their living prey. Opportunists are all those who want to exploit us: politicians, salesmen, missionaries, dependent family members, needy friends, rogue psychics and many others. You will find them in all walks of life.

When an opportunist strikes, at first, it may feel empowering or relieving, as if someone else had taken responsibility for you. It may feel safe and secure, but in actuality you are duped into a false sense of trust. Afterward, the sense of being taken in, duped or absorbed by someone is not always an unpleasant sensation. Do not give yourself into the hands of the unscrupulous.

We allow opportunists in most frequently when we are being pressed to make a quick decision. Poor choices made on the spur of the moment, without forethought or with insufficient information are one of the prime causes of psychic disruption. By accepting a new decision suggested by an opportunist you are simultaneously creating a contract with him or her. Do you really want to follow your decision through to the end? What will it involve?

• Submit your decision to the fivefold test of whether it gives you truth, beauty, health, happiness and light.

- If strong persuasion is being used on you, leave the persuader's presence and be alone to think things through.

- Ask yourself what are the ultimate consequences of your decision? How will it change the world around you? Does it harm you, your family or your society?

- See the Illusion/Reality checklist on page 13.

- Instead of entering into rapport with opportunists, your best defense is getting into rapport with your Advocates—add their beneficial power to your weakness and resist.

- Stage a revolutionary overthrow and evict your colonist with removal of intrusions.

CONFUSING THE ENEMY: CAMOUFLAGING OUR INTENTIONS

Opportunists and potential colonizers, like predatory animals, seem to know or quickly discover your weak points. We often reveal these weaknesses voluntarily in conversation. Sometimes we trail our coats and allow others to ride with us "for free." The antidote to opportunists is to be cunning and use camouflage, like the ancient Irish hero, Mongan, who confused the King of Leinster's druids, his opponents, by filling a bag with two chunks of earth—one from Ireland and one from Scotland—and then sitting on it as he traveled. The druids, who sent out their souls in search of Mongan, confusingly concluded that he must have one foot in Ireland and one foot in Scotland. Mongan escaped their notice by this clever ruse.

To be streetwise in our psychic protection and spiritual health, we must stop revealing ourselves and signaling our intentions so openly. Successful gamblers maintain "a poker face" so that their intentions won't be transparent to fellow players. Playing your cards close to your chest and not boasting about your hand might help you win the game. Not signposting your intentions to others and giving them advantage over you helps you confuse opportunists:

- When opportunists are stalking you, take a leaf out of Mongan's book and use psychic camouflage: call upon one of your strong Advocates to enclose you in his/her energy field. The would-be colonizer will perceive you to be a strangely powerful person against whom no attempt will be successful!
- Don't disclose too much about your affairs.
- In the vicinity of opportunists, keep quiet about what is worrying you most.
- Beware of signposting your distress or fear by telltale body-language: touching your nose, looking down, keeping your features tense, etc.

BREAKING THE CIRCLE

Gayle had been the coordinator of a meditation circle for many months. Gradually the circle had become more and more dependent upon her until she wanted out. She emailed everyone to tell them she was leaving, but was persuaded to stay for another term. When her mother fell ill, Gayle had to terminate her responsibility and told the group this at her last meeting. When pleading couldn't persuade her, the group employed guilt and recrimination, followed later by character assassination when she refused to return. One particular person had been so cruel and insulting to Gayle that she went away feeling quite sick at the malice directed at her. After several sleepless nights and resentful days, Gayle realized that she needed to do her own ritual of separation from the circle. She entered the Sanctuary of the Source of Life in meditation and called upon her Guardian Advocate, a Siberian Healer, to help cut her connections with the group. The Advocate shook powdered chalk in the air, which immediately revealed a cord running from Gayle's solar plexus and feet to the group. Taking the Knife of Separation, the Advocate passed the blade through a flame and then severed the cords, immediately sucking out any residues and then breathing onto the places where they had been connected and reweaving Gayle's aura with webs of colored light. This felt healthier immediately, but Gayle wanted to be sure that she didn't inadvertently harbor any resentment. Still in the Sanctuary, she mentally sat the most malicious member of the group opposite her, saying, "I acknowledge to the Source of Life that I've been harboring feelings of retaliation against this person. By my indecision, I've allowed feelings of obligation to stretch into chains of dependence." Gayle has to draw upon the help of her Advocate to stop falling into a stew of self-blame and anger again as she says this, for the words hurt. She turns her mind toward the Source of Life and calls upon the rose-colored light of unconditional love to help her continue, "I want to unconditionally let this person and the meditation group go." The light circulating her body now flows out and surrounds the person sat in the chair opposite. "May you and they go in peace." She asks her Advocate to help her act more decisively in future.

THE KNIFE OF SEPARATION RITUAL

Some connections are unhealthy for us: ex-partners, associates who sponge off you, people whose bad influence warps your behavior, a group you've left or family members whose dependent grasp is like death. All of these connections can potentially feed off you. When you've tried all the methods above against power-thieves, opportunists and others, and they still keep coming back and trying to reattach themselves, it is time for more drastic action:

- Go with one of your Advocates into the Sanctuary of the Source of Life. On a rack inside are many wonderful and useful tools and sacred objects that help maintain the universe. Your Advocate takes up the Knife of Separation, which pares away all that is unnecessary, and can cut through knots that hold you bound and ties of influence that chain you.

- Only your Advocate is authorized to use it and then only when it is needful. The Advocate wields the knife as tenderly and skillfully as a surgeon, but also with vigor and exactitude.

- The knife pares away and cuts bonds that stretch between you and any power-thieves and opportunists who are trying to connect with you.

- After this is done, immediately ask your Advocate to reweave your energy field (page 113).

FORGIVENESS RITUAL

Forgiveness is a primary form of releasing in which we let things go from us. Please regard it as a major form of psychic protection that will help detach you from intrusions and not merely as a religious practice to which you don't subscribe. If we continue to harbor hate, guilt, blame or resentments about someone or something, then we are inviting intrusions and residues of that person or situation to remain with us. Releasing our hatred and anger is often very difficult, because we want to hold on to our sense of injustice, to continue harboring revenge or capitalizing on the hurt. Dream-explorer Robert Moss recommends a form of the Iroquois "confession on the road," whereby you "go to a private place and give voice to all the guilt and bad experiences you may be carrying. You ask forgiveness of anyone you may have hurt. If you reach deep enough you may finally be able to forgive yourself."

Forgiveness is the most effective means of releasing yourself from long-nurtured hatred, anger, resentment and from a self-persecuting sense of victimhood. In the ritual below, don't engage with your anger, loss, or sense of betrayal. Restimulating these emotions will not in any way help you move on or change what has happened. You are not expected to change your hatred into love in this ritual, but you can draw upon the Source of Life to do this on your behalf:

1. Breathe, relax and establish your energy field. Enter the Sanctuary of the House of Life. Become aware of the unconditional love that the Source of Life has for you. Experience this as a rose-colored light. Breathe this into your body field and into your soul cauldrons.

2. Now visualize the person you need to forgive sitting opposite you. To this Sanctuary, all living beings find their own way, just as you have. But the reason that the person you need to forgive is here is because of the link between you. Now you have an opportunity to let go of this.

3. State your case something like this: "I call the Source of Life to witness that I have been harboring a sense of being wronged by [name]. In so doing, I have created links of hatred/anger/etc., that have bound her/him to me." Stabilize your breathing, calm any upset, by using the Well-being Breath pattern: Inhale 8; Hold in 8; Exhale 8; Hold out 4.

4. Become aware again of the rose-colored light of unconditional love that flows from the Source of Life into you and say, "Now I call the

Source of Life to witness that I let go of my sense of wrong and release [name] unconditionally. What's done is done. I no longer hold [name] to account. Go in peace!" Experience the rose-colored light circulating your system and see how it flows through you and out to the person you are forgiving, conveying the love of the Source of Life to him/her, and melting any old links of revenge or hatred between you. As soon as you experience this, the person in question is no longer sitting opposite you.

5. Now call one of your Advocates to come and be with you here in the Sanctuary. Receive whatever comfort and support your Advocates offer you. State your determination to change, "I have freely released [name] from my whole being. May there be peace between us."

TRANSFORMING PAINFUL EVENTS AND ASSOCIATIONS

Sometimes the pain, sorrow or fear of what we've experienced gets trapped, needing release and transformation. This pain is often imbued in or represented by an object, a letter, a photograph or a gift that seems to hold all the old anguish. Most times, we give these things away or destroy them, but sometimes, we retain a little souvenir of, say, a broken marriage because it also represents the love and joy we shared as well as the bitterness and reproach that followed. We can help that pain move on and transform in us if we change or ritually let the object go. By letting go of memory-ridden things, we also help the memories go free so that the pain lessens. The elements of air, fire, water and earth will help you transform memory:

- Make paper boats of old love letters and float them down river.
- Hang the object in a tree until it fades and disintegrates in the rain and sun.
- Burn biodegradable objects in a brazier or bonfire.
- Bury the object deep.
- If you have no object to destroy or transform, then you can make something that represents what you want to transform in your life.

Look through your house for materials that will help you make a thing of beauty: scraps of material, thread, wool, paper, crayons, paints, string or wood, or look in nature for fallen branches, seed-heads, grasses, flowers, etc. Make your object as wonderful as you can and imbue it with all the memories of grief and pain that you want to be rid of. When it's finished, return it to the elements. As you commit it to the fire or water, earth or air, state what you wish to transform and let it freely go with a few tears or a song.

SMASHING THE MEMORY

Every time Roy passes the corner cupboard he spies an ornament of a glazed duck that belonged to the aunt who brought him up with many little cruelties. He doesn't know why he keeps it, except as an evocation of his childhood place of play in the park, but it also reminds him of being shut up under the stairs when he was naughty, a memory which still makes him white with terror. His ambivalence prevents him from action until he loses his own temper with his children and finds himself threatening them with a stint under the stairs. In horror, he takes the ornament down to his garage and smashes it with a hammer. The shattered pieces only reproach him for a second. They become part of the rock garden he is making in the yard, where the glazed stoneware of the duck mixes imperceptibly with the colored gravel in the concrete. The ornament's remains help create a place of beauty where petunias and pansies grow, transforming the abandonment and fear.

PHOBIAS

Phobias are intrusive fears that have their root in us and that are activated seemingly irrationally every time we encounter the spider in the bathtub, the constricting space under the stairs, or the number thirteen. When we meet the object of a phobia, our fear gears up to get us out of there quickly, even though we may rationally know that the object is harmless. A dry mouth, a sense of going crazy or being in fear of death, heart palpitations and being unable to catch your breath are all symptoms. Something mysterious is going on when we suffer from such irrational fears, something that has taken root. Phobias can be caused through cultural, inherited, ancestral or reincarnational reasons, as well as being triggered by known events. Standard treatments for phobias range from the exposure method, where the subject is exposed to the object of their fear, to hypnosis and chemical solutions that suppress the symptoms. Use the removal of intrusion method, if it is clear that the phobia is an intrusion, as in the example below. However, if your phobia or fear stems from blocked up power within yourself, use the Power of Substitution ritual below.

THE WITCH CAT

Maria had a lifelong hatred and fear of cats, yet there was nothing in her experience to account for this phobia. Her Spanish mother finally told her that, while pregnant with Maria, she had encountered a feral cat that had badly scratched and frightened her. Full of superstitions, Maria's mother was fearful that the cat might have been the spiritual form of a witch trying to harm her child. This association and fear of her mother's had communicated itself in the womb to Maria herself who inherited this perceived threat to their mutual well-being and survival. Maria wanted to be rid of this phobia so that it wouldn't pass down to her own children when she had them. In this case, it was her mother's fear that was still lodged in Maria's being, so she used the Releasing Intrusions method. A lot of power came back as a result of this intrusion leaving her. While Maria will never own a cat, at least she is free of a fear that was never really hers.

THE POWER OF SUBSTITUTION RITUAL

We carry around a great deal of stuff we no longer need. Sometimes psychic disturbance is caused by our own unused power that has turned in upon itself and become grossly distorted and out of control. Having no means of escape, it can generate symptoms of physical, emotional or mental illness, which we experience as being psychically disruptive. It is not something that someone has done to us, but something that we have allowed to arise within ourselves. Sometimes it is a simple matter of transforming stagnant power into a condition of flow once more. One thing is sure, blocked energy is what ultimately leads to sickness, disorientation and death. But "what makes you sick or fearful also has the potential to make you well and courageous," writes healer Christopher Hansard.

Many people who feel under psychic attack are all for zapping, obliterating and wiping out whatever has caused their disturbance, but in such cases where our own dammed-up power has caused the trouble, we cannot zap ourselves! The shaman, Sandra Ingerman, explains, "You can't kill energy. You have to transform it." If you are able to put power in the place of fear, or to replace the old story that keeps pulling you down with a new one that builds you up, you will begin to feel strong and in circuit with yourself again. Transform your psychic disturbance by the Power of Substitution like this:

1. Center yourself and establish your energy field.

2. Ask Advocates to show you the spiritual form of your problem. *Do not interact with or be drawn into this form, just stay with your Advocate and observe it.* Now ask your Advocate to transform it into power that can serve you rather than hurt you.

3. If your Advocate is successful in transforming the disturbance into power that can help you, ask how you are to accept this back into yourself. Listen for any instructions that will help you manifest your power in a balanced way. Occasionally, as in the example below, power and soul come back during this meditation.

Do not use this practice if your psychic disruption is caused by an intrusion. Intrusions need to *leave* your body field, not be transformed back into it! Instead, use the Releasing Intrusions ritual, (page 112).

TRANSFORMING THE TORNADO

Hailey keeps getting panic attacks. She doesn't wish to use the prescribed medication, which she feels will just chemically subdue these attacks, leaving the origin of them untouched. She calls on her Advocate, the White Tiger, to help her transform the panic attacks. She sees a tornado-like funnel of scratchy gray mist that howls. White Tiger holds Hailey between his powerful paws when she begins to lean forward. "Beware!" he says, "It will sweep you into its funnel. Stay here with me. This tornado is made up of your fear, hurt and confusion that began after Donald rejected you and left you to manage by yourself." Hailey's boyfriend abruptly left her several months back without explanation: she hasn't made the connection between this traumatic episode and her panic attacks until now. She asks her Advocate, "Please turn this tornado into power that will help me." White Tiger roars a mighty roar that floods the scene with a serene gold light. The tornado stops whirling and howling. White Tiger breathes into the tornado and molds it into another shape. Under his mighty paws, the golden figure of a young girl forms. It looks very much like Hailey did when she was small. White Tiger says to Hailey, "Fear of abandonment is a memory buried deep within you. I promise that I will never abandon you. You can feel supported once more if you invite back the power and soul of your young self." She asks, doubtfully, "Are you sure it won't become a panic attack again?" White Tiger looks deeply into her eyes, "The ability to be adventurous and become reconnected to your power lies within you. Will you welcome it now?" "Yes!" Hailey breathes and draws the golden girl to her. As they join hands, White Tiger sings with joy.

MAKING SOUL SPACE

The way to avoid intrusive attachments is to be as fully inhabited as you can be. By taking up your own space in the universe, you allow no opportunity for invasion. Live your life to the full and beware of leaving voids where intrusions can lodge. By this, I don't mean "fill every minute of the day with activity," because we all need to pay time and attention to proper consideration, meditation, rest, etc.

Psychic disturbance doesn't just come at you from outside; it is also generated from within by allowing our souls to become fraught with clutter. We can seek remedy in spaciousness:

- Switch off from the continuum of daily life for an hour. The boredom won't kill you.
- Make space for silence and stillness every day for at least five minutes.
- Set aside at least one day in every seven to nine days when you have time for yourself.
- Declutter one cupboard, room or closet this month.

- Clean one room really well.
- Check to see if your shrine needs attention, change or cleaning.
- Slow down and perform one activity with care, attention and appreciation rather than hurrying on to the next task.
- Visit your soul cauldrons and check what needs clearing out (page 99).

BLUEPRINTS FOR BEING INFLUENCE-FREE

1. Maintain your center regularly.

2. Be circumspect about how you share your personal details and affairs.

3. Formulate your own opinions, tastes and interests.

4. Check your instincts before entering into any agreements or contracts.

5. Live vigorously and to the full.

6. Deal with residues daily.

7. Forgive and let go of people, events and memories.

8. Transform stagnant power into positive flow.

9. Cut loose from opportunists and power-thieves.

10. Practice spiritual hygiene.

CHAPTER 7

Mind Games

Fear is the mind-killer.

—Frank Herbert in *Dune*

CULTIVATING A HEALTHY MIND

A healthy mind is a flexible, agile mind. A closed, unexercised mind is a breeding ground for bad thoughts and massive psychic disruption. We play mind games all the time. When things get disordered in your mind, when it has been running a particularly detrimental program, the mind game you've selected can cause you considerable psychic disruption. If this goes unchecked, it begins to affect every part of your life and you feel driven to the edge. Secretly, we are all fearful about admitting to mental illness, because of the shame and stigma of being seen as crazy, and so we conform to the norm, in order to fit in. A little personal eccentricity is the sign of an individual following their own path: a blanket conformity with the masses is the sign of a fearful mind and a submerged personality.

When we cultivate a healthy mind we also cultivate our Wisdom Soul. The uncultivated Wisdom Soul is susceptible to the influences of other people's strong desires, rigid ideology or stubborn minds. The Wisdom Soul cauldron can also fill up with conflicting beliefs, negative thoughts and the delusions that we have grown ourselves. We strengthen our spiritual integrity and mental health by attending to what is true for us.

A healthy mind lives in tune with its own truth. When we focus on our own truth, we become visible and can be witnessed by the universe rather than invisibly overlooked and continually masking who we are from ourselves and others.

BELIEF AND DOUBT

The more people believe a thing, the more it manifests: the more you disbelieve, the more you doubt it. When everyone around you asserts that something is so and you don't experience this, then it may be that everyone around you is playing a mind game and living in a different shared reality. In the face of strong opposition, you can lose faith to such an extent that you begin to wonder whether you are not crazy or peculiar. Remember the little boy who blew the whistle on the naked emperor in the Hans Christian Andersen story of "The Emperor's New Clothes?"

The disapproval or disbelief of others can affect us considerably since there is a great social pressure upon us to conform to what others believe. For example, sharing your metaphysical experiences, spiritual realizations or psychic problems with the disbelieving only makes you feel mentally deranged. Yet speaking and being with people of the same mindset or beliefs as you is helpful. The group-mind of society, or a family or other group creates a contract of belief that we become part of as members of that group. But the beliefs of others are not necessarily our own.

Our habitual patterns of thought create beliefs that help us fix reality in conformity with the needs of our Personal Soul, which is susceptible to emotion, and of our Vital Soul, which is susceptible to sensation. To develop the Wisdom Soul is to expand this narrow view of reality. False beliefs, superstitions and irrational fears distort the natural wisdom that we were born with, and yet we tend to hang on to views of reality that actively harm us. Belief is a colonist. Some beliefs that we hold are actually based on memory distortions that have arisen in our early years or in circumstances when we were under stress, where we have misattributed causation to the wrong source for the wrong reason. Superstitions can arise from such distortions. Some minds are virtually turned to stone by beliefs that petrify them. Ancestral beliefs can become habitual and without personal meaning or power for us if we accept them from others unthinkingly. It is only when we ask, seek, question, challenge and live by what maintains the higher benefit of all that we truly believe. As a teenager you overthrew some childhood beliefs. As you grow older, you may need to check your personal beliefs. The great poet, William Blake, wrote, "I must create a system, or be enslav'd by another man's."

The self-doubting person is empty of self-belief. The ebbing of self-belief has created space for self-doubt to grow instead, like weeds invading the sunlit space of a once-vigorous plant whose leaves have begun to fall. This critical vacuum of emptiness is where opportunist and intrusive influences spring up.

Self-distrust saps your power and opens you to psychic disturbance. Doubts are merely leaking beliefs. Strengthen what you know is true by looking again at your code of honor (page 17). Faith and belief in ourselves and our abilities builds up the soul's defenses. Confidence is a matter of belief.

Try this checklist:

- What commonly accepted beliefs about reality tie you up in knots?
- What ancestral beliefs have you inherited that no longer serve you?
- How much of your belief system is yours and still useful?
- What beliefs have you begun to distrust and why? How are they hurting you?
- Where are you letting in beliefs that frighten or overwhelm you?
- What beliefs about yourself rest on baseless assumptions or outworn stories? See page 147.
- What beliefs cause you to feel excluded or substandard?
- How is your self-doubt impeding your growth?
- What mental residues of others attach to your thinking and slow it down?
- Which assumptions, perceptions and judgments are you carrying that distort the truth?
- What superstitions are you clinging to? Whose experience are they based upon?
- Revisit the source of your erroneous beliefs by tracing them back through your life. Then, one by one, submit them to the Pool of Change,

page 142. Trust grows by little steps. Set yourself one small task of self-trust today and trust yourself to carry it out.

CATCHING THE STAR OF DESTINY MEDITATION

Whatever beliefs, fears and memory distortions we hold about ourselves and life in general are reflected in our body field and aura, where they are clearly visible to opportunists who can take advantage of them to manipulate us. At any one time, we will be dealing with our own mind games by trying to bring them under control, retraining our minds and strengthening our Wisdom Soul. However, we can counteract the negative signal of our own brain waves by placing something stronger in our aura.

Every living being has a star of destiny shining upon him or her. Our destiny is our life-purpose, the reason why we were incarnated in the first place. It is a gift that we may chose to follow or to ignore, but it is not fated to come about without our full consent and effort. We may be aware or unconscious of this connection, but our Guardian Advocate can help us find and follow its guidance. Conscious connection with our star of destiny will help us mature our Wisdom Soul and clear the way for our life path:

1. Breathe, relax and be still. Call your Guardian Advocate to be with you. Be aware of the six directions about you and center yourself (page 106).

2. Direct your attention to the heavens above. In the dark night sky, there are many stars shining. One of them is your star of destiny. Ask your Guardian Advocate to show you yours. Now feel the ray of starlight shining down upon you, right into the crown of your head, and ask for the help of your star of destiny to protect and strengthen your mind.

3. Through the starlight comes a symbol of your destiny. As this powerful light beams down into you, catch the symbol of your destiny, placing it upon your brow, so it may constellate within your aura as a powerful new star that crowns you. Allow its light to infuse your whole being.

4. When you are in the presence of a strong, persuasive person who is trying to influence you, recall this symbol as a crown about your brows, and suck down powerful starlight into your aura.

OBSESSED WITH DISASTER

Donald's mother ghoulishly relished TV programs about disasters and misfortunes, habitually pored over accidents in the papers and related them to her acquaintances—she had no real friends as no one could bear her company for long. When Donald grew older he spent longer periods of time projecting "what-might-go-wrong scenarios." His teenage children had to report back home on time or he would start phoning hospitals and the police. His optimistic wife begged him to get help because Donald was becoming stressed and exhausted with "caring for" everyone in the household, rather than trusting everyone to get on with their lives. Donald's therapist helped him uncover that what underlay his anxiety for others was his mother's relish in others' misfortune. Just as she lived a life of disaster-anticipation, so he was living vigilantly to prevent accidents happening to his family. Taking it a day at a time, he began to substitute trust for anxiety.

NEGATIVE THOUGHTS AND THE FANTASY FACTORY

Our minds are powerful creative agents: they can create pathways to possibility, but if they are left to run unchecked they manufacture fantasies that fuel our self-delusion. Some of us are natural pessimists who always look on the dark side of life, but entertaining such negative thoughts and brooding upon them can create internal psychic disruption. Instead of a healthy mind, we sometimes make it a fantasy factory where we rehearse "the worst scenario," projecting the reasons why someone is late and opening a storyline that leads to mugging, rape or death, or to where the funeral will be held, the sorrow we will feel and so on. In such cases, we misuse our sacred creative ability.

Negative thinking can become a vine-like growth whose tendrils smother our mind. Being on the receiving end of the negative thoughts of others can also be very wearing. Negativity is not just caused by fear but is often an insurance policy against anticipated failure. Check your thoughts:

- Does your habitual negativity give you satisfaction? What effect does dismaying or frightening others do for you?
- How often are you anticipating the worst? Where does this negative thought come from? Is it yours or someone else's?
- What successes and freedoms might blossom if your negativity became positive?

THE BEAUTIFUL MIND RITUAL

We can retrain our minds to think in positive ways. The Navajo belief in living in a proactive and positive way called "the beauty-way" is a wonderful antidote to negative thoughts. Instead of entertaining the drawbacks or disadvantages, the Navajo people align themselves with their life purpose, accept themselves as they are, connect to their spiritual sources and act and speak in positive ways.

If you are fighting negativity, use this ritual to help you:

1. Relax, breathe and call your Advocates. Center yourself in the six directions (page 106) and attune to the great powers of the Source of life: life, light, love and law; in the east, south, west and north; and to the power of wisdom above and truth below.

2. Facing each direction in turn, send away your negative thoughts down the pathways between you and six great powers. These flow into the directions, and are received and transformed by the powers. On each pathway sense, see and feel how your thoughts are transformed by the great powers of life. As you receive your transformed thoughts back from each direction, say, "I receive the beautiful power of life/light/ love, etc., into my mind and Wisdom Soul."

3. At the end, say, "beautiful life before me, beautiful love behind me, beautiful light and beautiful law beside me, beautiful truth beneath me, beautiful wisdom above me, and all my beautiful thoughts in peace and harmony once more."

SELF-PITY AND VICTIMHOOD

When something goes wrong, we cry, "Why me?" The problem with negative thinking is that it can foster fear and open the way for such events to happen. Self-pity encourages victimhood, and once that is imprinted in your aura most opportunists and abusers can detect it at twenty paces. If our experience of life has been difficult, we are likely to believe that the world is a hostile and dangerous place. But if we become accustomed to suffering or overly attached to the benefits that arise from being a victim, we are playing mind games with our own power.

Victimhood is compounded by negative thought, leaving the individual feeling helpless, dependent and without resources. But victimhood can only come about through our collusion with an opportunist. Allowing ourselves to become the victim that the aggressor perceives you to be only strengthens their hold over you. Feeling superior to the perpetrator is a common mind game that we enter into with victimhood. Victim superiority can become like body armor that never allows you to creatively move on. The feeling that you are a better person than your attacker may make you feel more powerful, but it also masks the fact that you yourself are capable of similar attacks. Actually, we are no better than those who perpetrate psychic disruption.

Brian Keenan, the Irish hostage held in captivity in Lebanon, refused at all times to become a victim. However much he was beaten, he would not allow himself to be humiliated but withstood their assaults. "In that resistance, I would humiliate them." Maintaining a dry wit and irony, he preserved his own image of himself and refused to take on the mantle of victim. Commenting on Keenan's mode of survival, Thomas Moore says, "A little clean, honest wit can save you from the heavy seriousness that gives life a tragic tone." The ability to laugh at yourself and be philosophical about situations that go wrong is the gateway leading out of the field of self-pity and victimhood:

- Seek the companionship and solidarity of a peer group that believes in and stands with you.

- Gain strength by seeing yourself as a person, not a victim. Don't collude with the attacker's view of you. Also, maintain a level playing field by honoring your true self-image.

STOPPING THE TRAUMATIC TAPE-LOOP

Whether we witness an accident, have a narrow escape, receive a sudden shock or terrible news, the images of these events continue to whirl through our consciousness in alarming ways. Long after the traumatic event is over, it repeats because it is caught in our Personal Soul and is imprinted upon our imagination, and becomes a memory in our Wisdom Soul and in our Vital Soul, creating aversion and fear. You can use this method also for evicting troublesome mental tape-loops of anxiety:

- After major trauma, it is normal to experience this tape-loop. Talking it out to a friend or therapist helps discharge it. However, beware of keeping it a cocktail party story long after the event.

- Remove the tape-loop by doing the Releasing Intrusions method (page 112). Visualizing taking out the old tape and replacing it with a new, unused tape will also help.

- Gather your souls back together. See page 91.

- If any part of your body feels burdened or heavy, ask your Advocate to draw out the pain by placing its hand over your own as you rest it on that part. Sense, see and feel the burden leave and the strength of your Advocate come into you to help strengthen you.

- Practice centering yourself every day and strengthening your connections to the powers of the Source of Life. See page 106 and above.

- Concentrate upon reestablishing your connections to the universe (page 14).

CLEANSING THE MIND

"Canst thou minister to a mind diseased?" Macbeth asks the doctor about Lady Macbeth, whose nocturnal wanderings and obsessional hand-washing are the legacy of her complicity in the murder of Duncan. Sometimes we despair of our mind's unruly activity. The thought-forms that we engender in our fantasy factory can become so powerful that they take over our lives. They become powerful in the first place because we lend our mind-power and imaginations to their creation. We enforce them by brooding upon them. Breaking up destructive thoughts and habits requires:

- A conscious decision to change and the engagement of your will, passion and power to maintain it.
- A neutral assessment, exploration and understanding of the habit or thought's causation.
- A determination to take responsibility for the restructuring of mental pathways.
- The release, transformation or self-forgiveness of blame and guilt.
- A reduction of stress with rest, reflection, refueling and tranquility.

You can scatter the images and thought forms that you have created by envisaging a large wind machine or a chopper with a funnel. At one end you feed your thought form into the funnel and the turbine at the other end chops it up and casts it to the four winds. Or picture a giant eraser that rubs out the image as if it were a drawing.

SELF-ESTEEM

Our self-worth and honor are our glory. But when self-esteem goes out of balance, due to deflation or inflation, it can involve us in mind games of unworthiness and self-hatred or else of prideful ego and relentless self-promotion. These are mind games about how we take up our proper space in the universe, which is where we started in Chapter 1. Insecurity or a sense of invulnerability are the common causes of self-esteem mind games.

Low self-esteem is generally a sign of power and soul-loss; while a self-promoting esteem is generally a sign of power and soul theft. The strategies for returning power and soul and for giving these back to their proper owners are the correct procedures for dealing with both. We have all played one or both of these mind games. Low self-esteem makes us dangerously vulnerable, wide-open to psychic persecution and victimhood. Rampant self-esteem makes us dangerous and predatory, for when it becomes a weapon to pull others down, you become a psychic predator.

A balanced self-esteem is one not easily defeated by setbacks or criticism, but open and assertive, self-reliant, able to see the funny side and confident without being overbearing. This checklist is for both extremes of the esteem register. Most of us fall somewhere in the middle.

- Are you lacking in confidence? Or are you supremely up for things?
- Do you feel you're a failure? Or do you think people around you are failures?
- Are you full of self-doubt about your competence? Or is nothing beyond your skills?
- Do you call yourself names or berate or belittle yourself? Or are you always praising yourself or boasting about achievements?
- Do you feel guilty when you say no to people? Or do you ruthlessly dismiss the needs of others?
- Do you wilt under criticism or opposition? Or are you impervious to criticism and game for a fight?
- Do you concentrate on your mistakes? Or do you laud your successes?

If you feel that you are unworthy or are always running yourself down, how can you honor yourself? If you feel that you alone are chosen above all other mortals, how can you be part of the everyday world? Real life lies between these two extremes. The remedy for rampant self-esteem is humility, the ability to give credit where it's due and the realization that you are not the supreme being, but only part of the universe. This requires that we give back what has inflated us, returning the power and soul of others, giving thanks to the Source of Life. Those with low self-esteem need to call home their power and soul:

- Forgive yourself, see below.
- Love yourself by establishing and living by your code of honor (page 17).
- Do the Restoring Your Image ritual, below.

RESTORING YOUR IMAGE RITUAL

"We possess beauty when we are true to our own being: ugliness is going over to another order," wrote Plotinus, the Neoplatonist philosopher. Other people's fears and projections about you can make you feel ugly and very strange, especially if you receive them and take them on. The effects of this can make you anxious, self-doubting, open to power-theft and to loss of self-image. Those who have been belittled and disbelieved by others over a long period begin to lose their own self-image and take on the projections of others. We can also project a self-image that has little to do with the reality of ourselves, in order to impress or just to survive in difficult circumstances. Whether your image of yourself has been eroded or usurped by a false mask, you need to restore the beauty of the original image. It's possible that parts of your self-image may be scattered in places of humiliation, pain or loss, but you do not reassimilate these qualities. Here is the sequence:

1. Do the Soul Cauldrons meditation (page 100), this time tipping out any false images or usurping impressions of yourself. Or, if you prefer, perform the Beautiful Mind ritual, above, substituting your "original image" for "thought" throughout.

2. With a saucer of water before you, immediately follow this by calling home your scattered image from the six directions, just as you've called home power and soul in Chapters 4 and 5. Your Advocate takes a collecting net and brings home your true image and pours it into the saucer. When all directions have been searched, anoint your face with the water, saying, "I welcome back my true and original image. May the

Source of Life and my Advocates help me honor the true image that is my birthright." Thank your Advocates and dry your face.

3. If you have been abused or violated, then use the reconsecration ritual (page 214).

As our image of ourselves returns and we begin to inhabit it with vigor and joy, so we become less susceptible to the fears and projections of others.

FALLING FROM GRACE

It is human and normal to continually fall out of a state of harmony. We do not remain in a state of perfection. This is an important truth for the maintenance of psychic health. We do not get fixed, become perfect/whole/healed and stay that way. We have to return to what we discussed in Chapter 1: showing up, persevering and persisting. By returning to our code of honor, by examining how we stray from it and by living it, we restore balance once more. Because we continually fall out of harmony we should not regard ourselves as fatally flawed or irredeemable. When we fall from grace, we can seek to return to it. This is what keeps us on the road. By seeking balance and unity once again rather than struggling on as a lost soul alone, we become reconnected to the Source of Life. Mistakes happen to everyone, so admit your error and move on from it, and be patient with yourself and your efforts. If you slip back again, keep up your determination to change. Follow any mistakes or slip-ups by achieving one small, easily implemented goal or break down larger goals into smaller segments.

Whether your mistake was small or severe, whether it hurt one person, many or just your own pride, you need to seek self-forgiveness. None of us has lived a perfect life, but changing our intentions is possible. This is especially true if our motivations have been self-serving, malign or predatory. Change this yourself. Don't wait for change to arise from your stagnation or inertia. Don't wait for others to bring you change.

FINDING SELF-FORGIVENESS

Frank was responsible for running down and severely injuring a pedestrian in his car when avoiding a traffic accident. But by mounting the left pavement rather than the right, he hit one person instead of many people in line at a bus stop on the opposite side. He admitted his guilt and was duly fined, but felt horrible. The injured man and his family did not want to hear from him or receive any help. With no access to forgiveness, Frank began to blame himself and to become severely depressed, brooding on the details of the accident continually as well as speaking and thinking of himself with self-hatred. A counselor helped him come to terms with the shock of the experience, but his depression and sense of guilt did not alleviate. Finally he came to see me and I helped retrieve lost power, stop up the leaks and reveal his soul path to him once more. This began with forgiving himself and being witnessed as a responsible and careful person once more.

GUILT AND SELF-FORGIVENESS

Guilt and the self-punishment that accompanies it are mind games of psychic persecution. Guilt saps self-esteem very quickly, clogging the way with remorse, regret and false beliefs about yourself. Self-blame and guilt can provide easy footholds for psychic persecution by others. The mistakes we have made in the past can work for us in two ways: they can provide useful lessons on how to improve our life and be more careful and discerning about our intentions; or they can burrow more deeply into us and become accusers.

Guilt and blame are sometimes tricky to tackle because, although they are intrusions, they are also resonant with our conscience, the insightful faculty of the Wisdom Soul. Our own moral sense is a powerful inhibitor of harmful behavior; when we have transgressed, we feel it in our Wisdom Soul. Guilt knocks you off center so much, that if bad things subsequently happen to you, it is easy to say "I deserved it." The human need for punishment is a religious inheritance that has been strongly imbued in us over many generations. This misperception is a distortion of a radical law of the universe, which works on the principle of balance. Guilt can affect you as follows:

- Makes you over-conscientious, over-scrupulous and over-responsible.
- Reinforces negative self-beliefs and low self-esteem.
- Immobilizes and petrifies you into inactivity.
- Freezes you and causes you to ignore emotions.
- Creates scenarios of self-punishment.

Treat the intrusive parts of your guilt as such by removing them (page 112). Transform the stain of guilt in the Pool of Change ritual. Use the Forgiveness Ritual on page 120, adapting it to forgive yourself.

THE POWER TO CHANGE

Sometimes our power structures seem under assault when we are brought to a new threshold where change and adaptation are required. Being creatures of habit, human beings like things to remain the same and will kick and scream to keep them static, but that is not how the power-rhythms of the universe work. Attempting to hang on to old structures and supports, when these are threatened with removal, can also cause problems. Change terrifies us.

If you catch yourself accommodating lots of compromises that restrict your freedom, inspiration and action, then you are caught in a power loop. It may be through fear of change, but it can also happen that very conscientious people who have to complete all their tasks, no matter what their state of health, fall into workaholic states where their own power preys upon them.

Change is opportunity. Its winds bring fresh gift and opens new doors, but only after you have swept away the old, decaying and used-up chances, only after you have closed some doors behind you. Maintaining old power structures that are worn out is exhausting and can lead to major illness if pursued.

Fear of the unknown lurks at thresholds. But where there is fear, there's power. Fear and power are the two faces of the same coin: when one is face up, the other is face down, unable to function. This is why we experience powerlessness when fear rides us. But when power is uppermost, then fear has no power over us at all. Stale energy cannibalizes itself, spinning into chaos. Ask yourself:

- What is stuck?
- Where do you need to change?
- What are you holding onto that is finished and done?
- What is making you burdened and unhappy?

POOL OF CHANGE RITUAL

Use this ritual when you want to change a habit or thought:

1. Choose at least one habit or thought that needs to change in your life.
2. Breathe, relax and call your Guardian Advocate.
3. Sense, see and feel a pool before you that wells up out from the heart of the earth. In its center is a vortex or whirlpool.
4. Throw in what needs to go or change. If it is an abstract concept or idea, ask your Advocate to show you what shape it will take. Throw that thing, habit or thought into the central vortex until it is sucked down.
5. After the waters have settled, ask for something to come and infuse your life with new purpose and healthy balance.
6. Receive out of the pool what comes. Ask your Advocate if you are uncertain about what comes or the advisability of taking it on. Ask for instructions on how this will change things in your life.

AUTHORITY AND AUTHENTICITY

Learning to trust the wisdom that is inside us will help our lives immensely. But our upbringing has often led us to seek authority from others or from powerful institutions, and to neglect our own wisdom. We discover our own authority when we begin to live authentically. We do this when we consult our own needs, desires and inspirations, when we disconnect from narrow frameworks or rigid structures that have straightjacketed the mainspring of our lives. These sets of rules may have become so constraining that we have no freedom whatever. When we free ourselves from the habit of such behavior, our confidence increases and our own lives are lived powerfully and authentically. "You have to be faithful to the mystery taking place in your heart, rather than to any idea or system that would try, with the best of motives, to disempower you and make you theirs." You have lived for a long time and your experience is valuable. Allow what you've learned to be a teacher that expands rather than narrows your world.

BLUEPRINTS FOR A HEALTHY MIND

1. Take the initiative for your thoughts and intentions.

2. Clear outworn beliefs that you no longer hold.

3. Control the fantasy factory by creating positive mind-paths.

4. Train and strengthen your mind.

5. Check that your beliefs are yours and not really someone else's.

6. Evict mental tape-loops, negative thoughts and anxieties regularly.

7. Be true to yourself with spiritual integrity.

8. Trust the wisdom inside you.

9. Deal analytically and calmly with things and people that try to influence you.

10. Store good memories to be a continual source of help, and transform the difficult ones.

CHAPTER 8

Power of the Word

A word spoken by chance might have strange
consequences. It would suddenly come alive,
and what people wanted to happen could
happen—all you had to do was say it.

—Nalungiaq, an Inuit woman,
collected by Knud Rasmussen

WORDS OF POWER

Words make things happen. Many of the world's sacred myths and scriptures relate the creation of the universe from the spoken or sung word of a divinity. Our ancestors recognized that whatever was spoken had effect, which is why they had such a high regard for the truth. Although we no longer live in an oral society, the power and influence of the word is still very strong. It has its own magic, which can bless or curse. Every word that comes out of our mouths starts as a thought that is motivated by our intentions. When we utter that word it goes somewhere and shapes our universe. When we utter words with passion and focus, the effect is much stronger than careless words uttered without thought.

The power of silence is as strong as the allure of words. Silence is the place of creative origin from whence intention springs forth. We seldom seek silence, preferring instead a steady stream of chatter from our mouths or in our minds. Restraining our tongues and our intentions can sometimes keep the world a safer place, but refraining from speech when we should have spoken may make it more dangerous. Neither sound nor silence is better than the other: they just are, until our intentions alter them.

The Source of Life dwells in a place where silence and sound are equally balanced. Sound emerges from silence and is received back into silence again. The power of inner silence is what we learn from meditation. Instead of doing and speaking, we enter into the state of being and listening. When you are overstimulated, when the inner monologue is overwhelming, when hurtful words are screaming in your mind, seek silence and learn the poise of stillness.

In this chapter we will explore the way we use words, what we mean by them and what effect they have on the universe. Words are powerful tools for creation or destruction, for blessing or cursing. Let us explore how we can use them better and how to neutralize their destructive effects.

WORD-TOOLS FOR AVOIDING PSYCHIC DISTURBANCE

Some words are essential tools in the psychic protection toolbox. If we use these in a timely fashion, we avoid any amount of trouble for ourselves:

- "What, where, who, which, when, why?" Rather than meekly submitting to something you're not sure about, ask searching questions to get more information.
- "No" and "yes." Your ability to assent or dissent is the key to the boundary gates of your soul. You alone have the power to utter them and so prevent entanglements.
- "I don't have to accept that!" When you're told something about yourself or a situation, you don't have to take it on.
- "I'm sorry." When we say or do or assume the wrong thing, when we've overstepped the mark, this apology begins to restore things to balance.

WHAT DO OUR WORDS MEAN?

Irony is a device used to make light of pain and disappointment: "Well, that was a great day!" when actually it's been overshadowed by chaos and delay, or "So he's a great friend" when someone lets us down. But the facetious use of words really avoids the truth. The same goes for the white lie. When you praise a present you truly hate in order to spare the giver's feelings, you use it as a means of avoiding embarrassing truths and to avoid social offense. It is a diplomatic form of speech that we must use seldom. Lying warps our life path. Our own truth and integrity are the manifestation of our wisdom upon earth; lying interferes with the way we contain and live by that wisdom. Lies are brambles that we weave with our mouths: they can entangle ourselves and others. Lies distort the truth and open a storyline that we will be forced to dance along in the future, when we will have to stand by our word or be proven a liar. We lie to protect ourselves, to cover up our faults, to gain advantage, to pretend knowledge we don't have and to deceive others. Lies are ways of mentally accommodating one set of circumstances while living another set. We speak of creating "a tissue of lies" and that is a very accurate metaphor, because it films over the truth and obscures it. But if we continually lie and live a lie, both our language and our lives will become meaningless and obscure to us.

The way that we use speech alters our surroundings. If we encourage the proliferation of negative thoughts, the words that come from our mouths can act like curses or else become self-fulfilling prophecies. When we say, "I'd like to kill her!" or "That'll never work!" what are we intending, what is the effect? Monitor your own speech over the course of the day and listen to what comes out.

- How are you manipulating words to mean something different and how are people manipulating your words to mean something else?
- How are your words blighting your own or other's lives?
- What are your complaints about? To whom or what is your criticism leveled?
- How often do you lie, fib or bend the truth? Where are your lies leading you?
- How do you talk about yourself? Are you pulling yourself down or building yourself up?

- What or whom are you gossiping about?
- What part does exaggeration play in your speech?
- What are you continually denying?
- What swear words are you using? How often do they pepper your speech?
- How often do you fill silence with trivial words?
- What effect are your words having around you?

THE STORIES WE TELL ABOUT OURSELVES

The stories that we believe and tell about ourselves often keep us in bondage. Many are untrue, and even if they were true once, most aren't applicable any longer. We can discern remnants of old scenarios and stories by listening to the "always and nevers" that pepper our speech and make us whiny. "I never get to sit next to Molly"; "It's always me who has to clean up." These always and nevers are the evidence of superstitions or warped memories of ourselves that we are harboring.

Whenever anyone meets Sally for the first time, they are likely to hear about her last operation; within ten minutes of speaking to Joe, you will know that his son died in an accident years ago. Some people's lives are defined by the illness or misfortune they have suffered. This will usually emerge as an opening gambit of conversation, as a means of introducing others through the medium of their own self-pity. Loss defines some people: their inner monologues and spoken words often reveal the losses, misfortunes and resentments they are carrying. These are the bleedings of inner wounds that have not been healed. But such stories can also signal the more serious fact that they have become inured to their misfortune, have become comfortable or found it convenient, especially when they become the center of attention as a result of it. Their misfortune gives them status.

Many people have become so identified with their sorrow that it is virtually holding them together and any attempt to get them to loosen their grip upon it is seen as a rank betrayal or a murderous attempt. We clutch our wounds to us. If this is your problem, read Caroline Myss's book, *Why People Don't Heal and How They Can*, for that will give you great support to change.

- If you are perpetually running yourself down, read about self-esteem in Chapter 7 and use the Restoring Your Image ritual.
- Investigate the sources of your own uses of "nevers" and "always." Use the Pool of Change ritual (page 142) to cast these in and receive the abundance of new possibility.
- If you have become fused with your losses use the Power of Substitution ritual on page 124 or see page 112.

STOPPING THE INNER MONOLOGUE

The stories about us and our lives can spiral around in a vicious inner monologue that usurps any other reality. The problem is that these stories are invariably false, exaggerated and unhelpful. The inner monologue is the way that we entangle ourselves and spin stories that entangle others. So much energy is invested in keeping these stories spinning like a top, that we don't notice how we lose power. But as Daan van Kampenhout states, "as soon as the compulsive inner monologue is weakened, consciousness starts to free up for a new experience." We can stop the inner monologue by tracking elements within it to their source and reviewing the truth as it was then and as it is now, removing ancestral, family or authority instructions that are still causing you to think, react and obey outworn directives, by taking them to the Pool of Change (page 142) or by beginning to change your story by the power of myth-making, see page 149.

NOTE: We all have inner monologues with ourselves. However, if you are suffering from other voices in your head compelling you, please seek professional help.

ERIC'S SAGA

Eric's early life story was tragic. Abandoned as a child with a slight disability, he grew up in a series of unsatisfactory foster families that, one by one, returned him to an impersonal children's home. Eric's belief in himself was scarred by this continual abandonment, making him feel ugly and unwanted. Despite modest success as a craftsman and the love of a long-term girlfriend, his internal monologue was, "Nobody wants me." He rewrote his story as a saga: "Once upon a time there was a boy with a twisted leg whom nobody wanted. He lived on the beach all by himself, longing for a home of his own. One day, Vikings raided that coast and bore him away as a captive. On landing, the men were all for casting him away because of his leg, but the captain saw what clever hands the boy had, for he had been carving during the voyage. He brought the boy into his home and helped him set up a workshop. His carvings were soon sought after by many people. He fell in love with one girl who came to his shop and he carved her a marriage casket in secret. He proposed to her one midsummer's night at the fair and she consented, for she saw his kind heart and not his twisted leg. They lived long and had many children in the northern lands." This myth of being found, acclaimed, welcomed and married took his story beyond the present moment and resolved it. Eric's new affirmation is "I am welcomed, honored and loved in the heart of my community."

MYTHS THAT SAVE US— CHANGING THE OLD, OLD STORY

Whatever old story is circulating in us calls out to the universe for completion. Once the hammer of experience slams home the nail of certainty about us, there it remains, magnetically attracting the same old experiences. You can remove these old nails with the claw hammer and magnetic power of your rewritten myth, which is your new story. We can reverse old trends by transforming our old story into a myth. Here I am using "myth" in its original sense, as a saving story that sees past the surface into deeper places of solution, and not in the misapplied sense of "a fabrication or lie." This practice can also be used for transforming old, stale situations with associations and people:

1. Retell your story, but this time as a myth. The rules are that you must tell it in the third person rather than the first person and that you must

take it to the moment of crisis and into satisfactory resolution. Begin, "Once upon a time there was a young man who got everything wrong..." or "An old woman who answered a knock at the door..." Or, "There was a baby born to a couple who lived in the west..." or wherever your myth needs to start.

2. Focus on the main structure of your story. You may find that it comes out very differently and has all kinds of help in it. As your myth unfolds, there is another rule: *you must bring the story to satisfactory resolution.* This will inevitably mean that your story changes and that the mythic outcome resolves, heals, and transforms whatever has been troubling you. There are no rules to how you achieve that transformation—you can employ whatever devices you wish. Of course, your story can be much longer than the example above.

3. Make an aphorism or affirmation of your myth to replace the old internal monologue about yourself.

WEAVERS OF WORDS

In J. R. R. Tolkien's *Lord of the Rings* trilogy, the wizard, Saruman, has a voice so smooth and persuasive that he can make day seem like night, and evil seem like good to the unguarded listener. The lure of other people's words can weave a heady spell, creating a labyrinth in which we can easily become lost. Quite apart from the flattering charm others bestow on us, we can also wind ourselves up in the spells that they spin. Charm and enchantment, flattery and compliments, beguilements and baloney, sob stories and scams, all draw us into someone else's story and away from our own.

The ability to discern the truth in other people's words can keep us safe from psychic bespelling. Weavers of words are sorcerers whose voices seem to promise all kinds of wonderful benefits. Charismatic preachers and politicians, wheedling relatives, exploitative employers and promotional advertisers can all involve you in their concerns if you allow their words to take root in you. Not all that they ask of you is going to be beneficial, essential or even necessary. They may be drunk on their own words and ideas. They may just be trying to guilt-trip you into submission. See Guilty Persuasions on page 166.

CHAIN LETTER GUILT

Evita receives a chain letter from a good friend claiming to be for the benefit of "Welfare for Women." Promising her $2,000 in six weeks, it asks her to send $20 to the woman listed at the top of ten names and addresses. In return, she must send the letter to twenty other women of her acquaintance, putting her own name at the bottom of the list, or the wrath of the Goddess will fall upon her if she breaks the chain. It further gives a grim little example of someone who failed to obey these instructions and whose life descended into poverty and despair followed by suicide. The letter frightens Evita into looking through her address book for twenty friends and acquaintances. She knows that they will be mad at her for involving them, but she is down on her luck and needing some money. While she is dithering about it, her friend Marion calls and asks if she's received a silly chain letter. They discuss it and, encouraged by Marion's no-nonsense scorn of such things, Evita feels strong enough to burn it over the sink. She washes her hands afterward and tunes into her Source of Life for support and encouragement.

SCAMS AND CONFIDENCE TRICKS

Scams and confidence tricks are traps set for the gullible. Scams come in all shapes and sizes, from the sweepstakes letters to fixed machines at fairgrounds to the multimillion dollar defrauders who persuade gamblers to part with well-earned cash. In every case, the trap is baited with something very desirable. People of all ages are susceptible to scams, but particularly vulnerable are those who have a generous heart, the self-confident but inexperienced young, the experienced but lonely elderly, and those who view life through rose-colored glasses.

If you own a credit card or have ever filled out a consumer research survey, your personal details, including your income and credit-worthiness, will be on file somewhere. A scam artist may well already know the size and number of rooms in your house, the ages and number of your children and whether you smoke cigarettes or use tampons. These details help profile you.

Chain letters and "offers," which hold you at ransom by threats of personal loss, ill-luck or death, are the equivalent of blackmail. Put them in the trash. Emotional blackmail from fraudulent charities may cause you to reach into your pocket as you read their sob-story literature.

Complex scams by confidence tricksters, which draw people in over a period of time, may be more difficult to deal with, as they tend to become emotionally charged and spread their tentacles over your life, but they work in the same way that blackmail and gambling works, gradually emptying your bank account until some mythical "one last chance."

Your prime weapon is the knowledge that no one gets something for nothing and that you will lose something.

Give the scam into the hands of your Advocates for removal, if it has become intrusive.

RESCINDING YOUR OLD WISHES

The wishes we made in the past can take up disproportionate space in our lives, blocking the way to our achieving the things we want to do now. As with any intention, a wish is a stone that displaces the water in the pool of life. The ripples of that wish-stone keep spreading wider and wider until the wish is achieved or exhausted. When we obsessively promote our heart's desire, we are issuing a prayer that goes out through the universe. Whether we make an idle wish or one we want with our whole hearts, our wish is still out there and may come true in ways we had never intended, or too late to be of use to us. As we grow and change, so our wishes change. Canceling the old wish makes more space in the universe and puts us on track with our present needs and desires.

- What old childhood, teenage or young adult wishes are still circulating? What would their fulfillment do for you now?
- Use the Curse Canceling ritual on page 157, focusing on old wishes.

WORDS THAT HARM

"Sticks and stones may break my bones, but words will never hurt me," we chanted at school to fend off insults in the playground. But words can slide deeply into our souls and fester there. The most painful words are those that have some truth in them, for they salt the wound. In our electronic world, the power of the written word or letter to hurt us has been transformed into the short, nasty email or the even shorter, speed-written text message. Written words are, for some people, even more powerful than spoken ones because the chance insult can fade and be forgotten, but the letter remains to taunt you.

The major forms of harm that our words cause come through gossip; condemnation, criticism and detraction; curses and self-jinxing; and insults that label people.

We are good at insultingly labeling people as "losers," "idiots," "druggies," etc. In traditional societies, it is generally recognized that it is someone's *behavior* not the person himself that wears the label. However, in our society, labels stick. Condemnation cancels someone's flow, holding them in a tractor beam so that they cannot move on and inhabit other forms. Criticism deconstructs people's achievements. When we deny someone their space on earth, we become psychic aggressors.

All these harmful usages of words are in fact power-theft, which can lead to more serious soul-theft. By behaving in these ways we create complex webs of psychic persecution where we put people down in order to enhance ourselves. The ways to modify all these harmful words, whether you are giving them or getting them, is to return to Chapters 4 and 5, and use the power and soul returning rituals appropriately. The words that lodge in us can worm deeply within us and become false beliefs about ourselves. See page 129.

GOSSIP

Gossip is nothing more than words out of control. When words are manipulated by gossips, they can be experienced as stains or streaks of dirt by those against whom they are directed. Whispering campaigns soon change opinion, helping us recategorize someone, smear their reputations, sometimes causing them to be endangered, dispossessed of their rights and liberties or even killed. For gossip to flourish, it needs to be passed on.

It helps us feel superior to consider someone's misfortunes; we gain status from having a new snippet of gossip to pass on or we snigger at the celebrity's downfall, our rival's humiliation. As you see, gossip is the means of diminishing someone and of enhancing ourselves.

In *Othello*, Shakespeare's powerful play about suspicion and jealousy, Iago complains,

Who steals my purse, steals trash ...
But he that filches from me my good name
Robs me of that which not enriches him
And makes me poor indeed.

The loss of one's good name is devastating. It happens to people who are innocent as well as to those who have committed misdemeanors or crimes and been punished for them. Taking away someone's good name is something each of us does when we gossip. We are detracting others and bathing in the reflection of our own glorious goodness. Restoring your reputation in the community after the detrimental gossip can take years, unless you move away and make a life elsewhere.

- Treat any gossip against you as a residue that you cleanse away every day.
- Use the Restoring Your Image ritual (page 138).

TAKING BACK THE CURSE

When I was a teenager, my boyfriend of many years left me every summer to be with a new girlfriend. He always came back to me every fall. One summer, I snapped. On seeing him at the beach with my rival, I became furious and cursed him, tearing my hair and shrieking. I can't even remember the words that poured from my mouth, only that it was a serious wish for him to suffer as I was doing. I didn't see him for two years after that but he eventually found me and begged me to remove the curse, since several things had gone very wrong for him. I did not know then whether my words had been the culprit, only that *he believed* my words had cursed him. I immediately took back the intention of my words and prayed that he should be released from what had been said. This dramatically taught me that our ill wishes have effect, especially when we send them with anger.

CURSES

At some point we have all lost our tempers and spoken words in anger that we afterward regret, but we have seldom considered what harm they might cause. Words spoken with passion have a way of winging to their destination with deadly accuracy. All words have the potential to be blessings that heal or curses that wound. Formal curses do not have to be laid by a sorcerer to be effective:

- "He'll never amount to much!" says a father about his shy son.
- "You probably have about another six months to live," says the doctor to his patient.
- "I've been praying for that horrible marriage to fail," says the jealous mother about her son's marriage to a woman she didn't approve of.

The first two don't seem like curses to us and the last one sounds actively malicious, yet all three are potentially deadly curses that can come home and change someone's life. The son might become depressed at his father's estimate and fulfill his expectation. The patient might fulfill the doctor's prognosis and head for the grave even sooner. The young couple might argue bitterly and separate.

How do we overturn the power of the curse? We find clues in folk tradition. In the British folk song, "The False Knight on the Road," a little boy on his way to school encounters an armed magical warrior. Their interchange is instructive for us, for the warrior curses the boy, but the boy finds a way of turning the curse into something else: "I wish you in the sea," says the warrior. "And a good ship under me," says the boy. "I wish you in the sand," curses the warrior. "And a good staff in my hand," ripostes the boy. If you are cursed by someone, you can immediately turn the curse on its head, field it to one side or transform it as the young boy does here.

If we take our examples above, we can see what a difference our own attitude to life makes. The shy son may not be so extroverted as his father, but he can have a strong determination to succeed in his chosen career. Those who find the doctor's diagnosis unacceptable can sharpen their will to live, if only to outwit his prognosis. The young married couple can draw even closer and share their strength to fend off the jealous mother.

Self-jinxing is a complex word game that we play by turning the power of life against ourselves. This is when we contemplate the next action and say, "I won't be able to do it," or "I'll be lucky not to be sick on the way" or some other prophetic words that pave the way to disaster. Instead of positively approaching an event, we project back to a time where something did go wrong: our words merely perpetuate its trajectory. Some defensive people are actually so aware of the power of words that they refrain from speaking about how an impending event will go, or refrain from talking about a project in hand, for fear of jinxing it:

- To remove a curse that you have uttered, use the Curse Canceling ritual on page 157.
- To neutralize curses that have targeted you, find cunning ways of transforming the words to benefit you, or send them back down the

six pathways to Powers of Life to transform, as in the Curse Canceling ritual, or use the Pool of Change (page 142).

- To disempower your self-jinxing propensity, begin to change your old story of woe into a positive and supportive myth, as on page 149.

CURSE CANCELING RITUAL

Hurtful words and curses have a long echo that reverberates ages after they've been spoken. To cancel curses that you've uttered use the following ritual:

1. Consider those against whom you have idly or seriously wished harm. You may not be able to remember everyone, but if you have some names, write them down.

2. Breathe, relax and invoke your Advocates. Establish your energy field and center yourself.

3. From each of the six directions, call home the detrimental words you have uttered, from before, behind, right and left, above and below. Your Advocates catch these words in a fine net. Say, "May these words be neutralized and do no more harm."

4. When you've done this, turn to each direction in turn and say, "May these words be transformed into the blessing of Life, Light, Love, Law, Truth and Wisdom, for the benefit of all against whom I've spoken, especially [names]," and name those you remember. "May all these and those whom I've forgotten be blessed by the powers of the Source of Life." As you say this, your former words transform into the qualities you have mentioned. You may experience them becoming like vapor, mist, perfume, birds, leaves or many other things. They stream out of the net in their neutralized and re-empowered forms as blessings. Do not specify what kind of blessing they may now bestow; your Advocates and the Source of Life know this better than you do.

You can also adapt this ritual for rescinding old wishes that are out of steam by calling them home in the same way. When you've neutralized the wishes, turn to each direction and make any fresh wish if you desire.

PRAYER

"Prayers are simply a knock on the door, asking for attention from spiritual powers that may be able to help" (Daan Van Kampenhout). We have often confused prayers with magic word-formulas, when they are essentially the clear statement of our intentions. Immature prayer often manifests solely as a request or a demand, true prayer includes thanking and praising, attunement and alignment with spiritual sources, as well as asking and requesting. Prayer must partake of giving as well as receiving:

- Always pray in your own language, unless you are accustomed to praying in a sacred language such as Sanskrit, Arabic, Hebrew, Latin, etc. Intention is the most important thing.
- Use traditional and childhood prayers that are helpful and already known to you: their cadence will be comforting and reinforce a sense of protection, even if your beliefs have become a bit fuzzy since childhood.
- Create your own prayers, calling upon your Source of Life and your Advocate by name or direct your prayers through that name. See my *Celtic Devotional* for guidance on prayer creation.
- Do not use prayer-forms from traditions alien or unfamiliar to you. Your own words and intentions have more efficacy. Use modern speech to say what you mean, rather than archaic prayer modes, unless you find these helpful.
- In framing a prayer for yourself or others, don't specify a particular outcome, but ask the Source of Life to bring the help that is most needed. By defining and specifying a petitionary prayer we may be cursing, not helping. Analyze your motivations in requesting someone. For prayer to work, we must get out the way and do nothing. It is not our duty to fetch answers or solutions, only to make our prayer clear and be receptive to its answer.

Human beings love control. When things go wrong, we like to imagine that we can still make things right again if we make a bargain with God or with Lady Luck, when really we want to get our own way. This is spiritual blackmail and is a coercive way of manipulating the universe. We want to bribe God or Providence into giving us what we want, like a toddler who throws a tantrum to obtain a lollipop at the checkout. The Source of Life doesn't give us all that we desire, for which we should perhaps be thankful.

You can make your own prayer, like Will who works on an oil rig in dangerous and difficult weather. He half-sings, half-chants this prayer into the wind and no one hears him but his Advocates and the Source of Life itself: "In your hands, under your protection, within your embrace I am and was and will be." We need something quick and familiar from repetition when we are in danger.

"He who sings, prays twice," says an old monastic proverb. Underlying all words is the song. If you stop using your lips, tongue and teeth and allow the sound to arise from your lungs and vocal chords, you have the pure sound that is song. It just takes a little more breath to sustain it, that's all. Many people complain that they cannot sing. Believe me, if you can utter words, then you can sing. Sound, vibration and resonance are very powerful protections.

BLESSING FOOD AND MEDICINE

A Scottish Gaelic prayer requests, "Let nothing go down my body that will hurt my soul." The things that we take into our body by way of food, drink and medicines can be blessed before we eat or swallow them. The old-fashioned saying of grace is effective, not only to acknowledge and give thanks for nourishment, but to bless our food in ways that positively benefit us. It puts us into the right relationship with the gift of life that the food gives us. The same kind of grace can be applied to taking medicines. Bless your medicine before taking it and quietly envision the beneficial effect it can have on your body, or upon the illness or imbalance being treated.

WORDS THAT BRING HEALING

In the German folk story, *Mother Hölle*, the reward for good and bad deeds is bestowed upon the tongue of the courageous young heroine who wins the ability to speak gold whenever she opens her mouth, while her uncaring stepsister is gifted with the ability to utter toads and snakes. If words can wound, curse and bespell, then they can also heal. "Between curing and cursing, there is only a letter's difference," writes Dr. Larry Dossey. We rarely remember this healing ability is something that we each have and can use daily. The healing of words is found not just in great poetry, prayers or oratory, but also in our own mouths:

- Speak encouragingly to someone near you today.
- Utter a blessing for someone undergoing challenges and trials.
- Praise someone who normally receives no thanks.
- Write to someone who is struggling alone.
- Email or text some good news rather than dwelling on the bad news.

BLESSING AND GRATITUDE

O happy living things! no tongue Their beauty might
declare: A spring of love gushed from my heart,
And I blessed them unaware: Sure my kind saint
took pity on me, And I blessed them unaware.

—Samuel Taylor Coleridge in "The Rime of the Ancient Mariner"

These words spring from the mouth of the Ancient Mariner on his doomed voyage when he briefly forgets his own cursed predicament and sees the beauty of the water snakes. Their beauty and his blessed response create the breaking of his curse, and the albatross that he idly shot and which has been tied round his neck as a symbol of his error, drops from his neck and he is restored to himself once more. By being restored to the flow of life, we can also restore that flow. Gratitude is the bridge that marks the return to healing for all beings. When we thank, we give. When we are saturated with relief and utter a cry of gratitude, we give back to the universe. When we utter prayers of thanks we love the universe.

- Appreciate what is good about your life. Consider what your life would be like without these things.
- Make your own prayer of thanksgiving to the Source of Life.
- Offer song, praise, poetry and blessing to your Advocates in thanks for loving and caring for you.

BLUEPRINTS FOR TRUE SPEECH

1. Honor silence.

2. Think before you speak.

3. Let your tongue be the agent of truth.

4. If you can't say something encouraging, be silent.

5. Keep your promises.

6. Bless spontaneously.

7. Let honesty and compassion guide your words.

8. Give praise rather than detraction.

9. Let your words express what you mean.

10. Pray from the heart.

CHAPTER 9

People Problems

If I am to eliminate my own sufferings, I must act in
the knowledge that I exist in dependent relationships
with other human beings and the whole of nature.

—The Dalai Lama

CIVILIZATION AND STATUS

Psychic disruption commonly occurs when we succumb to the influences of other people who have forgotten about cause and effect,
who have no spiritual anchor, whose aim is fuzzy or self-serving.
Many people are confused about motives and outcomes, are quick to
cover up guilt and to manipulate; guilt and sly cunning impel them
to come out on top. At the other extreme, we know that humans can
also be selfless, compassionate, equitable and helpful.

Civilization has taught us the need for politeness and order in
a manner that fosters mutual well-being and the common good.
But we can maintain a civilized exterior while being psychically
disruptive to those about us, especially in a society that discounts
the effects of metaphysical reality. The way we control events
in our lives often results in evil effects for those we're trying to
control. We tend to behave in one of two ways with other people:
we absorb what they do and say, or we project our ideas upon
them. By now you will be familiar with the pattern of give and take
that governs psychic hygiene and what results when we ignore it:
the loss of power and soul or their theft from others.

The chief misconception around psychic protection is that
"everyone is out to get us," while we ourselves are paragons of
virtue. The truth is different, as Thomas Moore writes in *Dark Nights
of the Soul*, "Just as ordinary people can't seem to do all the good

they would like to do, so evil people can't be intelligent enough about their concerns to evoke genuine evil." Laziness and boredom usually win out over any planned psychic persecution. Perhaps we are too human to be wholly evil or good?

We must never forget that we humans come from the humus, that we share a likeness with all living creatures in taking our nourishment from the earth itself. Our instinct for interacting with each other is found in our Vital Soul, but it is our conscience, the faculty of our Wisdom Soul, and our compassion, a mature faculty of our Personal Soul, that enable us to be humane.

People only a hundred years ago sang a hymn with the lines, "The rich man in his castle, the poor man at his gate ... God ... ordered their estate," with a complacency that would now shock us. While we have begun to create a more egalitarian society, our place within it is often defined by age, sex, occupation, affluence, appearance, ability, intelligence, health and many other factors, which determine where we stand.

Throughout history, there have been movements, social experiments and revolutions to defuse the powerful glamour of status, but in nearly every one of them, the strong and aggressive, the characterful and persuasive, the well-placed and well-connected have risen to the top to claim the advantage. "If you're particularly charismatic or plausible you can gather a following fairly easily because, perversely, many people like to be controlled by someone else. It makes them feel safe and for a while gives the illusion of having no responsibility for their lives," writes Stephen Russell in *The Barefoot Doctor's Guide to the Tao*.

Human beings like to control their environment. Like all animals, we have a rating system that gives each community member status in the pecking order. There is a continual competition for the better and therefore more advantageous status—often at the cost of others. Our sense of well-being can be severely affected by where we stand in the pecking order of society. People with little power seek acquaintance with those in positions of greater influence. Powerful people find ways of engaging the support of the less powerful to enable their continuing lifestyle.

The way in which we fit into our society very much influences how we feel about ourselves and how others see us. Of course, we are much more than our job, age, sex or appearance, but these factors often determine how people deal with us. Look again at who you are (page 13) and aim to take up your place in the universe regardless of these exterior considerations of status.

One of the unkindest acts human beings inflict on each other is excluding individuals from the group or community. Everyone wants to be accepted and included within the social group and in order to stay within it we tend to compromise power and soul. We submit to the influence of others when we are full of insecurity and dependence; we exercise influence over others when we are resentful, overbearing and opinionated.

DEALING WITH PEOPLE

There are no walks of life, high or low, exempt from potential psychic disruption. People in authority or in occupations of trust, such as doctors, priests, policemen, politicians and leaders, should be trustworthy, but they are not always so. If we fail to notice the warning signs and choose to invest power in such people, we can experience difficulties. How can we deal with people and be discerningly, psychically streetwise?

- Overall first impressions are important. Someone may look handsome but be unscrupulous, or may appear unattractive or uncouth but have a heart of gold. The soul is in the eyes and voice but you should also check body language and see whether their deeds and words match. If you feel ambiguous, something doesn't match.

- Watch your physical feelings and instincts rather than how everyone else is behaving toward the person. If a person frightens you, pay attention to this fear and don't discard this information. If normally friendly children and animals give this person the brushoff or are reluctant to come near, this may be a sign that the person is less than trustworthy.

- When you first meet someone, you can tell immediately how they are by a firm or tentative handshake, the way they meet or avoid your gaze, or the way you are included or dismissed by their attention.

- To some degree human beings mirror what is around them. If we act with kindness and consideration for others, we are likely to find our respect reciprocated. If you behave as if everyone around you is beneath contempt, then you will undoubtedly encounter hostility and contempt in turn.

- If you give authority to someone to be in charge of your financial or legal affairs, be sure to keep copies of all agreements and review contracts regularly, especially if you are creating a living will or are entering a period of diminished responsibility where you and your goods may be preyed upon due to your illness or absence.

- When engaging an employee in a position of trust or someone to care for your children or your house, ask for at least two references and follow them up without fail. Don't trust their word. Get estimates of time and rates for proposed work from workmen.

- When dealing with invasive people, abusive superiors or people in authority over you, be polite, keep your physical distance and use the bodyguarding techniques on page 104. Opportunists will use a combination of voice, eyes and body language to reel you in.

- Be less impressed by charm and what is said by people than by their deeds and their outcome.

- Refuse to be rushed or pressured into snap decisions. Always sleep on things overnight and get sound advice from someone you do trust.

- With forceful personalities who tend to swamp you, hold your ground and keep your own views. Forceful people are not necessarily right in their views, just louder than others.

- Be polite and keep it neutral. Don't let your fear stampede you into verbal reaction or physical retaliation.

- When dealing with someone who seems unaware of their effect, you can state in a neutral, nonaggressive voice, "The way you speak to me makes me very angry" or "Are you aware of how insulting/upsetting/wounding/etc. that is?"

- Instead of being awed by someone into silence or compliance, speak the question that is in your heart.

- If in doubt about someone, ask one of your advocates to check him or her out by asking, "What are X's intentions toward me in this matter?"

TRUSTING OTHERS: LOCATING THE INNER BULLSHIT DETECTOR

Opportunists, salespeople and others will always attempt to create a rapport in order to create common cause or like-mindedness. Whatever their appearance and the extraordinary pull of what they are offering you, can you trust them?

- Try the inner bullshit detector test. Try testing it on a politician who's speaking on TV. Close your eyes and listen to the tone of the voice, not just what's being said. Now open your eyes and stop your ears, look at the person speaking, especially their eyes, gestures and demeanor: do voice and eyes match or are they just talking bunk?

- Does your mind feel peaceful, your heart feel warm and your belly calm?

- Are your guts shifting about uneasily, your chest feeling tight and your mind disturbed? The power in your soul cauldrons is warning you not to trust.

- Do you feel as if something is trying to worm its way inside you or that you are disengaging from your center and flowing out of your body field and soul cauldrons toward them? This is a sign that you're in the presence of a power-thief. See page 116.

GUILTY PERSUASIONS

How do people talk us into things we don't want to be part of? The chief persuasive weapon in their armory is guilt, which manipulates you by:

- Reinforcing your negative self-image, inflaming your guilt and invoking your self-judgment against yourself in ways that benefits the persuader.

- Threatening negative consequences such as expulsion, stigmatization, separation, divorce, violence, etc.

- Making you resort to irrational thinking that makes you blame yourself for supposed errors in the past and present or which you may commit in future.
- Weaving an imaginary scenario where you will be at fault for not accepting the proposal at hand.
- Harping on your known faults and projecting upon you responsibility for things in ways that make you compliant.
- Creating a moral absolute of "the correct or right way" that will paint you as betraying your duty for noncompliance.
- Pretending discomfort or sadness, pleading illness or incompetence in order to arouse your immediate action to relieve these conditions.
- Holding your secrets and shameful actions against you in order to blackmail you into compliance.

These guilt-provoking methods can press our buttons and lead us into collusion unless we stand firmly in our center. The guilty persuasions of family members are the hardest to resist because you are automatically wired to protect dependents and obey elders. Guilt is the winner's choice of manipulation because you do half the work for the persuader; *voila*, and you've caved in!

- Refuse to play the mind game of guilt by remaining centered (page 106).
- Don't collude with guilty persuasion in order to gain "a quiet life" or just to get someone off your back. Your collusion will ensure they will be *on* your back for some time to come!
- Check what actions you are carrying out in order to defuse the guilt that someone has given to you.
- Who is making you jump by manipulating your guilt? Why are you colluding? Who is getting what out of whom?
- To bring a cycle of manipulation to a close, take your guilt to the Pool of Change (page 142), then use the Knife of Separation (page 120) to disconnect from the persuader.
- In cases where you are being forced into criminal activity, are colluding in violence or suffering from blackmail, immediately seek police help and protection. The exposure that you fear by seeking help is not half as bad as the secret misery you will suffer by remaining in this cycle.

WHO IS THE ENEMY?

Few of us have outright enemies. Most of us have rivals, competitors, envious colleagues, manipulative family members, ex-partners, excluded friends and aggrieved others whose lives have touched ours abrasively. We regard these as enemies and treat them as such, a view that is often reciprocated. We reason that whoever is for us must be against our enemy; and whoever is of the enemy's party must be against us. So who is the enemy?

What you experience as the malice of your enemy is a source of great emotional satisfaction to the malefactor—literally, the maker of evil. But, wait a moment; don't we each share in that satisfaction when we are the aggressor? In *Dark Nights of the Soul* Thomas Moore says our great battle is "not between good and evil, but between really living and just pretending." In his opinion, "both the righteous and the evil avoid life." If we were truly living, we wouldn't have the will to be either superior or predatory to others.

Whom do you regard as an enemy? Which of your actions/behaviors trigger his/her enmity? Who is competing with you? Who is getting back at you? Against whom do you hold an implacable hatred or dislike? Against whom are you competitively pitting yourself? How long do you intend to hold your grudge and against whom? What effect is your enmity having upon the universe? These questions make us uncomfortable because they make us aware of the perpetuation of a cycle we have become part of.

Resentment is a seedbed for psychic disruption. The resentments we brood upon eventually hatch out into a monster. Revenge is a deep-rooted need to get even as well as to restore honor after losing face. Individuals try to get even in many petty ways, while groups and families can use vendetta, which persecutes and even kills those who wound the group honor. The urge to get even can eventually escalate into terrorism, which exacts indiscriminate revenge upon any convenient target.

By perpetuating the cycle of enmity with acts of petty revenge, by keeping score and maintaining malicious rivalries, we tie ourselves to opponents much more closely. Finding equilibrium in such charged situations of enmity isn't easy, especially when we are hurt and frightened. The scales of justice do not lie in our hands. Seeking to exact punishment is not our business. A streetwise saying bids us, "Love your opponent but lock the back door!"

Visualize your enemies and opponents as they were as children. If you want to be free from this revenge cycle, use the Forgiveness Ritual (page 120) and release your enemies from the bondage of your expectation, hatred and resentment. Use the Peaceweaving ritual on page 180.

POWER OF THE EVIL EYE

Soraya came to England from Africa as a brilliant medical student to study at a teaching hospital. Mysteriously, she would fall ill before each major exam and suffer feelings of inadequacy and insecurity totally at odds with her former confidence. Exams had been no challenge to her before. She tried all sorts of therapy to get to the root of the problem and was eventually referred to me. During the session, she made reference to a fellow student in her home town with whom she'd studied. Something she said alerted me, "Kagbe used to be my friend, but her mother stopped all that." When I investigated Soraya's body field, I found a tube leading into it. My Advocates showed me that Kagbe's mother, disappointed in her own daughter's achievement and envious of Soraya's success, had attempted a spell to draw off Soraya's gifts to benefit her daughter. The effect had disrupted Soraya so much that she had had little access to her own power. My Advocates rescued the stolen power and cut off the connection, sealing it with a strong, protective symbol to prevent reoccurrence. Soraya is now a doctor working in the Middle East.

ENVY AND THE EVIL EYE

In traditional societies there is a massive anxiety caused by the fear of being "overlooked" or, as we would say, becoming the object of someone's envy. Throughout the world, the evil eye is much feared.

If you go to southern Italy, Turkey or Greece, you will notice that boats, households and cars are defended by the symbol of the eye whose ever-open gaze quells envy. These talismans are set up to defend against the evil eye. Targets of envy can be anyone who's got what we haven't.

Envy is a murderous commodity and has been rightly feared throughout the centuries. Among older people in our society and throughout traditional societies worldwide, you will find a defense mechanism against envy that deflects your praise of their child by disclaiming, "Oh, the baby's just an ugly little thing"; if you admire an article in their house, it may well be offered to you. This strange behavior is about defusing the power of envy. By praising or admiring someone or something, even by pointing at it, you have "overlooked" it, meaning that your envy has surfaced.

We must be careful not to impute all our failures to the evil eye, because it can become a convenient excuse to blame others, but most of us are aware of when someone is envious of our success, gifts or possessions. Being on the receiving end of someone's envy feels like being stalked or staked out prior to a burglary: you can be aware of someone's burning envy scorching its way into you.

- Avoid boasting about your gifts, possessions, happiness, etc., especially around those who lack these things.
- Keep a close eye on work colleagues and others who have revealed their envious intentions to you. In their company, invoke an Advocate to "cover your back" and act as a rearview mirror so that you're not overtaken by nasty surprises.
- Use the Spiritual Armor Ritual (page 54) to protect yourself.

BLAMING AND SCAPEGOATING

"When you blame someone else for having written a rotten life-script for you it's easy to become self-indulgent, lazy, helpless, 'victim-like' and self-righteous" (Dr. Andrew Stanway). Blaming others is often at the root of accusations of psychic attack. Because we cannot explain what's going on, or cannot believe we invited in or brewed the psychic turmoil ourselves, we send the blame for it elsewhere and begin the psychic persecution of another. It is generally true that we blame others for what has been done, said or thought ourselves! Blaming makes us self-righteous and superior.

Petty blaming is a childish way we have of covering our own neglect. Ian forgets to close the back door and a stray cat steals the fish for supper. When challenged he blames his sister Kay, who left the house earlier and isn't there to defend herself. This behavior is but a short step from major demonization, where we project the blame upon others. The process of scapegoating—casting the blame upon others—becomes clear whenever we discuss psychic disturbance. It is always someone else's fault, never our own. Conveniently, we ignore the disruptions that we have caused or colluded with. The first way to tackle psychic disruption is to attend to our own attitude to truth and illusion, for culpability and blame coexist in all of us.

Religions have myths that tell how the problem of evil originally came into our world, how our story went wrong and how it can be redeemed: Adam blames Eve, who blames the serpent for leading her astray in the book of Genesis. These myths are an attempt to explain a cycle of evil that is connected by blame.

Scapegoating is the art of communal blame. In families and other groups, someone is made to take responsibility for what goes wrong. The scapegoat is the one who takes the blame when projects go awry. "It was *Pauline* who photocopied that document ..." "Uhhh!" everyone shrugs in mutual recognition of the fact that the inept junior is known as the office Jonah. Uncle Brian is labeled as "the black sheep of the family" because he bucks the trend of family conformity; all the family blame is placed at his door.

The communal need to dump all our stuff on someone is a recognized phenomenon worldwide. We can scapegoat countries, minorities and religions as well as individuals. Before people understood the physical universe with the help of modern science, sudden plagues, deaths of cattle or children were often blamed on witches, strangers or unpopular individuals who became scapegoats for the community. Modern people have not stopped behaving this way.

Scapegoats are also made out of whistle-blowers—people who uncover shady doings in a local business or national corporation. The media makes instant scapegoats of those who get themselves noticed by their achievements, overreaching pride or their incompetence. But scapegoats can also be made out of people who say nothing and who take on the blame.

All societies need fools and clowns who are licensed to harmlessly deflect humanity's shadow, who can deal safely with human ambivalence. In our society, we have comedians who are usually sharp observers of human nature. We need them to see the unseeable, say the unsayable and enact the undoable, just like the court fool of medieval times who was the only one who could bring the unspoken subtext to the court's attention with impunity. The fool is a licensed scapegoat, but some individuals take the fall or act as the butt of the joke for their group.

If you have been scapegoated and blamed for the mess others have made, you will feel as if you carry a great burden. Whether this burden has been unjustly laid upon you or whether you have colluded with the group opinion and taken it upon yourself, you can get out from underneath it.

- Who are you blaming? What effect does your blame have upon them?
- How are your projections upon others impeding their freedom?
- Reexamine self-pity and victimhood (page 134).
- When you have to be in a group that has scapegoated you, call on advocates to surround you with their powerful cloak. Remain true to your self-image.
- Make use of tribunals and arbitration bodies to enable your rehabilitation if you are scapegoated at work.

- If you have been scapegoated, perform the Restoring Your Image ritual (page 138).

GOOD COMPANIONS AND FALSE FRIENDS

When you wish to change, empathetic friends who encourage are better than negative ones who tear down your achievements. If you are surrounded by "friends" who pull you and your works down all the time, then you are being used as a punching bag, not a friend. To change our associates can be the hardest thing to do but when your psychic problem emanates from their careless behavior, think carefully!

True friendship is reciprocal and grows in trust and intimacy over time: it cannot just arrive. Some people whom we regard as friends are not really such, only acquaintances whom dependency and habit have given the appearance of friends. No friendship or relationship is entirely equal but we need to beware when over-dependency without loving return goes on for a prolonged period. It may have become time to sever the links between you. This is often painful when the person may have once been a close friend. Over time you may have changed or developed while the friend has remained where she was. Guilt often keeps the habit of friendship going when it's long been dead. The signs that things have deteriorated may be discerned from answering these questions:

- Who is getting what out of this friendship? Who is giving, who is taking?
- What does your friend do for you?
- What do you (still) have in common with this friend?
- Does your friend disparage or mock you?
- How far have you drifted apart since you first met?
- Do you experience a deep reluctance to see or engage with your friend?
- Do you fish desperately for topics of conversation that will keep you talking?
- Who usually contacts whom first? Is it always you or your friend?

- Are you being used as a convenience?
- Does your friend follow through on agreements or leave you to do all the work?
- Do you feel guilty or obliged when you consider your friend?
- Is your friend always trying to pull you down to their level or view or to engage in behavior against your personal preferences or better judgment?
- Are you a warehouse for power-theft rather than a friend?
- Do you continually *befiend* rather than *befriend* your friend?

If your answers above lead you to suppose that your friendship has gone super nova, or that it's become a habit and ceased to be a mutual friendship and it's time to close it down, then make it clear on both sides of reality. Some friendships and associations merely fall away into a lack of contact and die quietly.

- Check for any guilty persuasions that are impeding this separation, see above. The sense of obligation often binds us in stale associations "for old times' sake" and holds us back from using our energies elsewhere. Sometimes we feel emotionally blackmailed by the one who has a dependence upon us.
- Call home the power you've invested in this friendship (page 69) and bless the old friend.
- If the old friend mounts persistent attempts to reattach to you after all the above, only then use the Knife of Separation (page 120).
- Use the above for separation from clubs, societies and associations as well as friendships.

The loss of even a bad friend is a grievous one, especially if you were once close. All loss is a bereavement and should be mourned as such, to do honor to what you once shared. But when one friend leaves, another arrives (see page 281). Throughout our lives, we encounter striking individuals with whom we feel immediately at home: these are people with whom we have a soul affinity. When you're in their company, the conversation flows. Look at the criteria for accepting Advocates on page 27. This advice also applies to any new good companions that you may meet.

MINDING ANOTHER'S OWN BUSINESS

Denise was a retired care worker. Her desire to help people drove her to often step in whether she had been requested to or not. She became deeply embroiled in the affairs of a vulnerable elderly man, Sam, whose family had moved away. His family found out that she had been staying at his house to help out at night and that her natural concern for Sam's welfare had caused her to reveal the family's neglect to several local institutions from whom she'd sought support. The family saw Denise as an interfering old busybody who was after Dad's money. They forbid her to see Sam, put him in a home, and began a smear campaign to blacken her name. The dirt stuck and Denise entered into a series of low-grade but unshakable ailments that left her feeling weak in body and soul. The hurtfulness of the accusations made against her generous nature had the deepest impact, however. The shaman whom she saw understood how guilty Denise was feeling about Sam, whom, though he was now getting better care and attention, as well as some social life, she nevertheless felt she had betrayed. The shaman cleansed her of the intrusive accusations and restored the power she had lost. Through him, his spirits sent a message, "Be an advocate for the weak but always check with your instincts: How appropriate is your level of help? You cannot help everyone."

RESPECTING THE BOUNDARIES OF OTHERS

Psychic disturbance is experienced the minute someone oversteps your boundaries or attributes their own motivation to yourself: "We diffuse our feeling over others, and count on their acting from our motives," George Eliot says in her novel *Daniel Deronda*. If we stop projecting our thoughts and fantasies upon people and just see them as they are rather than how you would like them or imagine them to be, our relations with other people may improve or be seen in their true light.

Sometimes we can get involved with other people's business with disastrous results. This is largely a matter of boundaries. We see that someone is having difficulties, so we step in. Of course, if you see someone about to have an accident, you pull them back without asking, but life is not always so clear-cut.

When we see people in difficulties, we empathize and feel their pain. To relieve our own discomfort we may offer unwanted, inappropriate help. If people want help, they ask for it. You can also offer your help. But if they don't want it, or can't accept it, then they are unlikely to be able to benefit from the help offered. Observing the boundaries of another person removes most of the major causes of psychic disruption. Alternatively, you may find yourself being asked for help that you feel you cannot give. Maybe your instincts tell you that there is trouble ahead. Listen to them.

Consent is the key to the boundary fence that separates you from others. Generally speaking, if you have not been given consent, don't step in. Think about the following:

- What have been the results of your having done things for others without their permission in your life?
- Check how often you make assumptions for others.
- Ask family members, coworkers and friends to point out to you the times and places when you step over their boundaries.
- Before changing someone's life by stepping in, get someone's specific consent.
- Look again at your connections to people in your life. What is the special contract between you?
- Disentangle yourself from other people's affairs by removing your projections, influence and control over them through rituals that return power and soul to them. See page 66 and page 93.

GROUP-MIND AND THE ART OF CROWD MANAGEMENT

We have been speaking about our dealings with individuals, but we must discuss what happens when we are in a crowd and the group-mind is at work. The influence of the group-mind can be seen at any football game when thousands of supporters become fused together. The influence of the group-mind within a crowd can be both inspiring and chilling. Great orators can instill noble and honorable thoughts, charismatic preachers inspire feelings of spiritual connection, while dictators can inspire fear or blind obedience and rabble-rousers can direct the crowd to acts of vandalism, vengeance or murder. Mob rule is one of the most frightening manifestations of the group-mind.

It is hard to attend a sporting event and not feel some support for one of the teams or players. It is even harder to resist the music at a rock concert. If you've ever been to an auction, you may feel the sudden urge to bid for items you never previously wanted. If you enter a casino, your loose change suddenly wants to come out of your pocket and into a slot machine. Many unbelieving people have briefly "come to God" during the stirring ministry of a preacher and been bemused afterward. What made them go down to the front of the hall and witness? The group-mind made them.

When many people come together in a common cause, the power of mind is amplified manyfold like many instrumentalists in an orchestra under the baton of a conductor. The concert that the group-mind produces is very much tuned to the intent of those gathered there. It can be manipulated and guided by whoever leads or coordinates the event. The group-mind loves pageantry, spectacle and occasion because these speak deeply to the ancestral soul of the community or nation, but we should be clear about how group-mind can take us over.

Living in a community is very different from living independently. Monasteries, communes, camps, prisons, ships and army barracks require a different approach. Most communities are governed by very clear house rules, which have to be maintained by everyone for the well-being of the group. Living in such close proximity with others requires you to become part of the group-mind and soul of the community.

Different cultures and countries have different physical proximity boundaries. What may feel overfamiliar to you living in a northern country may be normal for someone who lives in a southern land. What you may feel is coolly reserved may actually be quite friendly for someone from further north.

Here's how to deal with boundary issues:

- If someone is getting too close, you can extend your hands in front of your body and make the gesture of cleaning off one hand upon the other.

- In a crowded bus, train or elevator when you are closely packed together, draw in your own body field as close as you can. Cleanse it from residues when you get home or in a convenient neutral area. See page 109.

- If you get panicked in crowds, check that you know where the nearest exits are. Keep a mini flashlight on you in the event of a power failure or emergency. Expand your body field around you and invite the Soul-Shepherd to conduct you to a place of safety.

- If things turn nasty in a crowd and you need to avoid the attention of aggressors, immediately call upon the Source of Life and seal your aura (page 52). Visualize a cloak of mist surrounding you, making you invisible.

- To avoid being drawn into the group-mind of any gathering you attend, keep yourself centered and alert. Do a self- and reality check periodically (page 34 and page 35).

- Ask your Advocates to show you how to weave your own peace cloak to wear when you go into crowds or situations where the group-mind is likely to be disruptive or aggressive.

WHEN PEOPLE ARE A PAIN IN THE NECK

The healer Jack Schwartz noticed that our sensitivity to people can literally give us a pain in the neck! He suggests this method as a first-aid strategy to help release the accumulated pain that gathers at the back of your neck after you've been with a difficult bunch of people and you've been trying to keep their influence at bay. The neck pain is often a result of the collision between your own defense, which is covering the entrance where your spine and head connect, and the attack of someone's power struggle to win you over or subdue you.

Place your right hand on your solar plexus and your left hand on the back of your head, resting just under the jut of your skull, over the occiput. Breathe gently and hold this position for three minutes. Then reverse your hands with left on solar plexus and right on the back of your head for another three minutes. The neck pain will now be released.

RELEASING HOPE IN THE UNLOVELY

Daily we may have to deal with people who seem beyond redemption, people who make us fearful and reactive, people whose presence or appearance revolts us. We only see them from our own perspective and never see what lies within. Some people are the way they are because hope has become trapped and died inside them. Old dreams have faded, passionate creativity has been crushed and stamina is low. They are struggling with things too great to shift alone. We cannot see into the hearts and minds of others, but we can be sensitive and aware of their hopes. Without being heavy-handed or being a do-gooder or giving away power, our kindness and encouragement can release hope in them if we recognize each person as having special potential.

Every person is worthy of respect, whatever their acts. Somewhere in everyone is the immortal soul that knows better. Our respect for others acknowledges their personal honor and their souls, even though the other may have diminished self-esteem or little sense of their own sacred self. Consider the needs and desires of others without giving away power and soul. "Approach everyone you meet as a beloved member of your family. This doesn't mean you must approve of them, or even like them. It simply means you treat them with the respect and kindness you would your own mother or yourself, no matter how scummy they appear," writes Stephen Russell, also known as the Barefoot Doctor.

Bless the unlovely, the unscrupulous and the unpleasant with this Buddhist blessing:

May all sentient beings enjoy happiness
and the root of happiness.

May they be free from suffering and the root of suffering.

May they not be separated from the great
happiness devoid of suffering.

May they dwell in the great equanimity free
from passion, aggression and prejudice.

You can name individuals or groups when you use this prayer. However, do not "send love" to the unscrupulous if you are being abused by them: this constitutes a giveaway when you should rather be protecting your boundaries.

PEACEWEAVING

Peace needs the pathway of our will to change.
Peace will not come to the troubled world
unless we first invite it under our own roof.

—Caitlín Matthews in *Celtic Devotional*

When considering our psychic protection, the tendency is for us to think of ourselves alone, but living defensively and seeing everyone else as a potential psychic attacker. This is a miserable way of life. We cannot live in sealed individual compartments away from others: we need friends, community and support. Ignorance and mutual suspicion may divide us from our neighbor, whether it is the stranger next door or the neighbor in the adjoining country to our own, but peaceweaving is something every single person can do. It starts with you. If you can daily hold the possibility that peaceful coexistence can happen between disparate groups of people, then you have declared a truce and opened a road to peace. The incredible power of the truth and reconciliation process that followed the reign of apartheid in South Africa is an example to the world of how peace can be obtained. You can weave a cloak of peace every day as part of your spiritual practice:

- Center yourself as usual (page 106). This time, offer peace to all directions as you turn, saying, "May there be peace in the east, south, west, north, below, above, within." As you turn to each direction, sense see and feel the peaceweaving running from where you stand to encircle and cloak the world.

- Ask your advocate to give you a sign or gesture of peace that you can make with your hands. One such gesture of peace is demonstrated by the Buddha of the all-accomplishing wisdom, Amogasiddhi, who makes the gesture of fearlessness, with right hand upraised at breast-height and facing outward. You can make this sign or your own in situations where things are becoming heated or aggressive. Visualize the Source of Life making this sign; then make it yourself in the six directions.

- When you, someone else or a place in the world is in emotional turmoil and yearning for unity and peace, pray to the Source of Life: "Source of Life, who harmonizes the whole universe with wisdom, love, justice and mercy, take from my/our/their heart/s all jealousy, indignation, rage and contention, and whatever may injure peace. Have mercy on those who seek mercy; give grace to all in need, and grant that I/we/they may recognize the wisdom of the sacred self both within my/our/their self/ves and in the souls of others that we may all live together in unity."

Our prayers irrigate the universe with loving compassion. Your prayer may arrive at its destination as a road under the feet of the lost, as a meal to one who is starving, as a beacon to one who is searching or as peace in the heart of a people at war.

BLUEPRINTS FOR HUMANE RELATIONS

1. Respect yourself and take up your proper space in the universe.

2. Respect others as you would wish to be respected yourself.

3. Follow your own standards and beliefs rather than be swayed by those of others.

4. Deal compassionately with the weak but stand your ground with the strong.

5. Be careful what you project upon others.

6. Be reciprocal in your dealings with others rather than vindictive.

7. Cleanly dissolve stale, unhelpful associations.

8. Seek out peers who share a soul-affinity with you.

9. Stop keeping score and getting even.

10. Declare a truce and bring peace.

CHAPTER 10

Home and Environment

Come you in and sit you down,
What you lost shall here be found.
Bowl and cup shall slake your lack,
Cast the bundle from your back.
No more wandering, no more war,
Come you in and close the door.

—Caitlín Matthews in *The Wanderer's Welcome Home*

THE LIVING ENVIRONMENT OF OUR HOME

Before we can consider the house where we live and its protection, we must acknowledge the earth as our first home. The living planet that wondrously supports our own lives has its own power and soul. But for many the earth is just a thing, not a living being. This misapprehension that our world is lacking in sentience, that it is just a resource to exploit, is causing great pain to the whole universe. If we behave without reciprocal regard for anyone, that person begins to feel exploited and neglected. Our planet is no different.

Many people are passionate about protecting our environment, realizing, almost too late, that how we live on our planet matters. But it is not just our misuse of the world's resources that is the problem; it is also the ways in which we behave that affect our environment. In our homes, offices and surroundings, levels of anger, resentment, despair, hopelessness and retaliation can pollute everything and everyone we come into touch with. When the living environment is disrespected and abused, the inhabitants of that place begin to feel abused or act abusively. Human beings are not the only ones who can lose power and soul. Such loss is recognizable in places where we notice how much the area has gone down through neglect or over-commercialization, through exploitation of natural resources, through the erosion of beauty and habitat.

Before we can consider our own family, we must acknowledge our wider family. We share the earth with many relatives, other species of life who have as much right to inhabit the planet as ourselves. The glad mystery of every living being is something we experienced as children when every animal, insect, plant and tree was wondrous to us. However, "we have silenced too many of those wonderful voices of the universe that spoke to us of the grand mysteries of existence" (John Lane). Every single place on earth has its own guardian spirits. In Iceland, the right of these guardian spirits to inhabit their place is actually protected by laws forbidding people from building just where they like. Icelanders know that if they disregard these spirits, accidents and other misfortunes occur. Anciently, we acknowledged this wisdom; recently, we have ignored it. Spirits of place cannot and should not be evicted because they live on that piece of ground. We must learn how to live with them as good neighbors.

These considerations dramatically affect the spiritual cohesion of the universe and impact upon our own psychic health, since we cannot exist anywhere else but Earth. The less reciprocal and attentive we are to the world-soul, the more we are likely to exploit and pollute our environment.

Meditate upon the Earth as a living being. Be aware of the world-soul as a cloak of atmosphere around the planet. Offer peace to every direction and bless the world-soul that cloaks you and all that you love.

DEDICATING A HEARTH SHRINE

The heart of every home used to be its hearth or fireplace but in the age of central heating and apartments, not everyone has a hearth any longer. However we still have a central living room, where we gather together as a family. Wherever you live, you can dedicate a hearth shrine that will focalize the sacred center of your home with protective love. In Chapter 2 you were invited to make space for your Advocate and Source of Life by creating a shrine, to strengthen you and make their presence more real to you. You may have set up a private shrine in your own room. A hearth shrine is something that everyone sees every day. If you share a space with others, your shrine doesn't have to be very obvious; it could be something as simple as a candle and a vase of flowers.

1. Clear a space in your main living room and physically clean it.

2. Turn and offer peace to all the directions (page 180). Then say, "May there be peace to the spirit of this place." Put a little gift to the spirit of the place upon the floor in a dish: a biscuit or piece of fruit will do. This offering is a courteous act of spiritual hospitality because you share your home with the spirit of the place that your home stands upon. Remove the offering the next day and throw it away without eating it yourself.

3. Bless the shrine with some sprinkled water, saying, "May the power of water, the mercy of love, bless this shrine." Be aware of water washing away any impurities and cleansing it.

4. Bless the shrine with incense or burn some dried herbs, saying, "May the power of air, the breath of life bless this shrine." Be aware of the wind brushing the shrine clean.

5. Bless it with a small stone, "May the power of earth, the stability of earth's law, bless this shrine." Be aware of the molecular pattern and shape of the shrine forming itself into a sacred receptacle that will hold the blessing of your shrine.

6. Bless it with a lighted candle, "May the power of fire, the illumination of light, bless this shrine." Be aware of the hearth-fire warming the shrine and sending illuminating protection to all parts of the house.

7. Set whatever you have chosen to place on your shrine and say, "In the name of the Source of Life, I establish this shrine to protect the heart of my home: may peace, plenty, health and joy dwell here."

8. Sit quietly by your shrine and commune with the sacred center of your home. Feel the power of your shrine pervading every room of your home.

9. Daily light the candle on your shrine and renew the blessing that lives in the heart of your home.

PROTECTING THE HOME

We are all security conscious when it comes to protecting our homes from unauthorized entry, but there are some things you don't want to come over your threshold that are not deterred by locks and alarms.

People who visit your house may bring residues with them and leave them with you—we sometimes bring these home ourselves from work or the supermarket; there may be the active malice of neighbor disputes swirling about; or the residues resultant from being near a main road. There are many ways of protecting your home:

- Traditionally across Europe, people have drawn threshold patterns upon the front and back doorstep of their homes to deter spirit intrusions gaining entrance. Ask your Advocates to show you a symbolic design that you can use. These patterns "tangle" intrusions and forbid them entry to your home. Renew them periodically every new moon. Use a traditional interwoven design such as a labyrinth or Celtic knotwork emblem to act as a protective emblem.

- Ask your Advocates to show you a sacred protective symbol to place on the way in or out of your house. Pious Jewish households have a mezuzah, a holder in which a scroll with sacred text inscribed upon it, is placed by their door, to be touched on going in or out. Catholic households often have a holy-water basin with which to bless themselves just inside the door. Hindu homes have a shrine to the deities venerated by the family with offerings upon them. If you have a strong faith, then you can utilize similar icons, emblems or objects as suitable protections. However, you cannot use such talismans with any effect unless you have a personal connection with and trust in those spirits whom the emblems represent.

- With the help of your Advocates, get to know the spirit of the piece of land your own house is built upon. This spirit may be willing to be a guardian of your home if you establish a good relationship with it. Each house has its brownie or house spirit who lives near the hearth or the stove. When you go out or leave your home unoccupied, it is on watch. Remember to thank it for its service.

- Here is an anonymous Latin blessing suitable for all homes:

  Pax intrantibus (Peace to all comers)

  Salus exeuntibus (Health to all who depart)

  Benedictio habitantibus (Blessing to all who live here).

HOUSE-CLEANSING RITUAL

Use this ritual to cleanse a new home from residues of unhappiness, violence or neglect before you move into it, as well as when you need to reconsecrate your home after a break-in. It can also be used for the eviction of intrusive spirits.

1. If you are moving in, establish your hearth-shrine first, installing some picture, object or symbol that represents the Source of Life to you. Do this with devotion and care, invoking your Advocates with loving confidence. Center yourself and surround yourself with the cloak of peace given by your Advocates (page 180).

2. Starting at the right-hand side of your front door, with some incense and a feather to fan it with, go round the whole apartment or house counterclockwise to sweep out and away every bad influence there. So, if you start in the hall, go down the right-hand side of the hall and then into the next room on the right and go right around that—making a complete circuit of your whole space—including cupboards, closets, etc. Continue upstairs. If you are dealing with residues, say or chant this prayer as you go around the house,

   Winter's sorrow, summer's pain,
   Visit not this house again!
   Underneath this blessed roof,
   Lives the law of perfect truth.

   If you are dealing with intrusions, in each room say loudly and confidently, "In the name of the Source of Life [and any other

Advocates you wish], I command all misplaced spirits to be gone from here. You are not welcome in this house. If you remain then [your Advocates] will chase and remove you. So be gone now!" Fan the incense into the room or space, expelling residues before you as you chase them out of your house.

3. Complete your counterclockwise circuit of your house or apartment, finishing at the left-hand side of your front door, and sweep out of your front door with incense anything you don't want in your house.

4. Now light a candle in the name of the Source of Life and go clockwise round your apartment or house starting at the left-hand side of the door, and bless every room and space, saying in every room, "In the name of the Source of Life [and whoever else you wish to help and protect you] I declare that this room is protected by [your Advocates]." As you bring the light of the Source of Life into each room, you can say or chant this prayer:

> *Health and blessing, joy and light,*
> *Dwell within both day and night!*
> *Advocates protect and keep,*
> *When we wake and when we sleep!*

5. When you're done, you can draw a protective threshold pattern in chalk upon your doorstep, saying, "In the name of the Source of Life, may no intruder enter here." Ask the spirit of your home to protect and guard it.

TRASHED

Alison and Richard came back from a lovely weekend away to discover that their house had been robbed. Apart from the theft of the electrical goods, their entire CD collection had been stolen, and the newly deco-rated nursery for their first child had been trashed. Although the insur-ance company eventually paid for replacement goods, some things could never be replaced, like the jewelry that Alison's grandmother had left to her. But the couple were devastated more by the sense of invasion and neither liked to be alone in the house for several weeks after the event. After thoroughly cleaning up and getting an overhaul of their security, Alison still felt very nervous and fearful for the safety of the child she was carrying. Richard finally called in the local priest to bless their home, especially the nursery, where the couple put up a Renaissance picture of an angel to keep guard. This blessing settled things down for the household.

RECONSECRATING AFTER BREAK-IN OR VANDALISM RITUAL

Whether it is your house that has been robbed or your car that has been broken into, or just some nasty act of vandalism that has marred your fence, the sense of violation is keen. Apart from feeling unsafe, you may also feel dirty. Use this ritual for reconsecrating any dwelling place, car or even shed.

1. Clean up any mess, repair any damage and remove things too broken for mending.

2. Do the House-Cleansing ritual above, except use water with a little salt in it for the counterclockwise cleansing rather than incense, and say, "In the name of the Source of Life, I wash away all hurt and trespass from this home with clean water." Sense, see and feel all violation leaving the room. For the clockwise circuit, use the candle and say, "In the name of the Source of Life, I illuminate this home with the flame that brings confidence and blessing." Sense, see and feel the power of the flame warming and comforting your house.

3. Go to your hearth-shrine and call upon the Source of Life to bless some essential oil. Now go into each room and behind each door, press your oiled fingertip to the wall saying, "This room is made whole and holy once again." Sense, see and feel the blessing of the Source of Life pervading the room. Finally, go to your front door and touch the lintels to either side, above and below, saying, "This house is made whole and holy once again. May all be blessed within this house! May peace dwell in this place forever more!"

4. If you are reconsecrating a car or other space, touch each part of the bodywork as you seal it with oil.

MORE SERIOUS INTRUSIONS IN YOUR HOME

More serious intrusions in your home are beyond the scope of this book. If your home seems to have intrusive spirits, you may experience some of the following:

- Movement of objects and furniture.
- Unexplained knocks and sounds.
- Glass shatters without reason.
- Stains, signs or writing appear on walls or in dust.
- Shadows or presences.
- A weighty presence on the bed.
- Voices and calls.
- Unaccountable smells and odors.
- Patches and areas of coldness.
- Pets see and react aggressively or fearfully to things that aren't apparent to you.

To clear such things away you first need expert spiritual back-up. Don't go in alone or unprotected. If this kind of spirit-clearing seems out of your league, then call in some expert help. For strategies to help the unquiet dead move on, see Chapter 15. But don't forget that some of the above symptoms may have ordinary causes.

HOW TO BE AWAY FROM HOME

One of the most destabilizing things is being away from your home and family. Cut off from your usual routines and surroundings and separated from loved ones, you may begin to stray from your center and become susceptible to psychic disturbance. You can make being away from home less stressful by some of the following strategies, which strengthen your connection to the universe in positive and nurturing ways:

- Take a traveling shrine that evokes your Source of Life: a folding photo frame with a sacred picture, a stone from your favorite place, etc.

- Bring something from your hearth: a family photo, a portable object to be your touchstone of home, a picture drawn by your child, a birthday card from your partner.
- Take one staple and portable item of food or drink as your "home nourishment." (Note: Some airlines do not permit certain foods unless they are factory sealed.)
- In your toiletries bag pack one comforting item that smells of home, such as your usual soap or an essential oil or bath-essence.
- Pack one uplifting and essential book, such as poetry, which gives you spiritual wisdom, insight or inspiration.
- Take your own music and the means to play it.
- Bring a notebook and pen for writing down your thoughts, keeping a diary, or storing reminders that will help you keep going.

Sometimes you have to be away from home for other less pleasant reasons, like going into the hospital or a stint in prison. You may also have to leave your home due to factors such as unemployment or house repossession and have to live in temporary accommodation or in a nursing home. When you are hospitalized or have to receive prolonged medical treatment, you no longer feel quite as at home in your body as you did when you were healthy. It is dispiriting to be both ill and away from home at the same time. When you are suddenly separated from home and family, and can make no provision as suggested above, these strategies will keep you together:

- Center yourself every day, paying close attention to the six directions and their relationship with you.
- Create a temporary shrine for yourself; if you are in difficult or confined surroundings, you can *draw* a shrine and keep the piece of paper in a book, which you take out when necessary. Or create a shrine from stones or other things from nature. If none of this is possible, then visualize your shrine being about you in the six directions.
- Reconnect with all your usual supportive connections. See page 14.
- Withdraw into the Sanctuary of the House of Life periodically for strengthening and advice.
- Connect with the spirit of the place you are now living in. See page 183.

- Ask to see an independent chaplain or one of a faith that you follow, to help you keep spiritually connected.

CEREMONY FOR GOING AWAY FROM AND RETURNING TO HOME

On my first visit away from my land I experienced a terrible disorientation and panic that spoiled my vacation. Someone correctly identified my panic as simple homesickness, though it felt much more serious to me. I now follow the ceremony below before leaving my country and on returning home, and I have never suffered from homesickness again. This ceremony helps prevent soul-parts straying off back home and leaving you vulnerable. In these days of fearful travel, this sequence creates a sustained ceremony that lasts from your leaving to your return home.

- Leave your affairs in good order, cancel local services and pack your travel shrine and comforts.
- In your yard or at your hearth, tell the spirit of your home that you are going away, why and for how long. Bless your hearth and garden.
- Tell very young children you leave behind that you will be away for seven sleeps or however long—they understand this better than long periods of time.
- Spend quality time with the ill and with elders.
- Say goodbye to pets, bless them and commit them into the care of whatever caretakers stay at home or come in to feed them. Tell all pets conveyed to kennels that you are returning; leave one item of clothing smelling of you with them.
- Sit down for five minutes just before leaving to appreciate your home and thank it for sheltering you. This also centers you before traveling.
- Call on your Advocates to accompany you on your journey and keep you safe.
- Bless your luggage as it is stowed for travel.
- On boarding your train, ship or plane, say goodbye to the spirits of your land/locality and bless them.

- Pray for a safe arrival and hassle-free journey through whatever element conveys you (earth, water, air), then sit back and enjoy the journey with your Advocates beside you as traveling companions.

- On arrival in a new place, greet the spirits of that place and tell them why you have come. Introduce your Advocates to them. Spend at least five minutes outside in your new place and appreciate it. Eat or drink something typical of the region, blessing your food, but don't stay up late on your day of arrival.

- Establish your room or space by setting up your traveling shrine, and give thanks for a safe arrival. If you feel uncentered, reconnect with your sources of strength and nurture, meditate, read something inspiring, listen to your music, have a scented bath or shower to relax. Gather your souls to you from the scattering of a difficult journey.

- On returning, thank the spirits of the place you have visited. Thank and bless the place and people you have been among (even if your visit wasn't very enjoyable). Leave the place as you found it or better.

- On the journey home, do as on your outward journey, greeting the spirits of your land.

- On arrival home, greet family members, pets, etc. Go into the yard and appreciate it, watering plants, touching trees, etc. Do one small household task to ground you, such as washing up or dusting. Light your hearth candle and tell your traveler's tales to the whole household.

- Wash off the effects of travel with a bath or shower. Eat or drink your favorite meal or snack.

- Give thanks to your Advocate and Source of Life for keeping you safe before you sleep.

UNNEIGHBORLY INTIMIDATION

Janis lived in the city in an apartment underneath the apartment of a woman whose unacceptable behavior arose from an undiagnosed and untreated mental illness. Over the course of several months, the woman upstairs threw waste down into Janis's ground-floor patio, shouted abuse and stuffed written insults through her mailbox, broke flowerpots and trashed plants, screamed, shouted and played music at all hours. Although these actions were annoying, it was the woman's unremitting malice that impacted Janis's health, which deteriorated to such a degree that she had to stop work. Police intervention never worked because the deranged woman uncannily knew when they were coming and behaved normally when they arrived. The rental agency manager was in cahoots with his troublesome tenant, who was a distant relative. It was going to be difficult for Janis to get corroboration for these misdeeds because her next-door neighbors didn't want to get involved and fall victim to similar treatment. Janis called upon her own Advocate to help her. Finally, she took her landlord to court for failure to regulate his unruly tenant. During the case, he agreed to settle and moved the woman in question to an apartment on the other side of the city.

NEIGHBORS

Of all the cases that I deal with, those involving neighborly disputes have often proved the most dangerous to clients. "Neighborly dispute" sounds mild and solvable, but in my experience it is more often a case of all-out war, with dirty fighting. For the vulnerable, such disputes can have a murderous effect upon their health and vitality due to the extremity and continuous impact of assault. Living under or over or next door to noisy or malicious neighbors can be so stressful that people fall seriously ill or mentally fall apart.

- Make yourself known to your new neighbors when you move in. Get a sense of who you're living next to.
- Be careful with your boundaries: what you grow in your garden and where it's growing, where you park your car, where your children play.
- Warn neighbors of any unusual or noisy events or about any building work you have planned.
- If your boundaries are transgressed, start by a friendly or at least neutral approach by bringing the offense to your neighbor's attention. If nothing is done, follow through with a personal call or polite note.
- If you share common tenancy duties in a shared block of apartments ensure that you fulfill your quota.
- If you are undergoing unneighborly disputes that do not seem solvable, call in an independent arbitrator to negotiate before you go to law.
- Avoid keeping score and getting even, this will only escalate matters.

- Ask your Advocates to speak with your neighbor's Advocates (yes, they have them too!) with the goal of seeking a peaceful solution and not to persuade, coerce or magically alter things.
- Practice peaceweaving with your neighbor in mind (page 180).

ROAD INTIMIDATION

A few years ago I was driving on one of the rainiest days of the year. Returning from an arduous speaking event, I was tired and feeling vulnerable. Across the back roads, I drove very slowly through the torrential rain, but once I joined the main highway home, the traffic was moving faster. Someone pulled in behind me and began to tailgate me. He was so close I could both see him and feel his frustration at my moderate speed. Slowly but surely, he intimidated me into raising my speed when I should have just held my own pace. As my car accelerated it hydroplaned, doing a horizontal 360-degree spin into the center ditch and hitting the car of the tailgater who tried to overtake me on the inside. No one was seriously injured, but my car was crushed both front and back. In a vulnerable state and in poor weather conditions, I had allowed someone to intimidate me into an action that was life-threatening. I now follow the simple checklist below.

DRIVING CHECKLIST

As the world gears up for faster and faster cars on slower and more crowded roads, consideration for other motorists seems to diminish. Many drivers feel that they are invulnerable when they become one with their car and that they are as powerful as their vehicle. We cannot entirely guard against the bad driving of others, but we can exercise our own care and precautions:

- ○ Bless any new car before you drive in it.
- ○ Create your own car-prayer on getting into and out of the car, something along these lines:

    Source of Life, help me be aware of the road and those traveling today.

    Advocates, keep me alert as I drive, protect me from the dangers of the road.

    May I arrive safely at my destination.

For your return home, add thanks to this prayer.

○ Always be in your body before you get into the car by doing a self-check first.

○ Say your car-prayer on getting into the driver's seat and extend your energy field to the size of your car.

○ Don't drive when angry or upset or attempt to drive if someone in the car is emotionally upset.

○ If the behavior of other motorists irritates or inflames you with anger, don't retaliate; avoid being competitive or retaliatory with other drivers on the road.

○ Hold a safe speed when intimidated by fast drivers.

○ Take frequent breaks at regular intervals on a long drive.

○ Turn off the radio, decrease volume or change channels to less stressful sounds if negotiating difficult intersections.

○ Test your attentiveness by checking your location, the color or make of the car behind you and on your state of body, mind and soul.

○ After witnessing an accident that has upset you, pull over at the next convenient place.

○ If your car is broken into or is involved in an accident, clean and reconsecrate it when it's been fixed. See page 189.

○ On getting out of your car, bring your energy field back to its normal size.

○ Bless the car with a protective prayer when you park and lock it, something along these lines:
> *Bide you safe and stay secure,*
> *While I go upon my way.*
> *May this blessing so endure,*
> *'Til I return by night or day.*

LIVING WITH JOYFUL PURPOSE

With the stress of travel, the fear of terrorism or burglary, we can end up living defensively, which is not healthy or advisable. When trust has been betrayed or when you have lived in danger for a long time, it may have become your usual mode to suspect everyone. Living defensively ultimately seals you away from even the most beneficial life experiences, including your joy. Live with engagement and relish, and share resources and strategies with others in your circle and community. Living to the full, rather than to the empty honors your precious human life:

- Live in tune with your self and your aims.
- Live in ways that reflect the balance and glory of the Source of Life.
- Live with joy and gladness for the small as well as the large benefits in life.
- Believe in the future and have something to live for.
- Be positive and active. This enhances life better than being defensive, negative or passive.
- Become part of the universe and see what you can do to serve your own community.

BLUEPRINTS FOR A SAFE ENVIRONMENT

1. Be at home in your body.

2. Have respect for the Earth and care for your part of it.

3. Respect the inhabitants of the Earth as your neighbors.

4. Maintain your own space impeccably.

5. Avoid infringing the boundaries of neighbors.

6. Give your home a heart by maintaining a hearth-shrine.

7. Keep centered as you travel about.

8. Live with joyful purpose.

9. Be actively part of your community.

10. Be reciprocal with and thankful to the spirits of your home and planet.

CHAPTER 11

Family and Ancestors

The individuals who are included in the family soul are present in our lives: they both bless and trouble us.

—Daan Van Kampenhout in *Images of the Soul*

THE FAMILY SOUL

The family is a continuous relationship, a meeting place for souls who share the same bloodline. We tend to think of a family as just being made up of members who are alive now, but the bloodline goes on before us into unimagined futures and stretches behind us into forgotten pasts. Our whole society is made of many families who are intimately related, but that is something we would rather not consider since our own family often seems troublesome enough. Some people just loathe their families and can't wait to get away from them, leaving home at the first opportunity rather than remain clinging to a raft of psychic manipulation, boundary violation and intrusive mind games. The family unit has frequently been used as a scapegoat upon which all blame can be dumped. I hope that you will find new and resourceful ways of looking at your family here and of bringing it strength and honor in which you can share.

A family is not a static unit, but one that is always evolving as we each grow older within it. From childhood and adolescence to leaving home we evolve into marriage, homemaking, child-rearing and a working life of our own, followed by retirement, old age and death. Our own role in the family is continually changing as the family itself reconstellates. The way we think and feel about ourselves and our relations is continually changing, while at the same time we flexibly sustain unchanging relationships that can evolve:

you will always be your mother's child, just as you will always be your child's mother, but the way you relate will hopefully change.

Mysterious and long-term difficulties of psychic influence can be traced to ancestral sources, but such influences are often over-looked when people go to therapists for help and clarity about a problem. It is assumed that, since the ancestors are dead, they can have no influence whatever. However, the family soul is a continuous presence that cannot be discounted.

We spoke of group-mind in Chapter 9, but we must also consider Family Soul. This is made up of many Ancestral Souls of one bloodline and is a guiding presence in family relations. Some parts of the Family Soul act like an unruly mob; while other parts are wise and resourceful. We will be drawing upon the help of the latter in order to help heal the former because some of the greatest psychic burdens can be lifted when we turn to heal the ancestors of our Family Soul who remain unclarified.

Very often the pains, abandonments and confusions that we experience are not personal but part of the collective experience of the Family Soul. We feel them as if they were wholly ours, of course, but when we explore our own family more deeply, we understand how much of our psychic confusion is shared. Our Personal or Ancestral Soul never leaves the family we were born into; it may return to be reborn to successive generations as a grandchild or great-grandchild, or it may remain in ancestral realms of the Otherworld. By attending to our ancestral line, we also heal ourselves and the rest of our family. Ask yourself:

- What is your sense of your family soul? What kind of character or features does it have?
- How do you feel about your family, both paternal and maternal lines?
- Do you feel at home in your family or alienated from it?
- What strengths/weaknesses run in your family and how do you inherit these?

If you were orphaned, fostered or brought up as an adopted child and know nothing of your birth family, use the Ancestral Hearth ritual, below, to help reconnect with your own bloodline.

THE FAMILY BALANCE OF POWER

In every family there are family spats, sibling frictions, fights between spouses and other wars of attrition by which family members attempt to gain power, force their opinion or win the day. These wars may be semi-humorous and good-natured, but some can be in deadly earnest and inflict serious wounds. People who live together can resonate together, but they can also hurt more because they know the right frequency. It is even more painful when someone from the family hurts or betrays you. Think about the power-struggle in your household:

- Who is hassling whom in your family? Whom do you hassle?
- Who has to be top dog? Who is the underdog?
- Who has to back down and concede in family arguments? Who always wins?
- Who is the conciliator and peacemaker?
- Who is your ally? Who is your chief opponent?
- Who is smoldering with resentment and anger?
- Who always has to be right/have the last word?
- Who is carrying the family burden, being the scapegoat whom everyone blames?
- Who always gets looked after? Who always has to cope?
- Who seeks approval to get love and affection?
- Who is nursing old hurts?
- Whose moans and complaints get dealt with quickest? Whose get ignored?
- Who has left the family, been excluded or wandered away? What gap/shadow/secret has that left?

Alternatively, write down your immediate family tree and write words under each person's name that you best associate with them, such as "always moaning" or "secretive." What role do they each play in the family? Who is allied to whom? Where are the connections weakest or strongest? What is your role in the family?

FAMILY BOUNDARIES

Where do you end and someone else begin? This is sometimes hard to tell when you've lived together so long. John and I have been together for nearly thirty years and it's sometimes easy for me to assume something on his behalf because we have inhabited the same space for so long. When I forget, he will remind me, as I will him. Consent and permission are important door-keepers of our boundaries in family life. Because you live in close proximity with each other, it is even more important that you respect each other's boundaries:

- Treat diaries, mail and personal documents as private to the owner.
- Don't eavesdrop on personal telephone conversations.
- Let people finish their sentences for themselves.
- Allow everyone to have their own opinion and voice.
- Knock on doors of personal rooms before entering.
- Avoid mind-reading intentions.

Firm boundaries are essential in a family, so that neither coercion nor anarchy can hold sway.

There are many family games that we play that manipulate and regulate other members. Many of these games are wound with love, guilt and expectation; here are a few of the ways we keep family members in order while transgressing their boundaries:

- Spoiling and rewarding to obtain love.
- Scapegoating one member to carry the blame.
- Smothering love and closeness that imprisons.
- Alliances between one or more family members that close ranks against others in the family.

- Pretended helplessness or technical incompetence to get attention.
- Verbal coercion or nagging.
- Power-theft by demanding and controlling members.
- Control exercised by continual reminder of past faults.

Look again at Chapters 4, 6 and 9 to see how better boundary respect can help your family.

THE LEGACY OF FAMILY IMPRINTING

We inherit many things from our family and upbringing, which we normally accept as the standard model of behavior and belief. Much of our lives are strongly influenced by family imprinting, though this is not so apparent until we mature and have children of our own, when self-comparisons between you and your parents naturally arise. Family imprinting works in negative as well as positive ways. We invariably state, in reaction to a parental model we've overthrown that we will never "do that to *my* children," yet we perpetuate a swing-boat of reaction. For example, my family home had few books so my own home is full of them. But family imprinting can have serious consequences that can alter the unfolding path of a child, as when Amy, who had to give up playing the piano due to difficult family circumstances, made her daughter Janet practice day and night as a vicarious vindication of her creative childhood frustration. Janet chose a nonmusical career but her resentment of those hours of scales and arpeggios has made her insensitive to the real musical talent of her own son, who is now in the same position of his grandmother when she was a child. Check what unconscious patterns and resentments you are replicating that still direct your life:

- What did your parents never let you do that you still resent?
- Did you feel loved and wanted by your parents?
- What made you most angry in your family?
- What were your parents good at/not good at?

- What are you grateful/resentful to your parents for?
- What parental creative frustrations were inflicted upon you?
- How is history repeating itself in your family?

If you detect any signs of victimhood in your answers, look at page 134. If you detect intrusive parental patterns still working through you, use the Releasing Intrusions ritual (page 112).

Apart from the family imprinting that we receive, there are ancestral patterns to which we often unconsciously conform. Ancestral patterns do not always manifest in everyone all the time; they may lie dormant until you reach a particular age or role in the family. The ancestral default switch may switch on to activate different ancestral expectations about patterns that frequently constellate in a family:

- **Conformist views about gender roles.** For example, in a family where traditionally the youngest daughter stayed single in order to look after her aging parents, Anne suddenly and mysteriously stopped working at her wonderful career when she was only 27 and never married.

- **Taboos about excelling or surpassing your forebears or changing the family occupation:** Traditionally this was seen as a form of ancestral disrespect. Connor refused to inherit the family moving business and went to college to study land management to intense hostility from all generations of his family.

- **The repetition throughout many generations of a pattern that replays itself:** a suicide in every generation would be a strong factor for ancestral investigation, for example, as would the recurrence of an illness, mental condition or form of behavior.

If your family imprinting goes back generations, use the Ancestral Hearth ritual to follow to help transform them.

PSYCHIC PROTECTION OF CHILDREN

One of our major sources of concern is for the safety of our children. While we can put up with things for ourselves, we will not tolerate trouble when our children are involved. We all want to bring up our children to be strong and positive so that they can live safely and with joy. Children are being exposed younger and younger to the difficulties of the world, if not in their environment and family circle, then through the medium of TV. The childhood innocence and carefree play of just fifty years ago is now only found in very young children as adulthood beckons them to early maturity. Here are a few general factors that will protect your children:

- Give your children not just food for their bodies but nourishment for their souls.
- Remember that while they are still in the womb, babies share their mother's body, nurture and influences. Do your best to clarify intrusions and heal imbalances in power and soul before you conceive a child. Ask your own Advocates to introduce you to the Advocates of your unborn child to find out how you can best raise your child with sensitivity.
- Imprinting by example and by encouragement helps maintain the boundaries of younger children. Poor imprinting can happen through your negative, fearful or overcautious attitude, as well as from TV, bad friends and associations, misunderstandings, neglect and lack of care.
- Help your growing child learn where boundaries are firmly but kindly, and by sometimes allowing them to make minor choices that are disappointing rather than just asserting your will for the better choice. Always giving children what they want is unhelpful both to you and to them. By continually giving in to the child, you allow your boundaries to be invaded while your child doesn't learn to form their own.
- Play with your child as much as you can. Play is the most formative teacher where imagination develops and where problems can be worked out.
- Include children in any family prayers and ceremonies; give them a role.
- Give blessing to school-going children as they step out of the door. It can be a nonverbal blessing, such as a kiss.
- Children are likely to be more psychically sensitive than you and notice "things that aren't there." Don't make a big thing about this so that the child feels either odd or self-important. If the child is frightened by things you can't detect, then it doesn't necessarily mean that those things aren't there. A psychic sensitivity is often at the root of terrors that the child learns to be silent about for fear of adult mockery or

disbelief. Use the strategies in this book for substituting powerful Advocates in the place of fears.

- Invisible friends are not imaginary to your child: they may be Advocates or they may be soul-parts that are not properly aligned yet. In imaginative children, the invisible friend is invariably an assistant who helps them explore and learn about the world. If it is helpful and boosts your child's confidence, then learn to accept the companion at the table and in the car. However, if the invisible friend is more of a scapegoat for your child's naughtiness, "It wasn't me who put the goldfish down the potty, it was Monty Monkey," then you will have to make it clear that invisible friend and child will be both punished in future.

- When children are the butt of bullying and mockery at school, you can do more than inform the principal. Help them to find Advocates who will reinforce their self-confidence and courage by finding a champion in a folk story or from a favorite TV show or film. Make this character figure in bedtime stories that you tell together.

NIGHT TERRORS

Night terrors seem irrational to adults because there really is nothing under the bed, and besides, the night-light will keep the child safe, won't it? The great expanse of night from bedtime until waking up stretches like a desert before a young child, for whom time is mysteriously incomprehensible. Night has no safe, familiar coordinates to it for a child, so you can help bedtime become less of an ordeal if you can familiarize your child with the work of the sun and moon. If they wake up and won't go back down, take them out to look at the moon and stars. No child is too young to learn these things.

Also, make the coming of darkness a time of comfort by regular routines and reassuring stories. Make a tape of yourself reading a favorite set of stories. This can be playing while your child is going to sleep as well as be of use if you have to be separated.

Keep a special activity for bedtime so it's looked forward to. You could have a shrine in the child's room on which familiar spiritual figures are deployed, if you follow a specific faith, where you can say prayers together. If you don't have a faith, then create something that draws on features of nature that inspire your child: a leaf from a favorite tree; a shell from a trip to the beach; a picture of an animal that your child loves. Place a photograph nearby of all the family together. Make up rhymes and blessings that your child can learn. Enlist the aid of stuffed toys as guardians with magical powers.

Listen seriously to what your child tells you frightens him or her. It may be simple shadows of familiar objects that grow sinister in darkness or less substantial fears. And listen to dreams and nightmares. If the nightmare is still lingering, help the child play it out with toys in the daytime, but this time supplying helpful toys that defuse the fear of the scenario and bring the story to victorious resolution.

Make a ritual game of making the room safe at night if the child fears intruders, monsters or other nasties: seal windows, doors, chimneys, under the bed, etc., with a protective blessing or talisman.

If a child keeps coming into your bed because of night terror, wean them back to bed on subsequent nights by reinforcing protective games. Attach a long piece of string to the leg of your child's bed at one end and to your own bed-leg at the other, taping any slack to the baseboard. Let your child know that this piece of string connects them to your protection. If you string a little bell at either end, the sound of this will act as a warning to whatever worries them that parents are ready to chase it away.

TEENAGERS AND GROWING UP

As children grow up, their physical development is paralleled by a soul development. We recognize this growing time as adolescence when children become irrational, stubborn, moody, outrageous and combative. In addition to bodily changes, the souls of an adolescent are beginning to come into a more mature state but they are not very coordinated yet: the evolving Vital Soul is hormonally upset; the Personal Soul is emotionally turbulent; and the Wisdom Soul is mentally confused, grabbing at anything that will bring solution or stability or help define what is going on. This creates the sudden mood swings and mental changes: adolescents can become overwhelmed, confused or gratified by the sudden access of power that they experience one day, yet enjoy exploiting that power the next to see what effect they have.

In traditional societies, this confusing period is marked by rites of passage in which adolescents are taken apart so that they can be initiated into adulthood by elders who set them many tasks and painful ordeals as well as educating them in the mysteries of life. In our own society, we have few rites of passage to help lead adolescents from childhood to adulthood, and so teenagers choose their own route, taking drugs, sleeping around, daring in all manner of ways to test the far extremes of their power. More acceptable initiatory routes include taking a trip abroad or doing volunteer work in difficult circumstances. This week, with parental permission, my own son received his manly tattoo that was his self-chosen rite of passage. It was painful and inconvenient, but he feels it has marked the end of his childhood and the beginning of his adulthood. When rites of passage are omitted, children can launch themselves into dangerous waters, becoming susceptible to random influences.

As your children become adults, bear in mind that they are not yours to shape and mold. They need their peers or adult mentors who are not their parents to help them along. You won't worry any less about them than you did when they were babies, but keep the following points in mind before you go into extreme psychic surveillance mode (see page 96):

- Give adolescents greater responsibility as they age to help them stretch.
- It is normal for adolescents to stray from the family faith and to choose atheism or an outrageous ideology, or else to gravitate toward the safe boundaries of a religion if the family has no faith, because their Wisdom Souls are trying to find a channel of manifestation.
- The strength of the sexual urges resultant from the alliance of the Vital Soul with the hormonal changes of their bodies is entirely susceptible

to the emotional influences picked up by the unformulated Personal Soul in all teenagers. Ensure that your child has a more than adequate sexual education so that the cause and effect of sexual activity is fully understood.

GROWING OLDER

Perhaps one of the most difficult times of adjustment is around retirement and old age. In traditional cultures, this is a time when someone is most respected as an elder and when their skills and gifts become benchmarks of achievement from which the young can learn best. How different is our own society where we honor youth and disrespect age, where the highly skilled must retire and have little chance to pass on their skills! As we now live longer with better health outlooks, it feels insulting to be discarded at the relatively early age of 60 or 65, a time when we want to slow down but not just stop dead. We need a rite of passage that takes us from an active work life into the dignity of age.

Getting older and losing your health and looks can cause many people to feel invisible and unimportant. The depersonalization of a retirement home or hospital may add to this sense of invisibility and lack of status as the care of elderly people is increasingly seen as the duty of the state not the family. Many of us fight off old age rather than seeking its treasures, trying to revert to a former youthfulness and to avert the evil hour of our deaths by being more active.

It is essential that we prepare for our death in good time, not only for the benefit of our family and partner, but also because we need to relinquish the influence and psychic manipulation that we have exercised in our family. Impending death in the family may be the focus for all kinds of psychic manipulation as family members make a bid for love and money. Whom does he love the best? Sometimes the will can itself be a means of psychically manipulating or punishing people from beyond the grave: "I leave the capital of my entire estate to Simon, providing he doesn't marry again." The reason why funerals are often full of suppressed acrimony is because there is an undercurrent of confusions about family roles and responsibilities, about who gets what and who will hold the balance of power after a family member has died.

- Begin to notice your own attitude toward elderly people.
- Respect the elders in your community and family. Serve them first and attend to their needs. This is the only way that we can change the ignoring of the elders in our society.
- Adjust your view of old age and envision what you would like yours to be like.
- If you are growing older and feel invisible, use the Restoring Your Image ritual (page 138) to enter your maturity.
- Prepare for your death; make an unintrusive will and delegate family duties to younger members.
- As you prepare to become an ancestor, visit the ancestral hearth fire (see page 211), to receive help and support from the root ancestor of your bloodline.

HEALING THE ANCESTORS

Roy had a checkered upbringing with a mother who had an untreated mental illness. After many years of neglect and hunger, he was put into care homes, and finally, into a foster family. He had no family history, no sense of family cohesion and support. His ancestors were mysterious and unknown. He had grown up with a desire to help children like himself and to be their advocate; despite his deprivation and lack of opportunities, he'd worked hard to gain a college education and get himself into a place of power and influence to enable this. But he was always aware of his own lack of family, concerned both for his ancestors' pain and suffering, which he felt within his own body, and for the heritage of any children that he might also have. He didn't want that bequest to fall upon them. I journeyed in spirit to help his ancestors enter into their own freedom. At first they came hungry and in severe want, having been displaced from their land and work, excluded and unwanted. As they were fed and cleansed of their pain and suffering in the Otherworld, so their souls began to move onward to a home where they could be peaceful. I asked for a symbol of family strength that would help Roy, receiving a musical instrument whose resonance would reverberate through the generations. Roy smiled when I told him this for it was the same instrument that he already played. Now he has the means to play and heal the hurts of his family at the same time.

FAMILY SHRINE

Daan Van Kampenhout says that "the strength the ancestors have to offer can be received by the living by simply giving the ancestors a place in their homes, and in their hearts." To your hearth-shrine you can add another component, the inclusion of your ancestors. This inclusion of your ancestors in the heart of your home is a fundamental witness of your belonging to the family soul.

- Place on the shrine photographs of ancestors and close family, or emblems and objects associated with them: the insignia of a naval command, a much-loved brooch worn by your mother, the toy of a brother who died.
- If you had "difficult" ancestors or acrimonious relations with your family, you need not place photographs on the shrine, but instead, select some object that represents *all* your ancestors.
- When you light your hearth-shrine, you make a fire for all your ancestors and descendants to gather around.

ANCESTRAL HEARTH RITUAL

Families go through a lot. Whatever you feel about your family, at least it has had the strength to survive, as you are the living witness. When your family is undergoing trials and tribulations, it needs that resilient spirit of survival to get through. Here is a way you can shake hands with the souls that have gone before you and receive their strength, even if you don't know your own birth family:

1. Center yourself and sit before your hearth shrine candle. Briefly cup both hands over the flame, so that you feel the warmth without burning yourself. Close your eyes and see this flame as the hearth fire of all your ancestors. Commune with the life-power within you, which you share with all your forebears and descendants. Now put your hands back in your lap and just watch the flame.

2. Extend your left hand. Sense, see and feel the strand of all your female forebears, all your mothers, stretching back.

3. Extend your right hand. Sense, see and feel the strand of all your male forebears, all your fathers, stretching back.

4. Now visualize between them your root ancestor—the source of your bloodline. This is a wise ancestor who watches over your family as an Advocate and can negotiate, heal and bring peace to family situations. Before your root ancestor burns the ancestral hearth fire. Your root ancestor sees you, and bids you stretch out your hands toward the fire. S/he imparts to you the strength of your family line in the form of a symbol.

5. Clasp this symbol and receive it by folding your hands over your breast to absorb its blessing. Thank the root ancestor and all your mothers and fathers. Feel their support for you.

6. With cupped hands and open eyes share this symbol with the flame of your hearth shrine, lifting the candle aloft, saying, "May the strong blessing of this ancestral emblem strengthen my family and help us find our way in this time of trial."

In your spiritual practice each day when you center yourself, see this symbol in each of the six directions as surrounding your home and family.

SHAME AND SECRETS

Every family harbors some secret about which it is ashamed. These secrets are usually about children born out of wedlock and the stigma of illegitimacy, which, until the last few generations, cast a long shadow. Such children were often treated differently as if it were their own fault; some were excluded, sent away or abandoned. Family shame also covers suicide, death or illness, especially mental illness, which carries another stigma. Or it can be about forebears who behaved in criminal or shameful ways. Shame and confusion are also inherited when someone has been orphaned, adopted or excluded.

The intrusive nature of secrets has the power to invade and eat their way through us, like worms. You may well be aware of something hidden in your family that is casting a huge shadow. Getting to the root of the secret is sometimes impossible because family members close ranks to hide it, often generations after the event. The further in time you are from the secret's origin, the harder it is to gain clarity and the more subversive and mysterious it becomes. Whether the secret is yours or another's, it creates disturbance in the family soul because we share the shame that it engenders.

- What old secrets are still in the closet?
- What is the family story or common theme that keeps repeating itself through the generations?
- Who is being protected by the secret? Who is affected by it?
- What shadow does the secret throw upon you and others? (This is a useful question if the secret is forgotten and may help you understand its nature.)
- What is the consequence of admitting to the secret? What is the consequence of keeping the secret hidden?
- What part are you playing in hiding the secret?

RESTORING THE FAMILY HONOR RITUAL

You can defuse a secret by dealing with it as an intrusion in the family soul that has to be first unmasked and its subject's true image restored. The subject of the secret has usually been excluded from consideration and cannot merely be disregarded. Uncle George's suicide, Grandfather Guiliano's mob activity, Cousin Martha's long-term stay in the mental hospital may be the secrets everyone's frightened will reflect upon the family, but in the mean time, Uncle George, Grandfather Guiliano and Cousin Martha remain excluded and shunned from the family soul. Whatever the cause of the secret, the family soul needs to be cleansed of intrusion and the subjects witnessed, forgiven and welcomed back as lost souls. When ancestral hearts, minds and hopes broke down, certain standards of honor may have fled the family soul. It is for us, the living, to redeem and take up the banner of our family honor once more. Collect what information you can about family secrets. Deal with one at a time. If the secret remains cloudy, do this ritual anyway, taking the shadow that it has cast upon you instead.

1. Using the Ancestral Hearth ritual as the basis, extend both hands to create the two lines of male and female ancestors and begin to walk before the ancestral fire. Call one of your Advocates to come with you with a large basket. As you walk toward the fire, any one of your ancestors who has been affected by the secret casts into the basket whatever residues they wish to be transformed.

2. Go to the root ancestor with the secret or shadow and ask permission to cast it into the fire. Your Advocate also puts on to it whatever residues are in the basket.

3. As the secret or shadow and its residues burn away, the fire dissolves its power to hurt, shame and humiliate, transforming it into the power to live again. The root ancestor searches the ashes and brings out of the fire an emblem of honor to adorn the family soul.

4. If there is something attached to the secret that needs apology or forgiveness, then call upon the subject and other family members involved in the secret to apologize or forgive.

5. All those in your family lines who have been affected by the secret now go to the fire and the root ancestor uses the emblem to cleanse their souls of shame by moving it clockwise around their aura.

6. When all have gone to the fire who need to be restored, thank your root ancestor and speak the names of any involved in the secret, saying, "[Name/s of person/s who have been shamed by this secret], as you are cleansed of shame, we acknowledge you as a member/s of this family once more. May the cloak of compassion surround the family soul as its honor is restored once more."

ABUSE AND INCEST

One of the most open secrets concerns sexual abuse and incest, which cast a long shadow not only over young lives but over souls as well. The many cases I have seen reveal that the abuse is well known about in the family but because of the collusion of shame, the manipulation of guilt and love, and an unwillingness to admit to what is going on, family members remain silent. Parental abuse of children violates what should be inviolable boundaries of care and protection, while, for the child, the abuse can become confused with love and upset the commandment to honor and obey one's parents. Many of those who've been so abused may attempt to break the silence and speak the shameful truth only to find that the family closes ranks and expels them from its circle, making forgiveness and reconciliation almost impossible.

Any act of violation breaks down boundaries that must be repaired but there is no point doing so if the abuser is still lurking within. Although years have passed and the abuser and victim haven't seen each other for decades, the abuser's presence may still be tangible in the soul of the victim as we saw in Sharon's case on page 111. This invasion may stand in the way of the person's recovery and render difficult any future sexual relationship. While psychotherapy can help put your head in order about abuse, it doesn't bring complete healing unless two factors are healed: the sense of violation in the soul and the sense of uncleanliness in the body. This is achieved through the following very powerful ritual of reconsecration.

RECONSECRATION AFTER VIOLATION RITUAL

This ritual is for anyone who has suffered any kind of violation or invasion. You will need incense, a bowl of water with salt in it, a glass of water or wine and some oil. If you need to cry during this, then discharge your sorrow freely. This ritual works well when shared with a handful of close friends, one of whom can perform it for you.

1. Remove any intrusions (page 112). Call home power and soul, as on page 69 and page 91. When you've done this, finalize your healing with a bath and this reconsecration.

2. Align yourself with loving trust in the presence of the Source of Life. Call upon your own Advocates to support and surround you and to act

as witnesses. Cleanse yourself with incense, saying, "I call upon the power of the Source of Life to help and heal me. With burning herbs I am cleansed; with sweet smelling incense, I drive pain and hurt from my body. With scented smoke, I hallow my soul."

3. Anoint your brow, cheeks, hands and feet with salted water from the bowl, saying, "With sweet water I cleanse myself of pain and wash away the tears of sorrow. With salt I am cleansed and made whole and sacred once again."

4. Holding up the glass of water/wine to the Source of Life for blessing, say, "Spirit that is ever holy and inviolate, please renew and reconsecrate my sacred center. Make me clean and holy once more. Help make me conscious of my man/womanhood as a thing of joy and beauty. Restore to me the image of myself as child, seeker, man/ woman and wise one." Bring the glass down slowly to touch your head, heart and belly, saying, "What is filled with light above shall be filled with light below. What is perfect in the upper realms shall be made perfect in the lower."

5. Now anoint your brow, breast, belly, hands and feet with the oil, as you say, "Fortified by this oil, made holy are my thoughts and all my dreams. Made holy is the heart within me. Made holy is my man/ womanhood. My hands shall heal the hurts of others and my feet shall walk forever in the light."

6. Drink from the glass of water/wine, saying, "I drink once more from the cup of life." Feel the blessing of the Source of Life passing through every part of you.

7. Call upon your Advocates to lead you back to the circle of life, and turn to each direction in a circle saying, "Now I return to my birthright and my blessing. Now I return to my native country, which is my original wholeness. I call upon my Advocates to witness that I am restored in body, mind and soul. Help me to go out into the world proud of my man/ womanhood, as I return to the circle of life."

NO MORE MR. FIXER

Jeff was the second of three brothers in a close-knit, multigenerational extended family, the Martins. Reginald, their father, the beneficent but controlling "head of the family," sorted out disputes and arbitrated in decisions for the whole extended family, whether they wished this or not. After their father's death, Jeff's elder brother, Bernard, succeeded to this role, becoming haunted and hassled by the responsibility. Finding it difficult to fill his father's shoes, he shortly afterward suffered a stroke and was unable to work again. This meant that Jeff was now looked up to as the one who made big family decisions and looked out for people. The unexpected responsibility of inheriting this role turned Jeff from a mild-mannered man into an angry and dictatorial character, just like his father had been on his bad days. Jeff's wife threatened to divorce him unless he came to marriage counseling with her. Through discussion and role-play, the counselor helped Jeff understand how he was conforming to an ancestral pattern of paternal care. Jeff wrote a letter to his forefathers, thanking them for all their guidance and sacrifice in guiding the family but clearly stating that he was delegating the responsibility for each branch of the family to the siblings and parents of the elder generation. In the future his care would be for his own branch of the family. He took this letter to the family plot in the cemetery and read it out there, before burning it in the grate at home. He then called together the family for a party and made this speech, "I'm not the man my father was; I'm just Jeff Martin. Anyone who wants my help can have it, if I'm able to assist. But I'm not the Fixer and I never will be. Those of us who are the oldest generation of Martins must now share the responsibility together for helping our families grow up, grow strong and find their self-reliance. The king is dead, long live the republic of Martins!"

ANCESTRAL ADVOCATE RITUAL

There can be no "them and us" when we consider our ancestors. What we suffer, they suffered. What we heal for ourselves, we heal in our ancestors. The Buddhist concept of regarding *all beings* as our mother can enable us to find compassion for those ancestors that irritate and anger us or whose behavior has hurt or violated us. By compassion we gather our ancestors and ourselves tenderly into one place.

For many people, any consideration of their ancestors evokes feelings of fear and danger. This may be due to the nature of the upbringing they have had where safety and security were unknown, or it may be due to a deep distrust of human beings at large. It is worth remembering that not all our ancestors were human. Our life comes to us via many species that preceded humanity. In traditional cultures, many families trace their descent from an animal that becomes a sacred totem animal whom the whole tribe respects. This meditation invites such an animal ancestor to help you without having to deal with specific human ancestors:

1. Center yourself and be still. Attend to your breath.

2. Bring to mind a tree that you know and love. This tree becomes your family tree. It is strong, graceful and noble. The roots of the tree represent your forebears, the branches of the tree represent your descendants. (You have descendants of your bloodline, even if you have no children yourself.)

3. Now, without dwelling on family entanglements, call upon the ancestral animal that guards your family. Ask it to show itself to you for the healing of your family tree. Without expectation or stress, allow that animal to appear near to the tree. Be aware of its guardian presence. It doesn't matter whether you are very clear about the animal at first. It may show parts of itself, you may feel its feathers, breath or warmth, or experience its loving gaze. Even if you experience the merest impression of an animal, ask immediately if it is your family tree's guardian.

4. If you don't get anything at once, try again. Practice this before sleeping and watch your dreams. Notice during the day whether animal images are showing themselves to you in subtle or not-so-subtle ways: the jaguar upon the car hood; a bird that seems to be singing only to you every morning; the gift of a card or object with an horse upon it. Sometimes these are clues and verifications.

5. Become acquainted with this ancestral animal. Put an image of it on your shrine. Pray to it to help your family tree and any entanglements, problems or bequests that flow into the present generation. Let the animal ancestor do the work while you do the praying and supporting.

6. Use this ceremony to help you clarify ancestral bequests: it works best when started under the full moon. Write down one issue that needs help or clarification and lay it on your shrine. Pray daily to the animal for it to help transform this issue and light a candle for at least five minutes while the moon is waning. On the night of the new moon when

there is no moon showing in the sky, burn the piece of paper. Thank your animal ancestor for help in healing or transforming this issue. Pray for the clarity and happiness of your ancestors.

BLUEPRINTS FOR FAMILY COHESION

1. Respect the boundaries and privacy of each family member.

2. Say what you mean: don't assume understanding.

3. Pose questions that help family members find their own solutions rather than prescribing solutions.

4. Acknowledge how family members each evolve. Don't keep them time- or role-bound.

5. Defuse arguments by moderating your angry or sarcastic tone.

6. Encourage family members to find their own place in their own way.

7. Your ancestors are also part of your family. Include and remember them.

8. Tend your family tree.

9. Clarify and heal any secrets, shames or ancestral bequests that still disturb your family.

10. Love your family unconditionally, however irritating they can sometimes be.

CHAPTER 12

Relationships

My true love hath my heart and I have his,
By just exchange one for the other giv'n;
I hold his dear, and mine he cannot miss,
There never was a better bargain driv'n.

—Sir Philip Sidney in *Arcadia*

LOVE'S STRANGE ATTRACTION

English is a language with a complex and exact vocabulary for many shades of meaning, yet "love" is the small word we use for emotions as diverse as torrid passion, filial duty, romantic attachment, spiritual regard and domestic bliss. Yet when love rages or when we lose love, our souls can be cast up and down quicker than by any other human emotion. In this chapter we explore how to handle our lives and the effects of love without psychically wrecking our relationships.

First love is painful, tearing open your secure world and letting in an unknown reality. It is so powerful and creates such irrational behavior that even the Greek god, Zeus himself, was terrified of it according to the myth of Eros and Psyche, because it is no respecter of age and position. Love comes like a raptor, swooping upon us whether we want to love or not, which is why the arrows of Eros, God of Love, are said to be randomly shot.

Socrates spoke about a Greek myth of how soulmates find each other because they were once part of a single soul that had been divided; the love between them is "always trying to make two into one and to bridge the gulf between one human being and another." Whether or not this is so, love is wired like the principle of electro-magnetism: like poles repel and opposite poles attract. This law also works well for human partnerships; for those that are based on opposite attraction often work better than those where both partners are alike. The power of complementary attraction draws together perfectly matched pairs, partners so dissimilar from each other that we gasp. "We unconsciously seek out a mate who has a near-exact mirror image of the dark part of our personality" (Dr. Andrew Stanway). Because we cannot fully accept and integrate this shadow side of us we seek outside ourselves for the mirror image. We will always attract partners who resonate to us and our interests, but we also attract those who supplement as well as complement our qualities, and who are looking for something they don't have. We see how optimists are most frequently paired by pessimists and sunny characters by depressive ones. These pairings often work out very successfully because the characteristic of one will balance the tendency of the other. However, some pairings can be deadly, especially where dominators are paired with victims and lost souls with rescuers. These kinds of pairings involve psychic power games in which love has little part.

People often say that love is an investment, meaning that what you put into a relationship is what you'll get out of it. But surely the mainspring of love is that you don't look for what you can get out of it, but what you can *give*? This is the true token of that famed and hard-to-find quality, true love. It is this desire to give to your beloved that keeps a relationship alive, because both partners are doing it. The beloved's desire is a command to her lover.

The psychic disturbances that surround relationships often feel mysteriously difficult to focus upon because they are hard-wired to our emotional circuitry, on which we have little perspective.

Most of the mind games that we play upon or with partners are ones that injure the relationship and will eventually kill love unless we deal with them. Here are the most serious:

• Anger, verbal and physical violence that make your partner fear you.

- Humiliating your partner by unreasonable expectations and perfectionism.
- Interference or encroachment of in-laws upon the partnership.
- Affairs that betray the contract of love.
- Possessive jealousy and lack of trust, which make a prison for love.
- Sexual confusion and promiscuity.
- Keeping score, which makes a battlefield of the partnership (see page 168).

POWER AND CONTROL IN RELATIONSHIPS

Like a family, a relationship is something that grows and changes as it matures. A totally balanced partnership is rarely experienced. One partner is nearly always leading or dominating the other. Between you is the negotiation ground for your two personal spaces to become merged into one. This requires give and take. Consider your own current relationship and the balance between you both:

- What is your relationship history? What kind of partners have you chosen in the past and why?
- What parental or other models (from magazines, films, etc.) are sabotaging your partnership?
- Why did you choose your current partner? What qualities attracted you?
- What do you expect and want out of your current relationship?
- What unreasonable expectations are you exacting from it?
- In what ways are you unlike/like each other?
- What do you contribute to the relationship?
- What baggage from past relationships do you bring to this one?
- What secrets destructive to the relationship are you keeping from your partner?
- Is your relationship a partnership or a competition?
- Are you friends with your partner?
- How dependable is your partner? Is your partner there for the important things?

- How much strain do work, children and other factors put upon your time together?
- What no-go areas don't you speak about together?
- How good a team are you?

A ROMANTIC COP-OUT

Shane was in a long-running production of a Broadway musical. He fell in love with Connie, one of his costars, and they married. They seemed well suited, but when the production ended, the dream-match also fell apart. During couples therapy, it transpired that Shane was in love with *the character* that Connie played, not with her at all! The character in the musical had all the qualities of Shane's ideal partner and that projection had disappeared now that Connie was playing the role of a policewoman in a tough TV series instead of her romantic lead on stage. They concluded that their two characters had more going for them than the two actors who represented them.

THE PROBLEM OF PROJECTION

We have all made inappropriate relationships at some time or another. Why do we do this? Within each of us is the image of an ideal partner. This image becomes the benchmark of what we believe our lover should be like, and we seek for someone who will mirror this image and embody it for us. This idealized image has been termed by psychology as the anima and animus: the anima is the ideal female for a man; and the animus is the ideal male for a woman. In young people, this image is projected upon pop stars, actors and other celebrities who become the "pin-up." But when we start looking for a sexual partner, we may end up falling in love with someone entirely unsuitable because we have projected our idealized image onto a living person who cannot possibly achieve the ideal that we've internalized.

Our ideal image matures as we do and can become fully integrated into our own personality in ways that make us more passionate, creative and spiritually aware. As you will have guessed from these qualities, the ideal image is a reflection of our souls. As these develop and as our life experience broadens, so our soul-cauldrons can receive and accept these projections as parts of our own soul once more. Then we begin to learn that the ideal image is not our partner's responsibility but part of our own self-acceptance. This integration usually doesn't begin to come about until we are in our middle years. It is part of our self-completion. See *In Search of Woman's Passionate Soul* for more about this process (see Bibliography on page 303).

- If you are starting a relationship, negotiate your love contract from your own center rather than from a place of projection. Over a week notice how often you project your emotion onto your partner.

- How are your old relationships being projected upon this one? With what result?

- In what ways do you project your ideal image upon your partner? What burden does that place upon him/her?

- Allow partners to be who they are, rather than whom you think they should be. To help see your partner the way s/he is and to remove any projections you've attached to him/her, use the Pool of Change (page 142) to send back false images. Ask your Advocates to show who your partner is.

- Look at the characteristics of your ideal image: which essential qualities do you yearn for, for your own completion? Center yourself and call these qualities home from the six directions.

THE TEMPLE OF LOVE RITUAL

In the Scottish folk story *The Black Bull of Norroway*, the heroine loses her partner to enchantment and can only find him again by entering a land only accessible by climbing a hill of glass. This is impossible and she has to apprentice herself to a blacksmith in order to fashion shoes with spikes on the soles to make this climb. Her apprenticeship to the blacksmith lasts seven long years and she is able to free her partner from enchantment only by her patience.

The ability to sustain a relationship is based on the way you mature together. In our quick-fix society, a relationship that isn't working is discarded and replaced as quickly as a broken radio is for a new one. Partnerships that last longer than a few months or years have to grow in order to remain contractually sound. We give up too quickly because we are often too lazy to put in the work that a relationship needs.

However a relationship starts out, you can be sure that it will change over time and that circumstances will arise that put strains upon it: illness, children, death, unemployment, social stigma, financial crisis and age are but a few. One of the favorite sonnets of Shakespeare to be read at weddings reminds us of the duty of constancy in the face of hardship:

> *Let me not to the marriage of true minds*
> *Admit impediments. Love is not love*
> *Which alters when it alteration finds.*

But all too often the demands of those alterations are enough to change your mind. "In a self-centered world many of us want to hear that we shouldn't be caring or self-sacrificing. But empathy and caring are good human characteristics we should nurture" (Dr. Andrew Stanway). We each have to find the patience to put up with our partner when the going gets tough: when your partner emotionally withdraws to deal with an internal crisis; when the household is under financial strain; when every day is a battle not to lose your temper.

Partnership is like a chariot with two horses pulling it. There is no such thing as a totally equal partnership: sometimes one partner will do more pulling than the other. When you feel up, he feels down; when he's enthusiastic, you feel reluctant; when she's determined, he's indecisive. Normally one partner encourages or influences the other and a balance is found. But you could be weathering more serious, long-term difficulties that require loving patience: severe depression, sexual problems, addictions or a profound lack of focus that leaves you feeling left out. When you are in the phase of your relationship where *you* are doing most of the loving and there is little coming back your way you need the renewal of love.

1. Center yourself in the six directions. Be aware of the great powers of the Source of Life about you as six great temples: below you, the temple of truth; above you the temple of wisdom; on the far horizon around you see, before you, the temple of light; behind you, the temple of law; to your left, the temple of life; to your right, the temple of love. You can visit each of these in due course, but today you need to visit the temple of love.

2. With your Advocates, pass down the path leading to the temple of love. Sense, see and feel how this appears and enter it. The first thing you notice is a fountain that wells up from a deep spring or well with steps down to it. There is a vessel beside it which you hold in the fountain. Pour the waters from the well of love over you as many times as you need. Whatever is hurting and painful within you is soothed by the waters. The places within you where the waters of love have become low or are drying up are refreshed and replenished. Each of your soul cauldrons receives the refreshment that it needs.

3. Go deeper into the temple. Within it is a central altar on which your own contract of love rests in symbolic form. What symbol do you see? Reach out and hold it within the fountain of love so that it is cleaned and refreshed. Replace it upon the altar with your own blessing.

4. There is a seat where you can sit and contemplate the altar and the fountain. Come and sit here when you have need. Return when you have finished.

POSSESSIVENESS

When love becomes possessive, then fear and distrust have entered into the relationship. It is no longer a contract freely entered into by equals but a form of surveillance. Possessive love doesn't just manifest as angry jealousy but also as a kind of loving plastic-wrap where one partner lives so close to the other that there's scarcely room to breathe. They both have the same effect. Treat possessive love as an intrusion that wants to steal your power and soul, and strengthen your boundaries.

Jealousy and envy are not the same thing. Envy involves one person being envious of another (see page 169). Jealousy involves three people. Jealousy is fostered by fear of abandonment, low esteem and a deep insecurity that you are not good enough; it can be further fueled by addictions. The fear is that a partner will seek out some "better" person to live with. Being subjected to jealousy usually brings this very thing about.

- If you are jealous, review Chapter 7 and use everything in it that helps your self-esteem.
- Why are you insecure about trusting your partner? Consider the effects that jealousy has had upon you and others in the past.
- What triggers jealousy of your partner in you? What is the root of your fear?
- If you are the subject of jealousy, discuss this problem with your partner, listening patiently to what may seem unfounded and mistaken views about you and your relationship. Gently hug and kiss them, neutrally refuting any accusations as untrue and restating your love and constancy.
- Use the strategies in the psychic surveillance section on page 96.
- If you have had an affair and want to repair the damage you've done, go to the temple of love and wash the symbol of your contract at the well.
- What are you psychically bringing home to your partner in this affair?
- What are the consequences of your affair upon your whole life?
- If your partner has had an affair, renegotiate your contract and establish some boundaries for the future.
- Look more closely at why your partner had an affair. What part of your relationship needs to grow?

ANGER AND VIOLENCE

Many of us store unrecognized anger just below the surface. Society bids us suppress our anger, and put a smiling face on our disappointments, pains and resentments. When anger is driven deeper in this way, people can eventually become volcanic with rage, enter into depression, express physical symptoms of illness or become passively aggressive—where they present a seemingly pleasant and reasonable exterior, while manipulating all around them with behavior that smilingly thwarts and disrupts things. Check:

- What is your family history with anger or violence? What are you angry about?
- What factors escalate anger and violence in you?
- Has your anger ever broken out into violence against your partner or family?
- What resentment do you harbor against your partner?

If you recognize suppressed anger in yourself:

- Identify and deal with issues in your past history that are creating angry reactions. Use Releasing of Intrusions (page 112), transform your anger by Pool of Change (page 142) or Transformation of Power (page 122).
- Learn to relax and de-stress.
- Communicate better rather than just losing your temper.
- Take yourself away from your partner when in a rage. Run, hit a pile of cushions, scream down the yard, cry and physically discharge the rage.
- Consider taking an anger management course for the peace of your family.
- If you are experiencing someone's rage or violence, then:
  - Examine what situations, subjects and tones of your voice trigger or provoke anger in your partner.
  - Listen empathetically without cross-accusation, nagging or counter-aggression.
  - Be responsible for your own safety and that of your children. Get out and find sanctuary if you need to.
- If someone in your past is still angry at you, assume your Spiritual Armor (page 54) and use the Knife of Separation Ritual (page 120). Do not enter into retaliation or revenge scenarios. If you can, use the Forgiveness Ritual (page 120).

ENDURING PAIN WITH PATIENCE

Love makes all things possible, we are told. This is nowhere more clearly seen than in abusive relationships. The excuses that people make for remaining in them include: "I stay for the children" or "Because I love him/her." Patience can be extended for too long. Fear of change, fear that you will lose your home, financial stability or children if you start challenging dysfunctional relationships often makes you decide to put up with emotional pain. But this will be stored in your soul cauldrons and color everything around you.

Living with someone who has addictions may not be as dangerous as being with a violent partner, but the strains can be just as great. The constant lying, deception, theft and unreliability; the sordid scenes of recrimination, disorderliness in front of neighbors and children, the continual round of promises and falls from grace can erode your resilience. The courage to change abusive relationships can come from the support of close friends and family, as well as from social and health experts. Change is a relay network: if you move just one piece on the board of your life it will move other pieces. Use the Pool of Change (page 142) to help you move on and find solutions.

- With abusive partners, center yourself and refuse to be their victim. See page 134.
- Give addictive partners your loving help but ensure they agree to seek addiction support. Neither of you can tackle the problem alone.
- Is yours truly a case of "I can cope with these violent/addictive bouts" or rather "If I don't escape this I'll die?"
- Do not compromise the safety of your body and souls out of love for an abusive partner. Get help for yourself.

BREAKING UP: DIVORCE AND SEPARATION

When love is not reciprocated and supported it grows either stale and cold or desperate and fiery with anger. When passions cool, some partners are happy to opt for security without progress,

where love subsides into habit. But is there anything more mean-
ingful going on in the partnership than a mutual dependency?
Affairs, violent abuse, living with a partner who makes no attempt
to grow or change, severe and irreparable differences of opinion
about lifestyle and the upbringing of children can all contribute
to breakdown. The place where love has dwelt can become a
corrosive cage of hate and loathing.

More psychic disturbance is suffered over split-ups and
divorces than anywhere else in a relationship. When couples
break up, they go through the legal wrangles about who will have
what, but the most important things they forget to return are each
other's soul-parts that have become meshed together in the partnership. Unless this is done, you remain yoked to your partner.
There are many other things that keep us together when we both
wish to be apart: feelings of fear, hatred, revenge, jealousy, etc.
all enmesh us in one weaving. Divorce can bring legal retribution
down on your partner's head, when you wrangle over possession
of things, children, cars, houses, money and assets. It can separate
the mutual friends of a partnership, and create professional no-go
areas if the partners have shared work colleagues or occupational
interests. Here are a few considerations around break-up:

• The wedding or engagement ring is an outward symbol of your love-
contract: when it's broken, the first reaction is to throw the ring away or
give it back. Before you do this, decommission it so that it bears no trace
of your contract. See page 273.

• The hurt, pain or betrayal that you feel is due in part to the love that you
had, and to the violence that is happening to the soul-part given to your
partner. Do the Lover's Separation ritual on the next page.

• Avoid involving mutual friends and colleagues in recriminating your
partner. Spreading the pain wider won't heal anything. Speak to one
trusted friend in confidence.

LOVERS' SEPARATION RITUAL

This is a ritual that can be performed alone or with a partner from whom you're parting.

1. Light a candle on a metal tray or dish between self and partner or a photo of your partner. Each say or address the photo, "I give thanks for the good times we have had, but they are now too few to gladden me. It is time to part."

2. You each say, "I freely give back what is yours/his/hers." Think what soul-qualities (not possessions) have been given you in this relationship. "Thank you for ..."

3. You each say, "I take back what I have given you/him/her." Think of all the soul-qualities that you have given that now belong back with you.

4. Physically give each other back a token or send back something given you by your partner as a witness of this exchange. If could be your rings or a small item of no monetary worth.

5. If you are doing this alone, go to the temple of love, and take the symbol of your contract from the altar. Cast it into the fountain of the well of love, saying, "My contract with [name] is over. I return it to the well of love. As s/he and I go our separate ways, may my love return unconditionally to this well. May s/he go in peace to seek love elsewhere." If you are doing this with your partner, take a strip of combustible paper and write both your names along it. Both holding one end of it, elevate the strip over the candle. When it burns into two pieces, drop them safely onto the tray, saying, "This contract is no more. Go in peace to seek love elsewhere!"

WHY CAN'T I FIND SOMEONE?

Molly was a beautiful woman in her mid-thirties. Her complaint was that no one seemed to want her. She had gone through all the right motions to find a partner, but no one wanted to go out with her beyond the first date. On the surface this seemed mysterious, since she had a lovely personality and no hidden defect or dependents in tow. I asked about her relationship history and discovered that she'd had a partnership with a man that had ended eight years before. He had left her over a long period, while traveling back and forth across Europe, so that she had been uncertain whether they were on or off, and she had been single since then. I asked her if she still felt engaged with that relationship, for it seemed that it had concluded messily and that there might be residues remaining. My own Advocates confirmed that a soul-part of Molly's was still with her ex-boyfriend, and we brought it home again. The reason no one had wanted to be with Molly was that potential partners were reading the "not available" sign in her aura. She did her own breaking the ties ritual, which finally concluded the old relationship for her. Now that the "available" light has gone on again, she has been seeing a new boyfriend.

MOVING ON AFTER THE LOSS OF A PARTNER

When you have lost a partner, whether it is due to death, divorce or break-up, it is normal to feel bereaved. A period of mourning is important, even if you split up acrimoniously, because you are mourning the love that you had and lost. If you cast yourself into the next relationship without this period, you are likely to drag your old baggage with you and act out scenarios, react to situations and emotionally shred your new relationship. Getting clear of the last relationship is essential if you want to form a new one. The love contract between your two sets of souls needs to be disentangled, for one thing. If your partner has died, the period of mourning will be longer, but it is still essential to recall power and soul for you to resume normal life again. It doesn't mean that you love your partner any less that you are contemplating moving on.

- If you are still yearning after an old partner whom you've lost or who's left you, call back your attention to the present moment. Look again at power and soul-theft in Chapters 4 and 5 to ensure that you are not psychically living out of that person.
- If your old partner is still inhabiting your thoughts and you have a sense of being under psychic surveillance, then perform the Lover's Separation ritual and call home power and soul.
- See more on Loss and Bereavement in Chapter 15.

SEX, FANTASY AND PORNOGRAPHY

The old '60s tag, "life is a sexually transmitted disease," reminds us that sex is as much an act of life as it is an act of love. Through the agency of another person you can enter the ecstasy of life and be in union with it. Sexual desire is the dynamic highway down which life makes its appearance. When desire is reciprocated, the ecstatic fusion is universally regarded as the erotic summit of human experience. However, sexual desire is such a strong drive that it sometimes runs counter to the balance of life and can become both abusive and addictive.

In sexual relations it is not just our bodies that seek union but our souls. From the standpoint of psychic protection, you cannot be more exposed to someone than in sexual union. It therefore follows that you must trust your sexual partner not only to be a responsible lover but also to be psychically impeccable. Casual sex with strangers may be exciting but you may pick up more than sexually transmitted diseases. Inhibitions fall away readily when casual sex is on the menu, providing the illicit spice of deception to a dull relationship. You are being at your most open and unguarded with a stranger, including emotionally open, needy and in a projective state. Sexual surrender lowers all thresholds. Most sex workers find ways of professionally distancing their emotions from the transaction they are being paid for.

Much psychic confusion arises in the discovery of our sexual orientation. Many traditional societies recognize not just man and woman, but man-woman in a male body and woman-man in a female body. With few exceptions, all human beings are born into bodies that are either anatomically male or female.

Our sexual fantasies are erotic thought-forms and imaginings that stimulate our sexual desire. Many men are attracted primarily to visual erotic images, whereas more women are drawn to erotic literature. Experts agree that sexual desire is as much a matter of the mind as it is of the body. You may argue that, because they stay in your head and don't get acted out, that your fantasies harm no one. In most cases this is so, but when our fantasies involve other living people, then that is another matter because you are invading someone else's space and using their image for your satisfaction.

Pornography is the explicit graphic depiction or verbal description of sexual, not necessarily loving, acts in order to stimulate sexual desire. It is about the pursuit of the unattainable. Pornography is different from erotica such as the Kama Sutra, which creatively stimulates the human imagination without appalling it. Pornography can plumb the depths of abuse and depravity, employing violent, exploitative and degrading images to stimulate. Pornography is one of the pollutions that sticks to the mind and which can become rapidly addictive. Violent images and thought-forms can be burnt upon the brain and spread throughout the soul cauldrons, imprinted upon the imagination, and spread through the whole system like mold through a building. Sexually addictive behavior that overwhelms and governs you needs professional help to remove its shameful and damaging effects.

- Explore your own attitude to sexuality. What part does it play in your life?
- What psychic dangers are you opening yourself to by sleeping with casual sexual partners? Cleanse yourself, seal your energy field and bless your aura after encounters.
- Ask your Advocates to teach you about the spiritual, psychic and physical impact of sexuality upon your souls. You can go to the temple of love and find a specialist teacher.
- Explore your own ideal image and integrate it as part of you rather than projecting it upon others.
- Practice sexual impeccability by avoiding fantasizing about other people. If this has been your habit, then use the Returning Power and Soul rituals in Chapters 4 and 5.
- To extract the sticky trails of pornographic image use the following rituals in sequence: Releasing of Intrusions (page 112), read how to cleanse your mind (page 136), practice the Soul Cauldrons meditation regularly (page 100) and finish with the Beautiful Mind

ritual (page 133). If guilt lingers, then use the Forgiveness ritual (page 120).

REPELLING UNWANTED ADVANCES

Fans with an unhealthy or obsessive regard often stalk celebrities. While you may never suffer from stalking, you may certainly attract unwanted attention from someone who has made advances you've rejected or from an ex-partner who is determined not to let you go. As we saw in Chapter 5, stalking doesn't have to be physical: we are quite capable of stalking someone with our soul.

Enclosed nuns are enjoined to keep "custody of the eyes," meaning that they must exercise control over their gaze. (No reading the newspaper that comes wrapped round the fish!) When we eye up some attractive person, what are we doing? Looking is one thing, but fantasizing about them afterward is something else. We are invading their body-space and seeking to possess what doesn't belong to us.

- Examine your sexual intentions. See page 219. Are you being sexually predatory or victimized?
- If you're aware of someone in your psychic space, use the procedures for Psychic Surveillance (page 96).
- If you're not available, make sure that sign is placed in your aura rather than a flirtatious availability.

CALLING THE RAPIST TO JUSTICE

Marta was a strong, self-possessed young woman until the day she was pulled off the street and raped in a dark ally by two complete strangers. From then onward, she began to feel like a victim. Two years later, she was raped again, this time by someone she knew very slightly. Revenge filled her whole outlook when she tried to bring a case against the man. Several other women had been date-raped by him but none had the courage of Marta who alone had decided to go through the grueling process of taking him to court. Since the case presented only Marta's rape and not the rapes of the other four women, which were inadmissible evidence, the man got off with a relatively light sentence, to her fury. It wasn't until Marta stopped harboring resentment about these unhappy incidents and sought reconsecration that she began to heal. She no longer feels like a victim and has regained her former resilience.

SEXUAL ASSAULT

Some people believe that sexual assault happens because of the mixed signals sent by a woman, the way she dresses and behaves. In some cases this may be partially true, but in actuality, sexual opportunists can instinctively recognize a victim in the same way an animal predator stakes out its weak prey. It seems to have little to do with appearance and a lot to do with what is held in our aura, a signal that we each unconsciously transmit. If there is a psychic openness or loss of power, a sense of victimhood or soul-loss showing in the aura, rape or sexual assault can result. In cases of sexual harassment and touching, some opportunists are literally just trying it on with the first available person, but most rapists are known to the women they rape, taking advantage of familiarity, intimacy or friendship with the victim. Many raped women never tell anyone about the assault, out of shame, keeping their secret for years.

The decision to bear the child of a rape is a very grave one. Many women choose to terminate such a pregnancy because they know that the child conceived from violation can never be blamed or resented for its existence. See page 286 for more about termination. Physical and psychological therapies can do much to repair the damage of sexual assault, but it is only when we expose the sense of violation to a ceremony of reconsecration that the healing finally emerges. If you have been raped or assaulted:

- Remove the sign of "victim" from your aura (see page 134).
- Expel the image and presence of the sexual predator from your being by the Releasing Intrusions ritual (page 112).
- Call home power and soul lost at the time of assault (see Chapters 4 and 5).

- If you are harboring feelings of revenge against the perpetrator, read page 52 and use the Knife of Separation Ritual (page 120).
- Finally, perform the Reconsecration after Violation on page 214.
- If you are able to, perform the Forgiveness ritual on page 120. This may be possible only after much time has elapsed since the assault.

MAKING LOVE LAST

The current myth that men and women are from different planets merely reinforces the irrational clichéd beliefs that have been traditionally held about the opposite sex. Relationship is not a form of warfare where we continually act out these old scenarios. What makes us ultimately compatible with our partner is about *resonance of soul*. It is our *souls* who fall in love, not just us.

Dion Fortune wrote about the need for a marriage to be consummated on all levels, not just body with body, but soul with soul. The different parts or our multiple soul long for this totality of fulfillment but seldom find it. If you have a predominantly physical relationship, then your Vital Souls are mated. If you include your Personal Souls, you will be romantically and emotionally mated. But if you also include your Wisdom Souls, you will be mated spiritually as well as physically and emotionally. This is ultimately what makes love last. In times of disruption when you are sexually out of action due to illness, disability or age, or when you are parted for long periods, or when you have differences of opinion, you will have more than one bond of love to connect you. This is something you can practice with a willing partner or alone. Please use it only if you are in a stable and reciprocal relationship and not for trying to ensnare someone:

1. Go to the temple of love together or alone. Sit opposite each other, or with your partner's photo opposite, on either side of the fountain of love. Meditate upon your soul cauldrons as on page 97.

2. When they are cleansed, your soul cauldrons begin to be filled up by the waters of the fountain of love that arise from the well. When you are both aware of a free flow of love through each of your own cauldrons,

visualize the waters of love going from the well to both your Vital Soul cauldrons and flowing between you both. The waters rise and flow into both your Personal Soul cauldrons, where the interplay flows between you. Then the waters rise and flow into your Wisdom Soul cauldrons, where they flow between you. If you are doing this alone, visualize the flow between you and your partner in the same way.

3. When the flow is fully reciprocated between you, running from the well through each of your cauldrons upward, you and the well become part of one flow. Stand and embrace each other, belly to belly, heart to heart, forehead to forehead. Kiss or make love. If you are alone, blow a kiss to your partner.

4. Allow the flow to recede to the well when you have finished.

BLUEPRINTS FOR LOVING RELATIONSHIPS

1. Be prepared to work at your relationship and help it evolve.

2. Remove the burden of perfection from your partnership.

3. Communicate regularly and say what you mean.

4. Have fun together and be friends.

5. Unpack the baggage from old relationships and discard old love stories.

6. Balance intimacy with doing your own thing.

7. Encourage each other by boosting each other's self-esteem.

8. Discuss your mutual contract as you get older, renegotiating terms if necessary.

9. Trust each other and be trustworthy.

10. Make up after any argument before you sleep.

CHAPTER 13

The Work of Our Hands

Give your heart to the trade you have
learnt, and draw refreshment from it.

—Marcus Aurelius in *Meditations*

WORK, IDENTITY AND SELF-WORTH

Why do we work? Usually, we do so to be financially secure, to
make our mark or to fulfill our creativity. But it may be because
we have to, to prove ourselves or to compete. Work issues take up
inordinate space in our lives and can color our lives for good or ill
because so much of our adult lives is spent working. We inherit a
whole raft of notions about work and how conscientious we should
be from our upbringing and the society that we live in. Examine
how you feel about it:

- What was your parents' attitude about work? How has this model
  shaped your own view?
- What is your attitude about your work? Are you conscientious, honest
  and committed in it?
- What is your attitude about your employer?
- How is your self-worth invested in your work?
- How do you value your work?
- What does work give you?

The way we feel about ourselves is greatly assisted by work and
our attitude around it. Work gives us purpose and the opportunity
to apply our energies and resources. Because our society equates
work with respectability, most of us connect self-worth and work
in one equation. Even as children we are asked, "What do you want
to be when you grow up?," as if our occupation and our identity

were the same thing. You and your work are separate entities. If we muddle these up we may be in an intrusive relationship with work or it with us. Work issues are often so related to our self-worth that we choose not to deal with them because they feel so intractable. The most damaging attitudes to work that are symptomatic of psychic disturbance include:

- Being a workaholic, where we totally enmesh our self-worth and identity with work and are obsessed by it.
- Dreading and fearing work, because we feel that our self-worth and identity are overwhelmed by its demands, so we attempt to avoid it at all costs, or need carrot and stick incentives to continue working.
- Enduring and resenting work, where our self-worth and identity feel demeaned by work, so that we are continually at war with our job and employer and never give our best but just fulfill the quota.

These attitudes suggest intrusion and power-loss. They may be inherited values we receive from our upbringing or they may spring from an abusive relationship between worker and employer. Look again more closely at who you are, without using your work as a defining label. If you take your work away from you, who are you? What is left?

THE WORKAHOLIC TRAP

At parties people come up and ask you what you do in an attempt to find out who you are. The identification of your status by the manner of your work does not reveal your personality or identity, unless perhaps you're a workaholic whose whole being is defined by overwork. Workaholism is an addiction to work, a condition where work has become an intrusion. Unfortunately it is a condition encouraged in many work places from executives who are expected to give their all and then some more, to the floor-workers who are often covering more than one job because of cutbacks.

As children many of us were given love and encouragement when we performed well, and felt less cherished when we failed.

Fear of failure may have its roots in reasonable ancestral anxieties about survival, or it may originate in parental anxiety to fully prepare their child for the wide world. Fear of failure is one of the biggest goads to workaholism.

"The greatest impediment to progress in life is success," says Bill Gates, the founder of Microsoft. Your addiction to success can be so overwhelming that, in order to keep up with your successful image, you scoop out energy and power from every available cavity of your life and submerge even your true identity in maintaining that image. We get what we work for; if you continue down this road it can lead to serious health problems, as well as fearful anxiety and sleeplessness, social isolation, marital problems and burnout. Work can be our compensation for being unloved, becoming the thing that completes us, with money, success, praise and respect taking the place of love. These questions are for the workaholic:

- What parental models of work influence your overwork: fear of failure, parental workaholism, unrealistic expectations upon you, family success image to support, etc.?
- How is your workaholism affecting your health, home life, partner, children?
- What rationalizations support your overwork: financial, to create a surplus against hard times, everyone depending upon you, because you always have worked like this?

Some strategies to help the workaholic include delegating a portion of your work to a colleague and eating regular meals without working during your breaks. For one day every seven to ten days, do nothing but play as a corrective to your condition. Spread your annual vacation time over the year rather than taking it all in one lump because you have to use it up. Also, invest your time and energies in something other than work: sports, hobbies, social activities, music, reading, traveling, etc. Do something for your own pleasure to balance work.

- Check how much success and perfectionism are fueling your work. See page 239.
- Treat your work as an intrusion that is filling the place of soul and power (page 111), then call back your power and soul (Chapters 4 and 5). Now begin to review your work attitudes.

WAGE SLAVES AND THE DAILY TREADMILL

It is said that the British attitude to work is more resentful and combative than anywhere else in Europe and that, despite the fact that Britons work longer hours per week, overall efficiency and productivity is lower than in many other countries. Many of these problems are about a lack of engagement and mutual respect between employer and worker. Instead of pulling together, we are actually at war with work, or under bombardment from its demands. Our attitude to work is what minimizes our output. Resentment and fear reduce our ability to engage with work: we withhold our services to punish our employer, reserving our energies for something better like our leisure time. Sometimes we endure work only because it pays us, falling into the perception of ourselves as merely wage slaves.

- What work did you want to do ideally? Would you have worked more willingly in that job?
- How proud are you of your current work performance?
- Do you turn in the minimum effort for a day's work?
- Do you turn sullen when criticized or when shown extra duties at work?
- Do you clock-watch or take sick days continually?
- How many ways do you avoid work when you are in the work place?
- In your work, what is your chief resentment, fear or threat? How much of your power is spent fighting employer, work place colleagues and work?
- What kind of culture dominates the management of your work place? And how are you perceived by your employer? See page 243.
- How reciprocal and respectful is your employer toward his/her employees?

If your attitude to work is to resent, fear or avoid it, then you are in a different kind of abusive relationship with your work. Unlike the workaholic who becomes symbiotic with his/her work by allowing it to become an intrusion, the resentful worker is threatened and oppressed by work because she feels it will take her power and soul. For most people, this resentment immediately arises from low salary, poor working conditions, low staff morale or the unrealistic expectations of employers, though it may also have its roots in parental work attitudes. If the employer doesn't value you, your self-worth and your work both suffer. There can also be more subtle causes that drive us to fear work: poor progress at school, the imposition of punishment when previous work was unsatisfactory, a low self-esteem about performance. Remember:

- You are more than a wage slave. Read Chapter 7 for more on self-esteem, and use the strategies you find there.
- Encourage yourself at work to give good service. If it helps, think about serving those who benefit from your work rather than your employers, if your relationship with them is abusive.
- Revisit your life purpose and vocation. What is your current life for? See below.
- Create your own work contract, which chimes with your personal code of honor. See page 17.

PROSTITUTE YOUR TALENTS HERE

One day last year, I visited two publishers who wanted to discuss book proposals with me. I was very short of money and badly needed some work. At the first venue, they didn't want what I had to offer but rather asked me to write a formulaic text for a book someone else had previously planned: I realized that the publisher merely wanted to exploit me and asset-strip my expertise. I refused the project. Heart in my mouth, I visited the second venue, Piatkus Books, to discuss the British edition of the book you are now holding. Not only were they pleased with the project, they were also happy to learn more about me. I expressed my gratitude for their willingness to see me, since so many publishers deal over the internet these days. My editor said, "But we like to know our authors: if we didn't get on, it wouldn't be a happy experience for either of us." My relief was huge, but what divergent receptions! It was chastening to realize how close I had been to prostituting my talents at the other publishing house, just for the sake of money.

THE CULTURE OF WORK

Different managements have different cultures. It is important to know what kind is prevailing at your workplace because some of your conflict may be with the employer's view of you. Six main types of work culture or management styles have been identified by Tony Humphreys. These are based around the following models and all come with easily identifiable metaphors:

- **The Armed Services:** in this set-up you are "one of the troops." Here work has a dominant and controlling chain of command. Phrases like "we run a tight ship here" or "time to send in the artillery" send the message that work is war, and the boss is "commander in chief."
- **Sport:** here you are a "team-player," not an individual. This is seen in the Japanese model of the cheerleading, team-building works, where morning assembly, company song or rallies weld the workers into one unit. Work is a game that must be won and the boss is "team captain" or "coach."
- **Clan:** here you are a "family member," whether you want to be or not. Loyalty to the company is central, family gatherings are essential and nepotism can be a problem. Work is a family duty and the boss is "mommy or daddy."
- **Mechanics:** here you are "a cog in the machine." The ethic has to run like clockwork, especially in factories. Time rules rigidly and workers who don't have stamina get fired quickly. Work is a production line and the boss is "the foreman."
- **Animal Pack:** here you are "a member of the pack." If you fail to be a ruthlessly efficient pack animal, you quickly become prey yourself. Work is "a big killing" and the boss is "alpha male or female."
- **People:** here you are an individual who brings valued skills. Work is an egalitarian exchange where the boss is just the boss.

As you will see from my own experience above, the first publishing house was predicated on the ruthless Animal Pack model, ready to tear out my liver and lights, whereas Piatkus Books is based on the egalitarian People model.

As a worker, there is little you can do to change the culture of your work place, but you can adjust your sights in accordance with the kind of work culture with which you have to daily engage. Remember that you are who you are, regardless of how your boss or management thinks of you. The chain of command in many of these models may be vertically downward, allowing for little response or feedback, so that the management is distant and indifferent to workers. If your livelihood is determined by loyalty to one of these work cultures, then become involved in your union and learn how you can negotiate a more egalitarian kind of feedback between employer and worker.

You have the right to be physically, sexually, emotionally, intellectually, socially and creatively safe at work, where you are free from danger, sexual harassment, mockery, humiliation, isolation and the exploitation of your skills. The best-run work places have arbitration points, union reps, tribunals or boards of inquiry that negotiate when personnel clashes occur. Family-run businesses often don't have these and may have the additional stress of relatives and emotional blackmail to deal with. People in self-employment who have to promote their skills to third parties may be vulnerable to their own anxiety for survival.

- If you feel you are being drawn into a distasteful or unethical work culture, call back power and soul and enact the Restoring Your Image ritual (page 138).
- Consider the relationship between your individual worth, your skills and the management. What kind of reciprocation is required of your work contract?

VICTIMIZATION AT WORK

Bernard worked in a public building where the boss took a dislike to him, giving him the worst tasks and the least favored hours. He would normally have appealed to the union representative to assist him, but the boss was also head of the local union. Many people at work could have spoken up for him as witnesses to the victimization, but they were too fearful of losing their own jobs. Bernard called on his Otherworldly Advocates for assistance. They said that the situation was stalemate. The only way out was to leave or to write to personnel requesting a transfer to another governmental branch. Bernard took this latter course and was duly moved, but he left very soon afterward to return to an occupation he'd left with great regret. He realized that giving up working on the land had put him in a vulnerable position of self-pity where he had become a prime target for victimization.

STRESSFUL WORK PLACES AND EXPLOITATIVE JOBS

The places where we work often contribute to our work attitude, especially if they are stressful or exploitative. Environmentally we feel unhappy in places that have been abused. If your job is structured in hierarchical ways, emphasizes the product over the welfare of employees, demands high work performance but penalizes failure, then you have a stressful and exploitative work place. By becoming aware of the spiritual impact of your work upon the community, you can sustain integrity for short periods in exploitative jobs, but not forever.

- In badly sited and environmentally difficult work places, make connection with the spirit of the land on which you are working. Do your best to do something reciprocal for the site where you work, even if it is a daily blessing of the place or the removal of trash.
- If you are exposed to high noise levels, factory conveyor belts or heavy machinery, then your whole being will resonate to its impact for several hours after work. It is essential that you seek daily silence or you sustain power-loss or become desensitized.
- If your desk is positioned with a door behind where you sit, and you cannot move it, then get a rearview mirror to put over it. This is surprisingly effective in checking things that go on behind your back.
- If you are afflicted by office gossip, reduce the aggravation by giving the gossip nothing to talk about. Don't leave personal or revealing material

about yourself or your family lying about. Try to receive personal messages as texts. Restrict incoming personal calls to the office phone to emergencies only.

- If you are suffering bullying, scapegoating or harassment, see page 170.

- If you have to be continually available to your employer even in your leisure time, for instance, if you are a security or care worker, ensure that you have a designated period when you are free of the tyranny of cell phones and pagers.

- If you are asked to do something at work against your integrity or code of honor or that is illegal, treat this as a direct attack upon your power. Consider carefully whether you can remain with this company.

- If you have difficult colleagues, read Chapter 9 and hone your people skills.

DECONTAMINATING PSYCHIC RESIDUES FROM WORK

When your work brings you into close contact with the general public, with stressful work conditions and the inevitable crush of the rush hour you can feel stressed and covered with the residues of other people's issues at the end of the day so that it's hard to tell where you begin and they end. Some occupations bring us into abrasive, intimate, emotional or psychic proximity with members of the public: customer service workers; telemarketers; police and traffic wardens have to deal daily with confrontational situations that are potentially aggressive from unpleasant and impolite or angry people. Emergency workers, morticians and health workers may have to deal with traumatic situations involving distress, injury and death. Others work with people in a physically intimate way, such as hairdressers, nurses, masseurs, dentists or doctors where people are feeling vulnerable, unsure about self-image or are in pain. Priests, spiritual counselors and metaphysical energy workers are brought into close proximity with those suffering from psychic disruption.

The nearer you are to those suffering from psychic disruption, the more you need to be aware of how to deal with its residues lest you become affected. The more we encounter physical, emotional or mental turmoil, the more impeccable we must be in guarding our own Vital, Personal and Wisdom Souls and keeping our cauldrons and energy field clean. It is hard not to let some people's distress affect you. While we experience compassion for such distress, our efficiency at work requires us not to be rendered helpless by it. If you find you have inadvertently brought someone's psychic disruption home from work, look again at Chapter 6.

- Keep your work area clear and clean. After difficult people have come into your home, office or work room—smudge, burn incense or spray around with your homemade cleansing essence (see below).
- If someone in your office is exuding a toxic atmosphere and you have to share their space, bring in an onion sliced in half about its waist and lay one half under the desk or in an unregarded place. Discard it at the end of the day and definitely do not eat it!
- Find a suitable indoor plant for your work place. Ask the spirit of the plant if it is willing to help bring life into your office and to help detox it. If one shows willing, buy it—you will find you feel a connection to one plant more than another. Keep up your part by good plant maintenance and feeding, dusting or washing the leaves if required. Neglect breaks the promised contract between you.
- On reaching home, leave your work issues on the threshold, cleanse yourself by showering and drink a long glass of water.
- If you feel seriously unclean, use the Removal of Residues (page 112).
- Learn how to close down and ground at the day's end (page 106).

- If you have encountered distress, create a ritual with the help of your Advocates that acts as a buffer zone between you and the traumas you may encounter daily.
- If you have abrasive or confrontational encounters daily, concentrate on your breathing (page 39), use Spiritual Armor (page 54) and perform Peaceweaving (page 180).

MAKING A CLEANSING ESSENCE

1. Obtain an unused, refillable spray bottle or perfume diffuser that will gently mist when you spray.
2. Boil some water, pour it into a bowl or jug, cover and let it cool completely overnight.
3. Buy a bottle of an essential oil that you think smells "clean." Sage, rosemary and lemon balm are good.
4. To spiritually charge the essence, call upon your Advocates and your Source of Life, and bless the water in their names. Call upon the powerful spirit of the plant that is the basis of the essential oil to help bring cleansing and clarity to everything it touches.
5. Now mix the water and oil by pouring one teaspoon of the oil to every cupful of water.
6. Shake well before use. Use the essence sparingly when and where it is needed. If you get into work early, you can spray the six directions around you before anyone else gets in!
7. Do not use your spray near highly polished furniture, clothing or uncovered food.

MENIAL AND UNCONGENIAL WORK

As teenagers, we took menial jobs to supplement our meager allowance or financial aid: assembly line, building work, shelf-stacking or checkout operation. We were glad to get the money and just as glad to leave the job. Later in life, you may find yourself having to resort to menial or uncongenial work, due to periods of unemployment, relocation, loss of partner, financial loss, illness or disability. In order to put bread on the table, you must work at something.

Low-paid menial work frequently carries a sense of diminished status. Yet even uncongenial work can gives us dignity and independence. Look at the experience of immigrants who often have a well-paid job in their own land, but who may have to take menial work because of their lack of language skills. Hard-working immigrants worldwide have thrived because they find all work to be honorable, so long as it's not exploitative. Your sense of self is never diminished if you give honor to the work you do and the people you serve.

- When you are served by someone, no matter how lowly the service is, look them in the eye and thank them, rather than treating them as inferiors. Return their sense of service to them in as honorable a way as you know how.
- If your employer is impossible, remember that the outcome of your work is not for him/her.
- If you have low self-worth at work, read Chapter 7 and use the self-esteem strategies.

REJECTION AND UNEMPLOYMENT

Life is unfair. Why was someone else chosen for the job and not you? Feeling unwanted and rejected is hard on all of us, whether it be a potential lover, job interview or something you really wanted. Rejection can lead to lowered self-esteem or to resentment, even revenge. Rejection doesn't necessarily mean that you're no good. It may be about the right fit, about office politics. Whatever the circumstances of your rejection, do not allow your anger and fear to become focused upon destroying yourself. You can manage your disappointment by channeling your anger into completing some long put-off activity at home or in the garden and by avoiding retaliation. Then reassess your skills, qualifications, good qualities and affirm these verbally and in print. Consider if there is still a chance of acceptance; what improvements/changes must you make? If you have been rejected six times by the same lover, prospective employer or funding institute, it is likely that their mind will not be changed whatever you do. If so, look elsewhere, try again, widen and persist in your search. Lastly, perform the Pool of Change (page 142). Throw in the old job application and ask for a new one.

To be gainfully employed and to be seen to work hard is the social expectation. To be idle is somehow shameful. Our self-worth declines when our usefulness is not validated by society; if we are not needed because of unemployment, downsizing, illness or retirement our self-worth can plummet. Many older people are finding it harder to get work if they suddenly appear on the market after several years looking after a family or elderly relatives; but it is often just as difficult for well-qualified people who move sideways into their own or other professions. People with valuable craft skills face similar rejection when their handmade products can be made more cheaply by factory production.

- Look for work that gives job satisfaction, even if it means taking a salary cut.
- Retrain or take a class to help equip yourself to be more flexible. Maintain your particular skills to a working level by practicing them where and when you can, even if it's only in your spare time. If you have found retirement stifling, look at voluntary agencies or community projects that could benefit from your skills. Look at ways of passing on your skills to younger people. Explore the fruits of retirement, elderhood and creative fulfillment.
- Do the Restoring Your Image ritual (page 138).
- Revisit the root ancestor of the Ancestral Hearth ritual (page 210) to ask for help and direction.

CLAIMING YOUR CREATIVE VOCATION

"What I do is me, for that I came," wrote Gerard Manley Hopkins. This close identification of self with work is typical of the creative vocation when we answer the deep call of our life's mission by discovering what we were born to express through our work. The creative vocation is one where our three souls resonate fully with our life's mission. Answering this profound calling, which discovers where our skills and the world's needs meet, is one of our biggest challenges in life but its attainment is somehow seen as a privileged vocation gained only by a few. Creativity is not something that just artists do; it is for you to implement wherever you work. How can we claim your creative vocation?

Each of us is here to be of service to the universe according to the gifts and skills we possess. Even when we know what and where this is, we may not be able to find the occupational opportunity immediately; it can be the work of years. We receive vocational messages all the time, bidding us to attend to our real work, but we ignore them out of expediency, fear of change, insecurity. You may be called to change and find your vocation, or you may ignore that call.

Conflicts at work and about work may be driven by our failure to discern and follow the gifts we were born with. Staying contractually bound to a job that doesn't suit you can be as bad as staying in a failed relationship: it is the source of great unhappiness and despair. Denial of your true calling creates psychic disturbance that affects not only yourself but everyone around you.

- What is it within you, what skills are people accessing when they call upon you to help them? What is it that you uniquely offer them?
- How are old work patterns wobbling or falling away right now?
- What story or new direction is calling you or attracting you? Check the clues.
- What recurrent dream is opening new vistas in you?
- Where are you discontent with your current work?

- Where do your gifts and the world's needs meet?
- Make work your prayer and service.
- Perform the Catching the Star of Destiny meditation (page 131). Every day, reconnect with the symbol that crowns you. Contact the fairy godparents who inhabit that star: they bestowed your unique gifts upon you. Pray for them to show you your creative vocation. Check your dreams and the kinds of opportunities that follow your doing this.

CREATIVE SELF-SABOTAGE

After book signings, some people shyly sidle up to me with a question that's been eating them for years, "How can I get my book published?" I ask where they've sent their manuscript so far and what response it's had. Invariably, the would-be author answers, "Oh, I couldn't show it to anyone" or "Well, I've not actually finished it." These people are unlikely to get published because they are unable to let their idea grow up or leave home. When creativity arises, we have to go to the edge and risk its manifestation. Fear of achievement is easily covered by excuses. However, when a deeply urged vocation is not answered, we begin to wobble. The fairy godparents who bestowed your gifts upon you at birth will often become demanding if you ignore their gifts.

Creative self-sabotage can emerge when old stories come back to haunt us (page 147). The inner monologue begins to whisper, "Are you really good enough? Is your work up to standard? Surely your plan is doomed to failure?" Do not let this voice overcome you but with the help of your Advocates, track it to its source before you fall into self-sabotage. What we call self-sabotage is actually assisted by a lot of hinderers who want to close you down. They may be:

- Ancestral, outdated or inherited social imperatives that demand you to attend to other duties, especially in the case of women who traditionally only raised children and looked after the home.

- Family members and parents who don't want you to become better educated or employed than them.
- Partners who see your success as threatening the status quo or the balance of power in the relationship.
- Colleagues who are frightened of how your plans will surpass theirs or else trespass upon their territory.
- The social convention that demands that you toe the party line and do things "properly," or conventionally and not spontaneously, naturally or by following your unique gifts.

If you detect any of the above, proceed as if these were curses that hindered you and use the Pool of Change (page 142). If they are deeply intrusive, remove these voices and call back power and soul.

To be fully creative, you must engage all three souls, which exchange and fire each other up: inspiration is received by the Wisdom Soul and passes down into the Personal Soul, which gets excited and passionate about the idea. From there it passes down to the Vital Soul, which has to provide the stamina to manifest the idea. Creative block happens when one or more of the cauldrons are blocked. It is perfectly possible for the Upper Cauldron to receive an idea and for the Lower Cauldron to manifest it without the interplay of the Middle Cauldron, but the effect is lifeless and uninspiring because none of your passionate engagement has entered into the creation.

Our self-sabotage invariably arises from the way we fail to coordinate the power, passion and intention of our cauldrons, for each of three soul-powers must be engaged for success in all enterprises. Here are a few examples:

- Henry has been excited about opening a wine bar, an idea he's cherished since leaving school, but he fails to check on zoning permits and licenses. The days go by and the enterprise never comes off. If you don't engage your power, you put off doing what intention commands and passion demands. A lazy Vital Cauldron ignores the Wisdom and Personal Cauldrons.

- Francesca has long dreamed of starting a health clinic for children, but years of working for Medicare have drained her. The clinic finally opens but she feels no sense of joy. Within a few months, she sells out to the other shareholders of the clinic. If you don't engage your passion, you achieve things without any satisfaction. A depleted Personal Cauldron bypasses the intentions of the Wisdom Cauldron and the manifestation of the Vital Cauldron.

- Sean leaves school and passes from menial jobs into increasing periods of unemployment. At the pool hall, where he spends much of his time, he boasts to his acquaintances of jobs he's pursuing in foreign countries where the grass seems greener. These jobs never transpire and it's not until he finally signs up as an army recruit that he begins to shape his destiny. If you don't engage your intention, nothing gets done. An unawakened Wisdom Cauldron is unable to get the attention of the Personal Cauldron's passion or the Vital Cauldron's power to help fulfill the plan.

Allowing the presence of skepticism, doubt or fear of failure into the process of our own plans only helps sabotage them. If you are overwhelmed by the size of your ambition, cut your project into smaller attainable portions: a little movement every day will move it incrementally forward. The gap between creative expression and livelihood is not unbridgeable if you maintain faith, commitment and dedication to your gift. Make a regular date with yourself to practice, work on, consider your creative skill and engage your souls fully. Read *The Artist's Way* by Julia Cameron to get you creatively back on track. Believe in yourself and evict any intrusive voices or imperatives that suggest otherwise. Ask the fairy godparents from the Star of Destiny (page 131) what is the contract that goes with your vocational gifts: what must you do to keep your gift honed? Implement at least one part of their advice and see the difference.

CREATIVE ENVY

When I first started my shamanic practice, I was unaware of how much creative envy there was in the world of work. I am wiser now, having heard of research assistants whose research has been appropriated by their professors in academe, of businessmen and women whose businesses have been poached from under them, of quisling employees who ferret out company secrets and reveal them to rival companies, of actors upstaged by envious rivals. There seems to be no area of employment that is free of it.

If you are on the receiving end of creative envy, then stand proud, because what you have and what you do is obviously exceptional because no one would be bothering you otherwise! In a climate of enterprise, advertisement and cutthroat business tactics, we cannot expect to be unscathed by creative envy at some point. The problem is that envy can be murderous in effect either to your career, or more seriously, to yourself.

- Ask your Advocates to warn you of envious intentions. You may be aware of psychic surveillance or a malaise that you identify as a profound self-distrust. Strengthen your self-esteem and self-belief. Rededicate your creative gifts to the service of the world. Ask for protective help from your Advocates and use Spiritual Armor when you are in the vicinity of the envious.
- Read about Envy and the Evil Eye (page 169) and use the strategies there.

MONEY

The major reason most of us work is to receive money in exchange for our services. Money is a manifest form of power. Like life-energy itself, it has to flow for it to work. Many people in the financial world are fully employed in helping this movement on the world stock markets where from day to day it appreciates or depreciates in value when compared to commodities and services. Money has a sense of self-worth too. It is quite extraordinary to see how different world currencies devalue at times of national crisis or lack of confidence, as the result of national power or soul-loss.

We inherit beliefs about scarcity and abundance from our upbringing. Regardless of how much money we have in the bank, we can be dogged by feelings of scarcity, like the classic miser who chooses to live in penury while he has millions in a suitcase under the bed. John Ruskin tells a story about a man who fastened a belt with two hundred pounds of gold on it about him just as his ship was foundering in the sea. Ruskin asks, "As he was sinking, had he the gold? Or had the gold him?" If we live in balance with the universe by being reciprocal with it, by engaging our creative skills and gifts in its service, we will never be in want or scarcity. There will always be enough, if we don't stockpile more than we need. Greed obstructs the flow of the universe because it is parasitic. Greedy people don't engage their own efforts but live off the fruits of other's work.

Financial dread keeps most people in thrall. In Charles Dickens's *David Copperfield*, Mr. Micawber's definition of security is: "Annual income twenty pounds, annual expenditure nineteen [pounds] nineteen [shillings] six [pence], result happiness. Annual income twenty pounds, annual expenditure twenty pounds nought and six, result misery." The art of spending more than we earn, borrowing more than we can ever pay back, is a recent occurrence that has been fueled by the accessibility of the credit card. So easy to use and so difficult to resist, we succumb to its temptation only to regret it. Most of us have a naive and trustful faith that there will always be enough due to our plastic friend: if one card gets maxed out, you can always transfer your "balance" to another one. Unfortunately, credit companies and loan sharks only help us weave a web of woe.

Considerations of money or the lack thereof can cause people to do very strange things that psychically and physically endanger them. Money can become inextricably mixed up with love, duty, punishment, self-sabotage, addiction and abuse of power, in the following ways:

- Giving money or possessions rather than love or intimacy to family and friends.
- Using the scarcity excuse to thwart family members, partners or others from fulfilling their desires or to threaten or punish them.
- Exploiting the skillful and gifted as slaves. If you have low self-esteem, you may devalue what your services are worth and be open to exploitative people who will merely prostitute your skills for their benefit. These are power-thieves and opportunists who will colonize you (page 116).
- Using the coercion of blackmail to extort money through guilt-manipulation of your shame (page 140).
- Borrowing more money to pay off a debt and gambling to create security.

To come into a healthy relationship with money we need to focus upon:

- How we value ourselves.
- What money actually represents.
- What we will and won't do for money.
- The power money has over us to corrupt our primal intention and alter our code of honor.
- Separate your identity from work and money, by calling back the power and soul you have given away to both, and by using the power of transformation to change your outlook (page 124).

BLUEPRINTS FOR VOCATIONAL SATISFACTION

1. Respect your unique gifts.

2. Honor yourself and take up your space in the universe.

3. Value the work of your hands.

4. Separate your self-worth from your work.

5. Engage vigorously with your work.

6. All work and no play makes Jack a dull boy.

7. Be faithful to your creative contract with life.

8. Play seriously, work playfully.

9. Let money be your useful servant, not your tyrannical master.

10. Spend the fruits of your labors wisely.

CHAPTER 14

The World of Spirit

The distance between our surface world
and the world of the spirits is exactly as
wide as the edge of the maple leaf.

—Handsome Lake, Senaca prophet

CONTACTING SPIRITS

By now you will realize how true these words are: the world of
spirit lies closer to us than we ever dreamed. Throughout this
book, I have encouraged you to find and liaise with your own
guiding spirits, advocates who are drawn to you by bonds of loving
soul-affinity, friends with whom you share a common wavelength.
However, many of us have been taught to ignore or fear those
spirits who live on the other side of reality. We may have been told
that all unauthorized spirits not sanctioned by your faith or religion
are demons who are out to injure you. This is no more true than if I
said all human beings outside your family are out to get you.

In disbelieving in other forms of life we may ignore their rights
and act offensively. When someone transgresses, hurts or insults
us, we feel annoyed, betrayed and violated. It is the same for beings
who have spirit rather physical existence. We share the universe
with many other life forms, which have as much right to live here
as we do. All around us live spirits of nature and of place, house
spirits, ancestors, planetary guardians, gods, fairies, angels, saints,
advocates and others. These spirits all exist in many different
conditions as we do: some will be on your wavelength, while others
may be indifferent to or prickly with you. At the very best we can
live together by being neighborly. If we cannot do that, then the
very minimum we can offer is our polite respect.

- Regard reality alternatives as a working hypothesis if you can't hold them as hard fact.
- Treat every part and inhabitant of the universe with respect. Consider how your attitude and behavior impinge upon those who inhabit both sides of reality.
- Be circumspect in the use of Ouija boards, automatic writing and channeling—don't open yourself to random spirits. This is like walking into the town square and stopping the first passerby to give you spiritual knowledge: you might get lucky, but the chances are you'll receive platitudes.
- Don't regard all spirits as automatically clarified and wise. Some are as long-winded and boring as people of your acquaintance.
- Challenge and question any new spirits that you meet in meditation. See page 27 for guidelines on accepting a new advocate.

You can spend too much time and energy exploring the world of spirit. Not only will you become a bit strange to those about you, you may become a New Age or esoteric bore whose vocabulary alienates your friends. The world in which you live is beautiful and has its own wisdom. The reason you were born in it has yet to be accomplished. Keeping checking with your Star of Destiny and reporting to the Source of Life, but don't forget that your home planet needs you too.

BEING PSYCHICALLY STREETWISE

These ground rules will keep you safe as you explore the world of spirit.

- Be as streetwise in spiritual matters as you are in daily life; there are no different rules. Your common sense works on both sides of the worlds.
- Just because someone's old/dead/reincarnated doesn't make him/her wise.

- Just because someone's considered spiritually enlightened doesn't make him/her ethical.
- Just because magic has been unauthorized for centuries, doesn't mean all metaphysical things are evil.
- Remember that people who deal in magic and spiritual matters are still ordinary human beings.
- Do not give away power and soul to metaphysical practitioners; ask for the help you need and use your own discernment.

WALKING BETWEEN WORLDS

When we cross the boundaries of our side of reality and enter the Otherworld in meditation or ritual, we walk between the worlds. From the perspective of the Otherworld and our advocates, we become visible to their side of reality when we pray or meditate. Mark your crossing over and your coming back with a simple ritual format every time you walk between worlds.

- On entering the Otherworld, say, "In the name of the Source of Life, I am stepping between the worlds: from this world to the Otherworld, from my world to your world, surrounded by the powers of life, light, love and law [visualize the four directions about you] guided by the wisdom and the truth that live forever [visualize the wisdom above and the truth below you]."
- When you finish your meditation or ritual, say, "In the name of the Source of Life, I now return to my own time and place: from the Otherworld to this world, from your world to my world, surrounded by the powers of life, light, love and law, guided by the wisdom and the truth that live forever."
- It is often helpful to envision a threshold, doorway, portal or gate through which you pass where one or more of your advocates help you make the transition between the worlds. You can make the gesture of opening or closing curtains to

signify what mode of consciousness you are in when you open up and close down.

RESCINDING THE INVITATION

Marian is a generous and good-hearted woman, perpetually open to influences of many kinds, mostly because of her intense interest in spiritual matters. She is frequently taken advantage of in daily life. Even when she walks down the street she is greeting every tree and flower. After attending a Buddhist meditation day, she comes away with an unwanted guest. The wrathful deity depicted in the silk hanging in the temple, seeing how welcoming she was being, just stepped into her and has upset her daily life with rage and emotional confusion. She has to see a spiritual healer to help move it on. On being challenged by the spiritual healer, the wrathful deity quite rightly answers that he was invited into Marian and that, as a dharma (spiritual duty) protector, he was just doing his work by cleaning her up, seeing as how she had repressed so much anger. The healer requests the deity to leave and gives Marian strategies to close herself down after any spiritual activity so that she's not continually open to every influence. They discuss the importance of clear intention and how the repression of hurt and anger under a mask of goodwill creates a seed bed for trouble. Marian learns to be more careful in her spiritual dealings.

PSYCHIC AWAKENING

"It is never well to learn how to open the door of the Unseen unless at that same time one learns how to close and latch it," wrote Dion Fortune in her classic book, *Psychic Self-Defense*. When I began to write this book, I went into a large metaphysical bookshop to see what was available on the market in this subject area. For every one book dealing with psychic defense there were about forty books training the reader how to be psychic. Few of these explained how to deal with the fruits of psychic sensitivity.

Many people want to achieve psychic powers but few count the cost. After reading the book, doing the meditation and taking the classes, some find to their horror that they have indeed become psychically sensitive and awakened and that it isn't as wonderful as they had been led to believe. They want it to go away again. Having been switched on you may not be able to switch off. Sometimes psychic awakening or sensitivity occurs due to illness, lowered thresholds, sudden shocks or being in certain places or company. You may be:

- Aware of people or objects or scenes that the five ordinary senses don't discern.
- Hearing voices exterior to your physical body that aren't there.
- Smelling fragrances and smells that have no ordinary source.
- Gripped by feelings, emotions or sensations that are outside or alien to your own experience.
- Aware of accurate and uncanny knowledge of things you do not personally know.
- Aware of spirits of discarnate or Otherworldly kind.
- Coming under the influence of a dictatorial spirit.
- Becoming spiritually inflated: feeling a need to change your name, wear robes in everyday life and be surrounded by magical impedimenta (see Overshadowing later in this chapter).
- Aware of any of the above on the cusp between waking and sleeping.

Do not assume that you must automatically be suffering psychic disturbance or attack if you have any of these symptoms. Because our multiple souls work in sophisticated ways to pick up information that is beyond the ordinary, everyone to some extent has the ability to be psychically sensitive some of the time and may be psychically accurate on rare occasions. Some people don't want anything to do with this ability, especially if their background forbids "psychic dabbling." Indeed, some people spend a good deal of their time blocking out what happens naturally to them. The truth is that few people are happy to be psychically awakened. You can:

- Practice your grounding procedures.

- Stop stimulating your sensitivity by refraining from anything but daily spiritual devotions: no high-powered meditations and rituals, just ordinary activities.
- Restrict your meditations to walks in nature and simple, physical, repetitive tasks like tending your garden or cleaning the house with intention.
- Get some training to bring your newfound abilities under control.

THE BINDING SPELL

Janice's long-term boyfriend left her after promising to marry her. The next week, in an attempt to cheer her up and get help, a friend took her to visit a well-known witch. He heard her story sympathetically and showed her how to create a spell to make her boyfriend come back. "Take these two needles and place the end of one into the eye of the other, and bind them together with red silk: that'll bring him back." He also gave her some words to say. She listened, fascinated and horrified. This was such an easy way to make things turn out right. But despite her grief and loss, Janice couldn't bring herself to perform the spell. She buried the needles and thread in her garden.

METAPHYSICAL ETHICS

We all inherit an ambivalent attitude to metaphysical matters because of the religious disapproval of anyone seeking to make spiritual transactions outside the church. After centuries of metaphysical sanctions we have entered an era of freedom to explore the world of spirit for ourselves. While this is seen by some as a license to throw off all restraint, the practice of metaphysics does have its own ethics. Today, powerful esoteric skills are often taught without any respect for ethics, grounding or spirituality, available to whoever can pay. In an increasingly secular world, many of us long for the sacred and the mysterious, instinctively knowing that life has a richer density than the giddy, consumerist world around us. How can we navigate the world of spirit and not come off worse?

People's expectations of metaphysics are not unlike their attitudes to money-making scams: they often expect something for nothing. They forget that magic is the art of making changes in accordance with the will of the universe in ways that don't harm anyone. That takes time, effort and perseverance—something few people seem to have in this instant-gratification age. In order to make these changes happen quickly, they think it's all right to resort to a little light persuasion. This is where magic becomes sorcery, when we try to bend the laws of the universe for our personal gratification.

Magicians and metaphysicians must have respect for the great guiding powers of the Source of Life: life, light, love, law, truth and wisdom, which you have yourself been drawing upon throughout this book. These powers provide the ethical framework for all transactions. Here are questions that you can answer whenever you need reminding of where you must ethically stand in any matter:

- Does this bring life or death to any living being?
- Does this bring light or darkness to any living being?
- Does this bring love or hatred to any living being?
- Does this defend or transgress the boundaries of any living being?
- Does this uphold or bend the truth of the universe?
- Does this reveal or hide the wisdom of the universe?
- How does this serve the universe?

By "living being" I intend to include all life forms and places on both sides of realities, not just people.

TELLING WISE TEACHERS FROM CHARLATANS

In the medical profession, license to practice is given to only mature, able and ethical individuals but few esoteric practitioners or spiritual healers have a certificate. How do you know they are capable and ethical? Skilled, ethical metaphysical practitioners and teachers do exist, but for every one of them there seem to be many unskilled or unethical others who have learned very little and immediately begun to teach that little to others. How we tell a wise teacher from a phony or fraudulent one is not always easy when the glamour or charisma of the spiritual publicity machine surrounding them is shining in your eyes. Ask around about someone. Examine the fruits of their work rather than be dazzled by their website or operation. Good teachers attract mature and balanced people. Poor or unethical teachers produce spacy, paranoid and ungrounded students.

How do you feel when you meet a teacher? Does s/he refuse to answer reasonable and clarifying questions, but rather swathes everything in a veil of mystery? Unwanted lecherous advances are made no more acceptable because someone is deemed "spiritual." The abuse of students by spiritual teachers and gurus is not acceptable. Large financial commitments, as opposed to reasonable fees and dues, are never a requirement of any initiation.

Wise teachers always show respect for others, have humility, do not claim to know everything. They have human faults and failings like everyone else. Regard and contrast the public and private lifestyles of the teacher: are they consistent? Is the teacher modest, truthful and wise? Test their true worth by asking yourself these two questions that reflect your instinct: "Would I invest my life savings in a joint account with this person?" "Would I leave my children overnight with this person?" If your reaction is "No!" then you have your answer.

BEACH BOY BLUES

Ray was told by a psychic that his surfboard company had no hope and that he should liquidate the business and seek work in financial services, for which he had been formally trained, where she said he would be highly successful. Egged on by his wife and mother, who were enthusiastic clients of the psychic, Ray foolishly took this catastrophic advice. Years later, when I saw him, Ray had become terminally discouraged.

Submerged in his conventional job that had not fulfilled the predicted success, he was at a dead end. It was clear that he was in mourning for his old company, but it was almost too painful for him to think or talk about it. Ray had lost both power and soul over the years, and these were returned to him. Two months later, he had regained both his confidence and his creativity, and we were discussing his future with renewed hope. After a hard year of working overtime, the extra money had given him a safety net to leave work and restart his business. He has exchanged his suit for a beach shirt and jeans.

DIVINERS, PSYCHICS AND MEDIUMISTIC SERVICES

We all need another perspective on a problem when we are low, confused or bereaved. This is when we approach diviners, astrologers and mediums to help us get a handle on what's happening and how to get out from under it. The problem is that we may be tempted to invest psychics and others with god-like powers under which we just lie down and bask. Dependence upon psychics or divinatory systems can lead us into passive living. No matter how good or ethical psychics and mediums are, you need to stand on your own feet and submit all advice to close scrutiny. Beware of any psychic or medium who asks you to have blind acceptance of karma/fate or makes guarantees and promises about results. Check your own greed and impatience to accept unethical propositions such as getting rich quick, making your boyfriend come back to you or influencing someone to do something. Practitioners who inculcate fearful messages and implant the need for you to return on each subsequent visit want your money. (However, ongoing help, therapy or tuition may take several sessions, but this is normally discussed and agreed on a first visit.) If you are offered enlightenment or other marvels "in a week" or suspiciously short time realize that this is impossible! All spiritual improvement is based on changing your present habits and upon persistent efforts and practice. This is the "spiritual" equivalent of the "crash diet": unfortunately you won't get spiritually wise overnight.

The question of payment for spiritual services often creates confusion in some people. They are aware, rightly, that spiritual services come from spirit and cannot be priced, but because a practitioner charges for services doesn't make them a charlatan. If services, time, tuition or products are part of some metaphysical transaction, then remember that the practitioner has to live and pay for these things from their own resources. In traditional cultures, there is always a proper exchange, whereby a gift is given to spirit and some material thanks given to the practitioner. If inordinate fees are being charged well beyond the service given, then you must be the judge of whether it is worth it or whether someone is just out to make money. Be aware that:

- Divination and astrology only show us a snapshot of what the near future can offer; it is not written in stone. Don't try to fulfill the predication or divination like poor Ray above.
- If a diviner has frightened you with a prediction, get a second opinion without telling the second diviner what you have been told.
- Phone diviners and psychics are not necessarily bad or misleading, but if you need their services, you would be better advised to pay for a proper session rather than rack up a huge phone bill.
- If you are continually using a medium to speak to a deceased relative, it is time for you and the dead person to move on: you have your own lives to lead.
- At readings, seances and consultations always prepare some questions you most want the practitioner to answer.

FATE, DESTINY AND BLIND OBEDIENCE

One of the most irritating questions arising from New Age thought is the accusing, "Now why did you allow that illness/insult/accident to happen to you?" The myth that we make our own reality is a pervasive one that leaves many people feeling guilty or doomed. Actually many factors enter into the making of every moment.

When people put inadvertent events down to karma they often enter into a sad fatalism. Fate and destiny are two very different things. The path of Fate is unswerving and inevitable, but Destiny is a web that we must be forever weaving. The way we live today is what affects the way we live tomorrow. Make a conscious choice between cruising the undeviating freeway of Fate and creating the itinerary that your Destiny is revealing daily.

The true spiritual path never asks blind obedience of you, though it may well test your trust and ability to surrender. The world of the spirits is a frequency that we can tune into; while we can ask spirits to help us in necessity, we do not put all the responsibility upon them to keep us alive. We must do our part and exercise both our free will and common sense.

Superstition is an idol that displaces your real wisdom. It is the shadow of a belief that most people don't believe in any longer. People who dispense with spiritual belief invariably observe superstitions religiously as if touching wood and not walking under ladders will keep them safe. Oh, and by the way, welcome to Chapter 14! (Did you even read the dreaded Chapter 13?)

Regardless of what the psychic predicted or advised you, you remain a free agent with free will; you are not doomed or fated. I've seen many people who've had a reading and are now trying to tug the ends of their life into the predicted pattern laid down for them rather than using the gifts and opportunities that come along.

- Try to get through the day without resorting to bargaining with the Source of Life.
- Visit the Star of your Destiny (page 131) and speak to the fairy godparents who endowed you with your unique gifts. Ask them to help you weave your destiny with confidence and not be shackled by fatalism.

WHAT DOES IT MEAN WHEN ...?

I was teaching at a college of metaphysical studies where the temporary cook came running in one morning in psychic terror that she had received a death omen. A dead crow had landed on her trailer roof: what did it mean? Without missing a breath, and knowing that crows roosted over her caravan, I responded, "It meant it was old." She was very grieved at my levity in response to her heart-stopping event, but a reality check seemed called for to defuse her terror. The search for hidden symbolism and meaning in ordinary events is a common preoccupation of the New Age. If you ask what a broken leg means, it probably just means someone was clumsy. Such superstitious nonsense encourages us to live in defensive and negative ways, tying us up in unfounded terrors.

Looking for signs and wonders in everything that happens around us can become a predictable waste of time rather than the significant event we hoped might elevate our dull lives to a new status. Some people live their lives by hidden significance, numerology, the turn of a tarot card or some other aid to spiritual understanding. Instead of using these means as an occasional help, they can become a full-time crutch impeding free spiritual progress. There is nothing wrong in using divination in times of darkness and uncertainty, but we must live our lives from the ground up rather than from the sky down, if you see what I mean.

- Begin to investigate how reality works for you and create a spiritual but grounded practice that is streetwise and helpful.
- Avoid passing the buck on to signs and divinations by taking responsibility for your own intentions, actions and words.
- Keep things ordinary rather than working them up into psychic hype.

FATA MORGANA

Diana was a pleasant, middle-aged Wiccan who started to channel a spirit called Morgana. Within two months, Diana had legally become "Morgana Starwoman," a spirit whose imperious personality became increasingly dominant until the old Diana was a distant memory. So enamored were her coven that they became slaves to Morgana's orders. When the coven assembled, it seemed to amplify the spirit overshadowing Diana, and to create considerable disruption at any public event or conference. When coven members were away from Morgana's influence, they were much more normal.

It was one of these who came to me for help. Adrienne's "service" to Morgana had made her unreliable at work and put strain on her marriage because of the amount of time she had to dance attendance. Before she'd formally left the coven, Adrienne had already carefully removed any personal things from Morgana's house where the coven met before making her announcement, but she had received letters, phone calls and emails denouncing her as a traitor and calling down all manner of threats and curses should she not return immediately. I advised her to destroy or decommission any items she had received or used with them. I also retrieved a soul-fragment, which Morgana had been keeping. We discussed how Adrienne could protect herself from their intrusive attacks. Maintaining her own center in peace, she cut off all contact with the coven.

OVERSHADOWING AND "ALIEN ABDUCTION"

When a personality is overwhelmed by that of an intrusive spirit we call it an overshadowing. Overshadowing happens mainly in the metaphysical world but can also be seen clearly in the world of celebrity, in actors, singers and performers where adulation goes to their heads, resulting in the inflation of the "Hollywood star" who has to have an entourage of sixteen people to accompany the star to the bathroom, and whose unique celebrity means that the entourage has to clear a bar or restaurant before the star can deign to drink or dine.

Overshadowing is not the same as possession in that the subject has initially allowed him or herself to be controlled by the intrusive spirit to do its bidding. The subject has usually developed a particular character trait that may be a real and useful gift on to which the spirit grafts itself. Overshadowing doesn't just happen in negative ways but also in positive ways to religious people and mystics, who may take on aspects of divine or saintly figures for which the subject may act as a mediator of healing or spiritual illumination. The fruits of such overshadowing are very different, creating feelings of bliss, calm and enlightenment in all who meet the subject.

Prime candidates for overshadowing include those who are naturally mediumistic as well as those who are drawn to metaphysical work, which is why such people should seek out the very best training they can from experienced teachers so that they know how to handle themselves professionally in such matters. Unfortunately, those who have a good opinion of themselves and who know a little about metaphysical subjects are often the ones who succumb worst to negative overshadowing. Signs that this has begun include:

- Lack of basic humanity or consideration for the needs of others.
- Excessive pride or arrogance.
- Insistence upon the spirit's own way.
- Tendency to enslave all employees, friends or associates.
- The intrusive spirit may finally swamp the human personality and overshadowing becomes full possession.

To avoid overshadowing:

- Be impeccable in any spiritual work that you do, carefully opening and closing.
- Do not randomly consult spirits by Ouija boards, or attend seances or spiritual meetings where your ego becomes inflated by spiritual influences.
- Get training if you are a natural medium who picks up influences like a sponge, so that you can handle yourself and learn how to control this gift rather than be controlled by it.

Over the last fifty years or so, reports of alien abduction and interference have become rife. I tend to agree with Robert Moss, "If they are alien in any way, it is only because they have become so alienated from the worlds of nature and dreaming." Stories of abduction and alien abuse are how people perceive their own power and soul-loss when they have no sense of how physical and metaphysical worlds make one reality; instead, they tend to perceive "the other" as living in outer space rather than the Otherworld. So it is that Otherworldly spirits have, since the last century, been seen by some as "aliens" who conform to a type our ancestors might have recognized as fairies.

- If you have power or soul-loss, concentrate upon retrieving what has been lost rather than focusing upon the story or scenario that created the loss.
- Read Chapter 1 again.
- Learn to live groundedly in this world. See Chapter 3.

DECOMMISSIONING OBJECTS RITUAL

The weapons handed in after a police amnesty are decommissioned and rendered harmless. Some objects that have been used for magical or spiritual purposes can be similarly decommissioned. However, some will have to be destroyed. The elements give you four different opportunities to neutralize the object in question: by burying it in the earth, by drowning it in the water, by burning it in the fire, or by leaving it in a tree or high place to let the winds blow it clean. In the interests of ecological responsibility, you must be sure that if you give back the object to nature, it is thoughtfully disposed of in ways that don't harm animals, birds, fish or the land itself.

Some objects can be returned to normal use by the following cleansing that should be done on the last day of the waning or decreasing moon:

- Center yourself and be aware of the great powers of the Source of Life in the six directions. Hold the object before you, saying, as you turn to the directions:

  Be you cleansed and be you clean.
  All the tasks you did are done.
  By Love and Life, by Law and Light,
  By Truth and Wisdom, be you bright.

- "In the name of the Source of Life, I return this [object] to ordinary use once more."

- Put it in a place where it can be exposed to the rays of the moon from new to dark moon or twenty-eight or twenty-nine days. If it can be put outside without damage to its usefulness, that is even better. At the end of this time, see how the object feels. If it still has feelings of the old purpose, then destroy it. If it feels OK, use it.

NIGHTMARE TEACHER

Anna studied with a high-powered spiritual teacher who refused to answer her reasonable questions about public teachings and who appeared in her dreams as a nightmarish figure when a student wished to leave her. Anna was quite proud of being this teacher's apprentice, yet was simultaneously terrified of her. I originally refused to see her, saying, "If you have problems with your teacher, then make a decision to challenge her or else leave her." Eventually fear won and Anna left the teacher and her group, and sought my help to break the links between them. The nightmares stopped.

DREAMS AND NIGHTMARES

Our dreams give all of us spiritual advice about what is happening on the other side of reality. The reason for this is that parts of your soul leave when you sleep, gathering information and traveling about and bringing you messages. Vital Soul dreams may include physical dreams of flying, movement or sexual union but can sometimes just be boring daily round dreams where we digest the day. Personal Soul dreams may include emotionally satisfying and love dreams, dreams where desires and longings are fulfilled.

Wisdom Soul dreams are what we call "big dreams," notable, uplifting, informative or prophetic.

Dreams give us clear signals and warnings, often a long time ahead of an event, a big decision or contract that we are about to be in danger or at risk, like the one I had the night before I married my first husband when I dreamt that all my teeth dropped out—a classic time and dream for such an event. The marriage was not a success, but I was too young and inexperienced to pull out at the last minute, even though my souls were shrieking the truth to me in my sleep.

For many people, dreams give the first signs that psychic disturbance is near. Recurring nightmares are signs that something is psychically disturbed. Your soul is trying to tell you something important or there is a traumatic event intrusively trapped in your consciousness. Disturbing images, sequences of being chased or hiding away may point to problems of intrusion. Recurrent patterns and tape-loop dreams that continually double-back on themselves may reveal that you are fraught with too much stuff that you need to discharge.

Remember that dreams speak in metaphor and pun, and are seldom literal in meaning. To interpret a dream, you must work from your own symbology and not from a dream-meaning dictionary.

- See the Restful Sleep strategy on page 75. Before sleep, meditate your way to the Sanctuary of the House of Life. Call upon your Guardian Advocate to come as a dream-warrior who will guard your sleeping.
- Thomas Cranmer's compline prayer from the *Book of Common Prayer* is one of the best night-protection prayers ever penned. Adapt it for your own use if you are not a Christian. "Lighten our darkness, we beseech thee, O Lord; and by thy great mercy defend us from all perils and dangers of this night; for the love of Thy only Son, our Savior, Jesus Christ."

· If you don't catch your dreams, begin to sleep with a notebook, pen and flashlight near your bed. Every night, center yourself and ask your Advocates, especially the Soul-Shepherd, to lead you to your dreams. Write down even small scraps of dream when you wake, or impressions, words or pictures. This encourages your dreams to become manifest to you.

Fear of nightmares may cause insomnia and poor health, making you extra vulnerable. To deal with nightmares:

1. Write down your nightmare: what action are you taking or avoiding in it? Who is your adversary?
2. Where is power or soul at hazard in your nightmare and in your life?
3. What fear are you facing? Use the Power of Substitution ritual (page 124).
4. If you have an intrusion on your hands, deal with it by using the strategies in Chapter 6.
5. Practice going into your dreams with one of your Advocates as companion.

BLUEPRINTS FOR ETHICAL METAPHYSICAL RELATIONS

1. Respect those who live about you in this spirit-filled universe.

2. Balance metaphysical activities with ordinary life.

3. Ensure you psychically close down after opening up.

4. Use discernment in your choice of psychics, healers and metaphysical teachers.

5. Test the predictions, advice or instruction from metaphysical people against your instincts before acting upon them.

6. Acquaint yourself with your Advocates and don't consult random spirits out of curiosity.

7. If you are metaphysically sensitive, get proper training to help you control and understand this facility.

8. Forge your own destiny rather than be petrified by fate.

9. Seek out your spiritual family: people with whom you share soul-affinity.

10. Ensure your spiritual practice is cooperating with the universe rather than manipulating it.

CHAPTER 15

The Unquiet Dead

No one told me that if I failed to close the doors
on the past, or at least learn to live with it, I
might never be able to get on with my life.

—William Horwood in *The Boy with No Shoes*

LIFE AND DEATH

"The belief of one man, one life, has imbued us with the idea of death as the supreme evil," wrote Dion Fortune. Modernist society would like us to believe that this life is all we have, causing us to live expediently and selfishly, without harmony or consideration for cause and effect. All who are born into this world will have to die to it. Or, if you prefer to think of this from another perspective: those who die to the Otherworld will eventually be reborn into it. Life is cyclic and what we perceive as death is a state of changing from one mode of existence to another.

Death is but a door, the other side of what we call birth. But while we have classes to help new parents prepare for the birth of their child, we have no classes to help us die. Since people now more commonly die in the hospital away from sight rather than in their own beds surrounded by family, we have become less familiar with death. We fear it for others and for ourselves, but we cannot avoid it.

Whatever parts of the soul animated our body depart from the physical shell. The physical elements of our body decay and return to the earth. The different parts of the soul go to their appointed places: to become part of nature, to become ancestors, to become reincarnate, to pursue purification or transformation. We cannot know precisely the route that each person's souls take after separation from the body, although many spiritual traditions have myths and maps that have been transmitted. The Tibetan Bardo tradition gives such insights, while the Irish Otherworldly voyage traditions provide us with a Celtic Book of the Dead.

Immediately after clinical death happens, which is when the brainstem no longer registers electrical impulses, the physical body begins to cool. The multiple soul parts have, until this time, inhabited and been wound with the body since conception and late pregnancy. Now they begin to depart. The Vital Soul, which has been wound in the bones and flesh, needs longest to leave, which is why, in many cultures, the body is invigilated and left for a fixed term for this transition to take effect. The process of burial or cremation enables the Vital Soul to finally depart to its abode to the well of souls in the house of life. The Personal Soul, which is wound in the bloodstream inherited from human, animal and even older ancestors, usually leaves to visit those places that have been personally important during life, before passing on to the ancestral realms. After death, our Personal Soul becomes an Ancestral Soul. Ancestral Souls may be in many different conditions: unclarified and confused, learning and searching for meaning, content and stable, actively involved in teaching and transmitting wisdom. The Wisdom Soul, which is wound in the breath of the Source of Life, leaves most easily when we cease to breathe. It returns to the place of its origin, the Source of Life, but may not immediately reincarnate in a new form.

The major issues around death which create psychic disturbance for the living include:

- Sudden, violent death or suicide.
- Abortion and miscarriage.
- Places where many people died together in accidents, fires, battles, plagues, etc.
- Ancestral imprinting and psychic bequests (See Chapter 11).

HOW WE DEAL WITH THE DEAD

Not everyone reading this book will be cut out for dealing with the dead and with unquiet spirits. If this is not for you, then seek the help of a qualified and ethical person, whether it be a friend, a priest, a healer or someone familiar with spirits. Few of us have great confidence about things around death and dying but that doesn't mean that we can't learn. Here are some things to consider about the dead:

- Do not attempt to deal with psychic residues or ancestral issues of the dead if you are frightened. Get help or let others deal with it.
- The recently dead may not know they are no longer living and can be confused, lost, frightened, angry, etc. Do not allow their state to influence your own. Keep centered and grounded.
- Deal speedily with the duties and residues of the deceased: the physical committal of the body, the settlement of their will, the dispersal of their belongings, etc.
- Commit to the elements the cremated remains of the dead and don't keep them in the home.
- If the deceased's will is manipulative, for example, if it withholds legacies unless you agree to be bound to restrictive obedience such as not remarrying, or continuing a family business, consider carefully whether you want to play this game and what it will mean to your life. Emotional blackmail is unethical whether it originates with the living or the dead.
- Resistance to the loss of someone near and dear to you can result in the retention of a dying person's spirit.
- Just because they're dead doesn't make them also wise or authoritative. However, the deep ancestors—those among the dead who have become wise and are now ancestral teachers—can help from their side of the worlds. See page 296.

- Be respectful of the dead but also be prepared to challenge any nonsense. The dead may not always be wise or clarified in soul.
- Heavy ancestral bequests and traumatically haunted places are better dealt with by the family collective or a small group rather than by the individual.
- By continually consulting mediums about the recently dead you may be impeding their journey.
- All dead people are our ancestors: pray for them, talk to them, help them by living your own life in balance and by dealing with ancestral issues that trouble the family.
- Celebrate the life of the deceased by creating something in their name: an annual event, a charitable donation, a community gathering, a tree planting.
- Tend the graves of the dead.

LOSS AND BEREAVEMENT

Loss leaves a hole that nothing can replace. Whether we lose our job, our health, our looks, friends, partner, country, money or our mobility, we feel the same as if it had died. We mourn it in the same way. After the death of a loved one or close friend it is not possible to make the feelings of loss and sorrow vanish in a few weeks or months. Bereavement is a natural process in which you undergo a period of mourning. It is not something we can fix or cure. Unfortunately our culture no longer recognizes or wears signs of mourning as it did in past ages, whereby black clothes or mourning bands proclaimed a person as especially in need of compassion and consideration. Recently bereaved clients have reported being told to "snap out of it" or blamed for "not getting over it" quickly enough at work after a bare month has passed since their loss. For the first two years after a major loss of a partner, child, parent or close friend, you will pass through many different states of anguish, pain and sorrow: these will not be unmixed by feelings of hilarity, guilt, forgetfulness, anger and depression. These feelings do honor to the one who has died and demonstrate the strength of the love between you, but sometimes we continue to carry a dead person with us, long after the mourning period, especially if guilt, self-blame and dependence are involved.

Missing persons leave a festering hole in the lives of their friends and relatives, who suffer a loss that feels like a death. More and more people go missing every year, unable to deal with the stress or misunderstanding of a family or relationship: just to know they are safe often outweighs the need to see them again as the time goes on. Treat the loss of a person as a loss you have suffered without putting your life on indefinite hold.

Anniversaries of losses often send a shadow over us, especially of the death of loved ones or of difficult surgery, serious accidents or a disaster. Rosemary experienced the death of both mother and father over one Christmas five years ago; she now has a pathological dread of everything associated with the holiday season and usually rents a room in a remote part of the country to be out of town and away from company.

Loss disconnects us from one of our major connections (see page 14). We cannot immediately return to the weaving of our lives when one major strand has been severed, we have to pick up the stitches and hold them as safely as we can until a new pattern can be found. This period of bereavement after a loss or death is a pilgrimage on which your own soul-parts are simultaneously traveling back home to you and visiting the places where the loss or loved one lived: you are searching for meaning and pattern. That new pattern takes a while to find, but it begins to reveal itself as the intense pain fades, as we cease to revisit the old places of connection and when new ones weave themselves into our lives. We want to be like Orpheus who traveled to the underworld to find his beloved Eurydice and bring her back to life, but we don't know the way.

- Seek help for depression after a loss and see a therapist or counselor with whom you can talk freely. Try to make minimal use of medication if you can, by seeking the healing of nature, the nurture of creativity and spiritual solace to help reconnect you to the universe after your loss.

- If you have lost something that cannot be replaced, go with your Advocates to the temple of life and ask for a symbol that will replace your loss. Create something beautiful with this symbol: draw a picture, tell a story about it, embroider it as a star in the heavens and sing it out as an elegy.

- If you have a missing person in the family, ask your Advocates for help, visit your ancestors and ask that they send the family strength and honor to assist the missing one. Pray for their safety and well-being daily. Look after yourself.

- When the anniversary of a loss comes around, mark it with a ritual of remembrance. Don't schedule hospitalization or serious life-changing events around that period. Gradually begin to separate the time of the year from the event. Be vigilant for signs of depression or vulnerability around that date: center yourself and call back power and soul.

- During the pilgrimage of your bereavement, spend time everyday meditating upon your ancestors and on the Advocates who form your spiritual family: sense their closeness at your hearth shrine. Speak what is in your heart; pray and seek strength. Take your pilgrimage one day at a time.

- If you are still carrying a bereavement well past two to three years, it is time to use the Committal ritual to help you both move on. (See page 293.)

BRING THE PEACE SOON

Eamonn lived in Northern Ireland and committed suicide after being intimidated by an illegal terrorist group. The investigation revealed that he had been frequently tortured by members of this organization, including having been shot in the knee. Committed to peace but unable to face his torturers one more time, or to give in to their intimidation and join them, he committed suicide. Just as Northern Ireland was regaining peace and pride again, Eamonn's short life had been woven around with the barbed wire of ancestral vengeance. His grieving family tried to honor his commitment to peace by inviting those from both sides of the conflict to his funeral. His sister has instituted an educational community project in his name to help young people in similar situations of sectarian conflict.

SUICIDE AND SELF-MUTILATION

Although you may have temporarily felt like ending it all and have even voiced such a wish, you didn't go through with it. Most suicide attempts are cries for help and are usually discovered in time. The serious urge to commit suicide is rarer and, as in Eamonn's case, is brought on by great extremity and the need for escape. Particularly vulnerable seem to be young men whose self-esteem and confidence have been eroded or are not quite resilient enough to stand up for themselves, boys who needed to be recognized as men in a rite of passage. Self-mutilation, while not life-threatening in itself, is believed to occur in one percent of Americans, predominantly occurring in women but the male self-harming rate is also rising. Self-mutilation is when people deliberately injure themselves; as with suicide, the triggers include low self-esteem, stress, abuse, distress, bullying, work and money troubles. It is done in private and seems to give the self-mutilator a sense of control over their feelings. People who self-mutilate or attempt suicide are not stupid, insane or attention-seeking but they do need help because they are laboring under the effect of intrusive influences that are eroding their own will to live.

If someone of your acquaintance has recently committed suicide, then be assured that it was not your fault that they did so. Suicide invariably provokes guilty feelings and self-blame in those who survive. The sense that you could have done more, shown your feelings better or extended a helping hand that night instead of staying in to watch TV weighs heavily not just on your heart but is felt by everyone who knew the one who died.

The ghosts of suicides are usually attached to places with traumatic memory. Spates of suicides in prisons, army camps or mental hospitals are not uncommon because these are places where coercive means, restraint, persecution or bullying is present. Some urges to suicide are actively prosecuted by unquiet spirits who want the company of other suicides: this can happen in such institutions or it can be experienced within a family where more than one relative has killed themselves. A family suicide pattern is indicative that some ancestral imprinting has left a bequest in your line that needs dealing with before it cascades down to future generations.

- If you are self-mutilating or have suicidal urges, enlist some help now. Call your local helpline if there is no one else to confide in. Read Chapters 6, 7 and 8 and utilize the strategies there.
- If there has been a suicide in your acquaintance, inquire if there have been other suicides at that place.
- In families that have more than one death by suicide, use the Restoring the Family Honor ritual (page 212) to lift this urge from your descendants.
- For all suicides, use the Committal ritual to come; pray the Peaceweaving Prayer from page 180, adapting it as necessary.

A GIFT TO THE WATERS

Gwyneth miscarried her baby at four months. It was so small and quiet a passing that she could not honor it with a funeral service where she could share her grief with relatives and friends. Nevertheless the loss of that baby daughter continued to eat at her and prey upon her mind: was it something she had done or had failed to do that caused the baby to leave her body prematurely? I journeyed in spirit to the Ancestral Soul of her baby to ensure that she was content. The facts were simple: Gwyneth's body had been unable to produce the right nurture to carry a baby to full term and the stresses she'd been under at the time were too severe. My Advocates suggested a ritual that Gwyneth could do to help let go of her guilt and grief: to take a baby's rattle to the sea, where she lived, and give it to her daughter, via the waters, as a token of her love and sorrow that they had not been able to be together. That was over a year back. Just this month, Gwyneth gave birth to a healthy boy.

ABORTION, MISCARRIAGE AND UNWANTED CHILDREN

Nothing stirs up more controversy than the issue of abortion. Whatever your personal opinion, there are many women who have had terminations and who suffer psychic disturbance as a result of it. The guilt and pain involved in deciding to terminate a pregnancy are severe and often recur. But the psychic disturbance doesn't just end with the mother.

The child that is conceived after an abortion or a miscarriage is often called "a replacement child." Some parents even call the next child by the previous child's name, which can create confusion. The ghost of the child that has died may be apparent to the "replacement child" as she grows up, even to the extent of becoming what parents call an imaginary companion. The living child may even address the dead child with his correct given name, even though the parents have skillfully hidden the death from their family. This is similar to the case of twins where one dies in the womb or shortly after birth and the other lives: a similar companionship is set up.

Some children were unwanted and attempts were made to end their lives: I have seen many such who, as adults, feel unwanted and who bear the scars of abortion attempts in their energy field, rather than on their bodies. They often feel that they are still fighting for life, are distrustful of their parents or have a sense of being unloved.

When a child is miscarried or terminated, it is very important to mourn its death as a loss and not to just carry on because subsequent children who are born to that mother may pick up on residues surrounding the previous child's death while in the womb.

- If you have had an abortion, use the Reconsecration ritual on page 214 to heal yourself and then use the Committal ritual to come.
- If you have miscarried, ask your Advocates what symbolic offering you can use to send your love to the child you've

lost, then do the Committal ritual to say goodbye. Go to the temple of life in the same way you entered the temple of love (see page 223) and seek a symbol to replace your loss before you try to conceive again.

· If you are aware of the presence of a sibling who is long dead, use the Releasing ritual below and then the Committal ritual.

· If you were an unwanted child, it is time to live in the present moment and welcome your life. Dispose of all the old beliefs and stories you've taken to yourself in the Pool of Change. Make a new story (page 149). Finish with the Rite of Forgiveness (page 120) in order to give closure to your traumatic beginning.

LAYING THE GHOST

Ghost-hunting may entertain us in films, but in reality it is an exceedingly unkind pursuit if it does not include some rite of passage for the soul that is stuck between worlds like a person in an elevator. The traditional expression for helping a soul pass onward is called "laying the ghost": literally, helping the unquiet dead to depart.

In a society that shuns discussion of death, it is possible to be both surprised and unprepared for its sudden coming. Many people who die suddenly may not understand that their body is dead. Instead of passing on to their places, they continue their life-round, going to work, doing the garden, keeping appointments that they made in life. When we become aware of the souls of the recently dead in this manner, we call them "ghosts." The most urgent task for such souls is to realize their condition has changed and to pass onward, leaving their earthly concerns behind. We should not try to hinder these souls in their passing by asking them to stay near us because of our own need, pain or sorrow.

Some ghosts have the compulsion to finish an unfinished task and will readily attempt to find someone living who can complete it. Be very careful: not all such tasks are legitimate. Just because someone has suffered death doesn't automatically mean you must obey. The ghost of a murdered person may demand the death or punishment of her murderer. The ghost of a manipulative old woman may seek to continue interfering with her family. The ghost of a ruthless sorcerer may attempt to deceive the innocent into believing he is a great teacher.

Ghosts are the shells of souls that have not passed on. Because of the way they have lived or because of unfinished business or unclarified intentions, their souls may not depart so easily. The Vital Soul is the soul-part most often encountered by the unwary because it takes the form of a ghost that can be physically seen or whose presence can be sensationally felt. Instead of passing into the world of nature or into a part of the Otherworld, an insubstantial form remains in our world. The ghosts of Vital Souls are often specifically located in places where they used to live, only appearing on the landing at home or the copy room of the office, for example. They are just there.

The Personal Soul may be experienced as an ancestral presence or weight that has fallen upon the family. We mostly experience this through our blood and have a sensation of ancestral haunting or of great turbulence. We may feel certain responsibilities or concerns, which until that time did not concern us. The ghosts of Ancestral Souls have more sense of agenda and frequently appear to family members or friends close to the family. If there are ancestral bequests still running in the family, you may be aware of more than one presence.

It is rarer to experience the disembodied Wisdom Soul, but it does happen, usually when the soul in question has unclarified life issues or fears about returning to source. In previous generations, this has been a fear of being judged or punished for actions that have brought evil to others. To avoid detection and any final accounting, the Wisdom Soul will hide, duck and dive in order to avoid being reincarnated. More rarely, some Wisdom Souls, who have gained metaphysical knowledge without equally developing a conscience, may seek to enter a living body that is unconscious or asleep in order to avoid this perceived punishment or accounting.

- You may be aware of the presence, voice, appearance or smell of the deceased. Use your protective and centering strategies; call Advocates to help them find their way. Use the Keystone of the Arch of Heaven prayer later in this chapter.
- If a ghost is earth-bound because of an unfinished task that can be ethically completed, such as the completion of a community project, then it is laudable to do so, but beware of agreeing to finish tasks that continue to manipulate the universe. See page 264 to test the criteria.
- If a ghost is earth-bound due to emotional or family ties, then the one to whom they are still attached may need to grant permission for them to pass on. See the Loss and Bereavement section, on page 281.
- If a ghost is seeking to find ways to prolong life here by living with you, firmly do the Releasing of Spirits ritual followed by the Committal ritual below. Do not encourage contact.
- Unquiet spirits can be mischievous, despairing, revengeful, lost and disbelieving that they are dead. Address them appropriately.
- Use the Committal ritual below.

RELEASING TRAUMATIC MEMORY FROM PLACES

Some places hold memory and residue of happenings that took place there, while others have concentrations of spirits of the unhappy dead that make us feel oppressed or ill. Residues of traumatic events often remain in memory at a location: the accident hot spot on a dangerous road where many people have been run down, the site of a factory fire where hundreds of workers perished, the battlefield where soldiers suffered carnage. The recent abuses of Iraqi prisoners by American troops in charge of the Abu Ghraib prison took place at the very place where the previous Iraqi regime ran a systematic program of torture of political prisoners. The memory of those terrible abuses still lingered there and I doubt that anyone psychically cleansed the prison before it was put to use again.

Certain high places become imprinted with the suicidal urge, like Beachy Head on the south coast of England where considerable numbers of people jump to their deaths from its high cliff. Situated on the cliff itself there is a pay phone with clear information about a support hotline and regular police patrols come by to dissuade any jumpers. Such places need reconsecration because they have become imprinted with the fear and despair of impending suicides.

Some places cannot be restored to usefulness because what happened there was too dreadful. Thus, the house in Gloucester where the serial murderer, Frederick West, perpetrated his crimes and buried the bodies of his young victims has been pulled down and has become a memorial garden where no one will ever build again. Similarly, the concentration camp of Auschwitz has been left as a memorial to those who died there so horribly.

Places like these need to be cleansed and reconsecrated in a special way because to decontaminate the land from the trauma you will also need to create a bridge into the Otherworld for those who perished untimely. Do not attempt to cleanse a place of traumatic memory by yourself if it is where many have died: this is best undertaken with the help of a group or community because it is too heavy a task for one person to do.

- Call upon the help of people who have an interest in the place: ex-workers of the factory, servicepeople whose regiments lost personnel on the battlefield, the relatives and survivors of an accident. With a priest or community leader to officiate, hold a simple blessing service to lift the trauma from the place and follow it by a memorial service for those who died.

- With a small group, center yourselves and meditate upon the seven powers of the Source of Life: life, light, love, law, wisdom, truth and peace. Have at least one person meditate upon one directional principle and ask for a symbol of cleansing and blessing for the site in question. For each direction create a series of seven small flags on which each power-symbol is drawn. Go to the place and hold or implant the flags on sticks in the ground. Call upon the directional powers to help take away the pain and anguish stored at the site. Sweep each flag over the site and bless the place. Afterward burn the flags and their sticks to discharge the pain; do not keep or reuse them.

- Adapt the Reconsecration ritual (page 214) for a place.
- Use the Releasing Unquiet Spirits ritual on the next page.

THE GREAT EATER

When Moira came to me she used to eat like a horse but remained stick-thin. No nourishment did her any good because of an ancestral pattern of unassuaged pain. Her grandmother confirmed what I found that, four generations before, the maternal line lived in abject poverty and suffered in the Irish potato famine. By releasing the spirits full of grief and hunger and by the saying of a requiem mass for the repose of their souls, Moira began to put on weight again. She also decided to give a monthly donation to a charity that helps feed homeless people as a practical way of helping the hungry today. She is no longer part of the ancestral spiral of pain that she has now helped transform. Her ancestors are at peace, and so is she.

RELEASING UNQUIET SPIRITS RITUAL

If you become aware of disturbance in a place, perhaps in a new home you've just occupied and suspect that it's caused by a ghost, use this releasing ritual. You will need a candle and a bell or a hollow metal object you can strike with the end of a knife.

1. Call upon the Source of Life and the six directional powers. Call your Advocates to help you. Light a candle, "In the name of the Source of Life, I light this candle as a guide to the lost spirit that is seeking to go the realm of his/her true abiding." Strike the bell.

2. Speak slowly, kindly and confidently, meaning each word as you speak it, "Lost spirit, by whatever name you were known by in life, now you

are called home to the realm of your soul's true abiding. Your earthly tasks are done, your struggles are over. Whatever caused you pain is now over and cannot torment you any more. Leave all unfinished tasks now and turn to the peace that lies waiting for you beyond the tears, anger and regret that you have suffered." Strike the bell.

3. Continue, "You have no need to fear punishment and judgment for your deeds: the Source of Life is merciful and will help you come into balance once again. See spiritual guardians coming toward you to help you find your way. See the dear and loved souls of your family and friends upon the horizon. See the animals that you loved yearning for your company." Strike the bell.

4. "Leave this place now and go peacefully with them. Allow them to lead you to your spiritual home. Peace be upon you and wrap around you. Depart peacefully from this place and pass to the realm of your soul's true abiding." Strike the bell.

5. Repeat the Keystone of the Arch of Heaven prayer. Strike the bell.

6. Firmly and compassionately ask them to go, "In the name of the Source of Life, may you now depart from earthly realms through the gate of this candle flame." Strike the bell.

7. Continuously striking the bell about the candle, say, "Peace be before you and behind you, peace be to your left side and your right side. Peace be above you and below you. Peace be within you and guide you to the place of your true abiding."

KEYSTONE OF THE ARCH OF HEAVEN PRAYER

This powerful invocation by R. J. Stewart is a wonderful liberating prayer and blessing upon the way for all unquiet spirits who are needing release, upon those souls who are prisoners or captives to states and conditions that they cannot shake off or escape. The Son of Light in the invocation is but one shape that the Source of Life takes in Western mythology. You may see him as the Liberating Child of any spiritual tradition, whose innocence bursts all bonds and whose truth is the promise of all people.

In the name of the Son of Light, the Son of Maria,
Keystone of the Arch of Heaven,
He who joins as one the forks upholding of the sky.
His the right hand, his the left hand,
His the rainbow letters all in rich fermented milk.
We will go in his name in all shapes of shapes,
In all colors of colors,
Upon the path to peace.
It is the Son of Light, the Son of Maria, saying,
"Ask in my name and it shall be given unto you.
Enter in my name and you shall in no wise be cast out."
Do you see us here, O Son of Light?
– Says the Son of Light, "I see."

COMMITTAL OF THE DEAD RITUAL

However much we love those who have died, it is important that we draw a line between our life in this world and their life in the Otherworld: incarnate human beings have to draw their living from this planet and not sojourn untimely in the land of the dead. The funeral service fulfills this function of demarking the separation between the two sides of reality, and enables both us and those we have lost to move on. Sometimes it isn't possible to have a funeral service because the body is missing or lost. In the case of ancestors who were lost, separated, unmourned and unloved, and those who died in war, accident, epidemic or anonymously in workhouses, prisons and other institutions, there was often no great send-off. This ritual gives closure, honor and respect to all such cases, as well as for miscarried children and unknown ghostly individuals who need to be released from their spiritual wanderings.

If the person or group for whom you are performing a committal had a strong faith then please utilize the rituals and ceremonies of that religion: a requiem mass, a Eucharist, a prayer service or other ceremony will help. If you use the following committal ritual, then include the names and divine titles that would be recognized by those you are working for.

The first song is the "Blessing for the Soul's Release," my translation of a Scots Gaelic prayer, which was set to music on Donovan's album, *Sutras*; the second is the "Soul-Midwives' Song," which I wrote for the Guild of Soul Midwives. You will need seven candles or seven tealights in glasses if you work outside, a bowl of water, a little oil, a paper boat, which you can draw or make by folding paper. Take this ritual slowly, especially part five; if you need to stop and reconnect with your Advocates do this.

1. Set seven candles as follows: one each in the directions at the room's edge and three in a triangle in the center: these each represent the powers of the Source of Life: Light, Life, Love and Law—these designate the circle about you. Set the fifth and six lights to represent Wisdom and Truth as the straight line at the bottom of the triangle with the seventh light, lit for the person you are committing, as the point of the triangle. Wisdom and Truth are the gateway through which the dead will pass. Ask your Advocates to stand with you as you perform this ritual.

2. Light the directional candles, calling their powers by name to be present with you in the name of the Source of Life.

3. Use the Keystone of the Arch of Heaven invocation to open your ritual, lighting the wisdom and truth candles when you get to the fourth line. Be aware of a strong gateway opening between them.

4. As you light the seventh light, say, "I light this candle to guide [the person] on his/her way." If you don't know the name of the person, use a name that comes to you as appropriate or else use a descriptive title, "the woman who died at the intersection," or "the children who died in the hospital bombing," or "the uncle who drowned at sea."

5. Say, "Dear [person], whatever caused your pain is now over and cannot torment you any more. Peace lies waiting for you beyond the tears, anger and regret that you have suffered. Be cleansed and healed!" Sprinkle some of the water on the paper boat.

6. As you say the following, be aware of how the departed spirit of the person lays down the burdens of life:

You go home this night to your home of Winter,
To your home of Autumn, of Spring and of Summer;
You go home this night to your lasting home,
To your eternal bed, to your sound sleeping.
Sleep now, sleep, and so fade sorrow,
Sleep now, sleep, and so fade sorrow,
Sleep now, sleep, and so fade sorrow,
Sleep, my beloved, in the rock of the fold.
The sleep of seven lights upon you, my dear,
The sleep of seven joys upon you, my dear,
The sleep of seven slumbers upon you, my dear.
Sleep, oh sleep, in the quiet of quietness,
Sleep, oh sleep, in the way of guidance,
Sleep, oh sleep, in the love of all loving.

7. Say compassionately, "Dear [person] be aware of your soul as free and healthy, strong and light. Be aware of the boat that is ready to take you to another shore where a new home awaits you. Your spirit can decide to leave this world now with its own Advocates and companions who assemble here to this central light." Mark the boat with a little oil at stem and stern. Be aware of Advocates coming near to assist the departed spirit.

8. Say confidently, "See the dear and loved souls of your family and friends upon the horizon. Leave this world now and go peacefully with them. Allow them to lead you to your spiritual home. Peace be upon you and wrap around you. Depart peacefully from this place to the place of your soul's true abiding."

9. Lift the central candle with one hand and the boat with your other, saying, as you move the boat between the gateway made by the Wisdom and Truth candles:

May you safely go to the bright realms of joy,
Where a greater life is breathing yet, to the home of your soul.
From all pain go free! May your burdens be few!
May your soul's companion lead you on across the wide sea.
May your heart be light as the waves bring you home,
To the shore of those you loved and lost, to their welcome so bright.
Be serene and sure, may your heart's hope be strong!
And your soul's own song go on before to the realms of delight.

10. Sit in silence to mark the committal and passing of this spirit from this world to the Otherworld. Then quench the central candle, saying, "The spirit of [person] has passed over in the Otherworld. May they rest in peace!"

11. Quench the other candles in turn, thanking each power for its assistance.

12. Take the boat into nature: bury or burn it, put it into a river or the sea, fly it away from a height, saying, "The physical vessel of [person] is no more. May the souls of [person] voyage safely to the Otherworld and be at peace."

REINCARNATION AND RESPONSIBILITY

We live in an age that is obsessed with the past lives of our many reincarnations. But it is evident that few people have the memory to recall these and even fewer have the common sense to deal with them when they do. As Robert Moss has sagely written, "If reincarnation is a fact, then we need to have developed the grounding and humor required to integrate the memories we may be able to draw from past or future lives."

Some people have been told by psychics about their past incarnations and the problems that they suffered in those lives. A sense of fate or karma surrounds them, and they often become fixated on past events. Whether these reported past lives are proven or not, they become very real for the subject, who can become neglectful of the present precious life that they are living. Human nature gravitates toward certainties and authoritative signposts that seem to lead us progressively forward. Stories of past lives, real or imagined, have a power over us that holds us enamored and bespelled.

In traditional metaphysical training schools, exploration of past lives is the last part of a student's education that enables them to live with responsibility. It is never taught as the first module because the salutary knowledge of our past lives cannot be forgotten or laid aside. The long route of our eternal Wisdom Soul to this moment is an awesome journey in which it has had opportunity to learn, change and implement the gifts and talents that are wound eternally within it for the good of all life. You might think it would be lovely to fully know its journey, but, believe me, you would not wish to have conscious knowledge of all of its sojourns. Sometimes forgetfulness is a great gift.

One of the greatest exponents of past-life therapy, William Baldwin, states that "the object of past-lives therapy is to enhance harmony in the present life by eliminating the residues from past lives." Where this is supported by a discerning and ethical therapist, I am sure that this is so. But I have seen many cases of psychic disturbance arise from someone's past-life regression session. With mature people of discernment, such work can be very useful. However, it has a way of appealing to the vulnerable and unbalanced as a quick solution to all ills; for such people it can become addictive and obsessive, more exciting to consider past lives than to live the life they have.

"Past-life memories are often the memories of dead people who remain attached to the living," writes Robert Moss, and we do well to distinguish between our own Wisdom Soul's journey and that of another person's Ancestral Soul. We sometimes experience our ancestor's pain and believe it to be ours, not theirs.

Morbid or obsessive pondering on the long dead and on the past can be a source of psychic disturbance. Historical reenactment seems to be a harmless exercise in historical research but some reenactors seem to be happy only when re-fighting the American or English Civil Wars. The restatement of past causes, lost or won, are not so far away from the toxic cycles of revenge of conflicts like that in Northern Ireland, where the restatement of old principles and scores are reenacted both symbolically in traditional drum-parades as well as in actual senseless acts of violence in the community as we saw above in Eamonn's case. Long-held grudges and conflicts can surface generations down the line.

The Source of Life enables us to balance past errors in other lives by giving us a unique and personally appropriate program of living right now, where we can explore the limits of wisdom, love, justice and mercy. But remember that reincarnation and many lives are not to be seen solely as a punishment for past actions. Our reincarnations are the sovereign path of spiritual manifestation when they are lived in alignment with the Source of Life, which uses our hands and feet to affect the physical world. Human beings as well as other life forms are blessed with the precious gift of life that can shape the whole universe, if we will only dedicate our Wisdom Soul to its purpose.

- If you are susceptible to psychic disturbance, then steer clear of reincarnational curiosity until you have strengthened and clarified your three soul cauldrons considerably.
- How much time have you spent inhabiting the past rather than living in the present?
- If you remember details ask, whose life memory is this? Mine or an ancestor's?
- Which soul-part has provided this memory? Is it from the cellular memory of your Vital Soul, the emotional memory of yours or another person's Personal/Ancestral Soul or the memory of your Wisdom Soul's long journey?
- Check the story/memory with your Advocates.
- Consider the story or memory that you have gained. Treat it as a teacher. What lesson does it teach you? What actions must you avoid in this life? What changes in behavior must you strive toward? What tendencies do you still bear?
- Don't burrow into your reincarnational life memory and live in it. Engage with your life now.
- If you have no memories, don't beat yourself up. Rather, look at the things you invariably find difficult. What recurrent problems and opportunities for change has your life consistently offered you? These are the factors that you need to master and deal with; these will rectify and balance the imbalances of a past life.

- What is your Wisdom Soul's eternal gift and task? How does that manifest in your life now?
- What responsibility does the knowledge of your past life/lives give you? How must you live now?

Let us remember, whatever our faults and problems in past lives, we now have ample opportunity for rectifying these in our current lives. Robert Moss reminds us that in metaphysical reality, there is only now. "If I 'was' the druid who refused to become the willing sacrifice in Scotland more than a thousand years ago, then what I do or fail to do in my present life will affect him, as much as his actions will affect me. If there is causality at work, it will flow both ways." This has been my experience of working both with ancestral and with reincarnational cases: in the Otherworld it is always now and the power to heal flows forward as well as backward in what we call time.

BLUEPRINTS FOR PEACE AND CLOSURE WITH THE DEAD

1. Mourn and honor your dead. Your grief and sadness honors the love between you.

2. Allow the recently dead to pass to their appointed place without hindrance.

3. Respect and remember your ancestors. They are still part of your family.

4. Deal with residues, ghosts and spirits compassionately but firmly.

5. Prepare for your own death spiritually and materially.

6. Ask the Advocates of lost spirits to reconcile them to passing on to their true abode.

7. Help those who died to pass with the Committal ritual.

8. View past life memories dispassionately; draw lessons on how to live now.

9. Have the same compassion upon the dead as you would wish others to have upon you when you next die.

10. Live your present life with engagement.

Afterword: Valuing the Experience of Psychic Disturbance

Don't forget in the dark what you learned in the light.

—Sandra Ingerman in *Medicine for the Earth*

This book has been about recognizing those places where we are vulnerable and protecting them better. However, psychic protection won't make you utterly invulnerable; it can only make you feel stronger and more resilient, make you more prepared and less unready. The places where we've received hurt or pain have another purpose that we seldom consider: they make us more human. We somehow don't relate to people who appear totally invulnerable; we may look up to them or look to them for protection, but they are not like us. Our vulnerability opens us to compassion, the ability to experience unconditional love.

Psychic disturbance often comes as a wake-up call to live in tune with yourself and not to be tuned to the frequency of another. Look back on how your understanding of it has changed since you've been reading this book. What has your experience of psychic disturbance taught you? It might be that you are:

- Less naively trusting but more trustful of your instincts and Advocates.
- Possessed of strategies that help you to perceive and manage it better.
- Able to create rituals that transform fear into power.
- Aware of how your multiple souls experience things and affect others.

- More focused upon your intentions and their effect.
- Less fearful of falling apart due to the influence of others.
- Able to have more control over what happens and how you react to things.
- Able to have awareness of how to stop creating psychic disturbance.
- Able to have greater trust in navigating your way through life.

It takes courage to feel your way through the darkness and trust the little candle flame of your protective strategies to illuminate your way. Do not be scared by leaping shadows, for these are but the silhouettes of your inner wisdom.

The great Buddhist teacher, Milarepa, said, "My religion is to live and die without regrets." By your responsible intentions, by your unique connection to the universe, by the eternal task of your Wisdom Soul, may you find a blessed balance that leaves no hint of psychic disturbance in the memory of any lives lived or yet to come!

Bibliography

ABRAM, David, *The Spell of the Sensuous*, New York: Vintage, 1997.

AURELIUS, Marcus, *Meditations*, New York: Modern Library, 2003.

BALDWIN, William, *Healing Lost Souls: Releasing Unwanted Spirits from Your Energy Body*, Charlottesville, VA: Hampton Roads Publishing Co. Inc., 2003.

BALDWIN, William, *Spirit Releasement Therapy*, Terra Alta, WV: Headline Books Inc., 1995.

BLAKE, William, *The Complete Poetry and Prose*, New York: Anchor Books, 1982.

CAMERON, Julia, *The Artist's Way*, New York: J. P. Tarcher, 2002.

CAMERON, Julia, *The Vein of Gold: A Journey to Your Creative Heart*, New York: J. P. Tarcher, 1997.

CHÖDRÖN, Pema, *The Places That Scare You: A Guide to Fearlessness in Difficult Times*, Boston: Shambhala, 2002.

DENNING, Melita and PHILLIPS, Osborne, *Practical Guide to Psychic Self-Defense*, St. Paul, MN: Llewellyn Publications, 2001.

DOSSEY, Larry, *Be Careful What You Pray For... You Just Might Get It*, San Francisco: HarperSanFrancisco, 1998.

ELIOT, George, *Daniel Deronda*, New York: Penguin, 1996.

FIORE, Edith, *The Unquiet Dead*, New York: Ballantine, 1995.

FORTUNE, Dion, *Esoteric Philosophy of Love and Marriage*, York Beach, ME: Samuel Weiser, 2000.

FORTUNE, Dion, *Psychic Self-Defense*, York Beach, ME: Samuel Weiser, 2001.

GRAY, W. G., *Exorcising the Tree of Evil*, Cape Town: Kima Global Publishers, 2004.

GRAY, W. G., *A Self Made by Magic*, New York: Samuel Weiser, 1976.

HANSARD, Christopher, *The Tibetan Art of Living*, New York: Atria, 2003.

HUMPHREYS, Tony, *Work and Worth*, Dublin, Newleaf, 2004.

INGERMAN, Sandra, *Medicine for the Earth*, New York: Three Rivers Press, 2001.

INGERMAN, Sandra, *Welcome Home: Following Your Soul's Journey Home*, San Francisco, HarperSanFrancisco, 1994.

KHARITIDI, Olga, *Entering the Circle*, San Francisco: HarperSanFrancisco, 1997.

LANE, John, *Timeless Simplicity: Creative Living in a Consumer Society*, Dartington, England: Green Books, 2001.

LINN, Denise, *Sacred Legacies: Healing Your Past and Creating a Positive Future*, New York: Ballantine/Wellspring, 1999.

MASEFIELD, John, *The Box of Delights*, London: Heinemann, 1985.

MATTHEWS, Caitlín, *The Blessing Seed*, London: Barefoot Books, 1999 .

MATTHEWS, Caitlín, *The Celtic Book of the Dead*, New York: St. Martin's, 1992.

MATTHEWS, Caitlín, *Celtic Devotional*, Gloucester, MA: Fair Winds Press, 2004.

MATTHEWS, Caitlín, *In Search of Woman's Passionate Soul: Revealing the Daimon Lover Within*, Boston: Houghton Mifflin, 1997.

MATTHEWS, Caitlín, *Singing the Soul Back Home*, London: Connections, 2003.

MATTHEWS, Caitlín and John, *Walkers between the Worlds*, Rochester, VT: Inner Traditions, 2004.

MATTHEWS, John, *Healing the Wounded King*, Shaftsbury, England: Element Books, 1997.

MATTHEWS, John and Caitlín, *Encyclopedia of Celtic Wisdom*, Shaftsbury, England: Element Books, 2000.

MOORE, Thomas, *Dark Nights of the Soul: A Guide to Finding Your Way Through Life's Ordeals*, New York: Gotham, 2005.

MORRIS, Desmond, *Body Guards: Protective Amulets and Charms*, Shaftesbury, England: Element Books, 1999.

MOSS, Robert, *Conscious Dreaming*, New York: Three Rivers Press, 1996.

MOSS, Robert, *Dreamgates*, New York: Three Rivers Press, 1998.

MYSS, Caroline, *Why People Don't Heal and How They Can*, New York: Three Rivers Press, 1998.

PENNICK, Nigel, *Threshold and Hearthstone Patterns*, Cambridge (Old England House, 25 Partridge Drive, Bar Hill, Cambridge CB3 8EN, UK), 2004.

PULLMAN, Philip, *His Dark Materials Trilogy*, New York: Knopf, 1996.

RUSSELL, Stephen, *Barefoot Doctor's Handbook for the Urban Warrior: A Spiritual Survival Guide*, London: Piatkus, 1998.

SCHWARZ, Jack, *How to Master the Art of Personal Health*, Grants Pass, OR: Schwarz Publishing, 1996.

SOMÉ, Malidoma P., *The Healing Wisdom of Africa*, New York: J. Tarcher, 1999.

SOMÉ, Malidoma P., *Of Water and the Spirit*, New York: Penguin, 1995.

STANWAY, Dr. Andrew, *Intimate Solutions: A 21st Century Guide to Managing Relationships*, London: Vermillion, 2005.

STEWART, R. J., *Living Magical Arts*, Poole, England: Blandford Press, 1987.

VAN KAMPENHOUT, Daan, *Images of the Soul: The Workings of the Soul in Shamanic Rituals and Family Constellations*, Redding, CT: Zeig, Tucker & Theisen, 2003.

Resources

When seeking a practitioner from this list, please use your discrimination and sense of affinity to find someone on your wavelength. If possible, speak on the phone first.

Addiction Support: Look in your local phone book for help with the addiction in question, or contact your local doctor or social services for a list of helpful organizations.

Exorcists: Every diocese of the Catholic, Episcopalian and Orthodox churches throughout the world keeps a register of exorcists. Contact your local diocesan office for more information.

Family Constellations: This therapy helps resolve ancestral problems. For a list of Family Constellation practitioners in the US, see www.systemicfamilysolutions.com/index.php.

Shamanic Help: Foundation for Shamanic Studies keeps a register of experienced practitioners to help with spiritual healing. PO Box 1939, Mill Valley, CA 94942, 415-380-8282, www.shamanism.org, email: info@shamanicstudies.com

Support Hotlines: There are two national hotlines that will listen to whatever you are experiencing. National Suicide Prevention Lifeline, 800-273-8255, www.suicidepreventionlifeline.org. National Hopeline Network, 800-784-2433, www.hopeline.com.

Also check your local phone book for listings of other support hotlines and resources.

Acknowledgments

This book could not have been written without the many students, clients, friends and acquaintances who have made me go and seek spiritual solutions to psychic danger and soul terror. Without them and without my good guides, teachers and spirits who gave me those solutions, you would not be reading this book. I would like to thank R. J. Stewart for his permission to reprint the Keystone of the Arch of Heaven Prayer on page 292 from his *Living Magical Arts*. To my dear teacher, Dolores Ashcroft-Nowicki, who originated the Reconsecration after Violation Ritual on page 214: I have done as you asked by giving healing and passing it on. Thanks also to Jane Gubb and Felicity Wombwell for their help and inspiration: if a lost soul ever needed a roadie, you would be equal to the task! Thanks to Gill and Helen at Piatkus for trusting the vision. Lastly, I would like to thank John for reading this manuscript and making good suggestions when it threatened to take over my life.

About the Author

Caitlín Matthews is a shamanic practitioner and the author of many books, including *Singing the Soul Back Home*, *Celtic Devotional* and *Sophia: Goddess of Wisdom*. She teaches and lectures worldwide. At her shamanic practice in Oxford she sees clients in need of spiritual healing; she can also refer prospective clients to other trained ethical practitioners living in the United Kingdom. To receive this list write to her at BCM Hallowquest, London WC1N 3XX, UK. Enclose a stamped envelope (only within UK) To find out more about her courses, books and events, visit www.hallowquest.org.uk.